Data

SYSTAT® 7.0 for Windows®

For more information about SYSTAT® software products, please visit our WWW site at *http://www.spss.com* or contact

Marketing Department
SPSS Inc.
444 North Michigan Avenue
Chicago, IL 60611
Tel: (312) 329-2400
Fax: (312) 329-3668

Preface

Release 7.0 is the most comprehensive expansion of SYSTAT in its entire history. The core of this expansion is the incorporation of the supplements that used to be sold separately in DOS versions (LOGIT, PROBIT, SETCOR, SURVIVAL, TESTAT, SIGNAL, and TSLS). These modules were rewritten and adapted to a Windows environment, given *quick graphs*, and revised to be more consistent with the other SYSTAT modules. The other part of this expansion is a number of routines that I have been waiting until Release 7.0 to include in the main package (POSAC, TREES, CONJOINT, CORAN, and PERMAP). Like some of the other routines in earlier versions of SYSTAT, I wrote these for fun rather than for anticipated markets. These new procedures are documented in *SYSTAT: New Statistics.*

The other major development is the addition of bootstrapping to almost every SYSTAT module. We have implemented this capability with a one-pass algorithm that does not require extra data sets to be made. Bootstrapping and related computer-intensive methods are receiving a lot of attention among statisticians. For many technical reasons, bootstrapping has been late in coming to comprehensive statistics packages. I hope that its introduction in SYSTAT will make bootstrapping more widely available to researchers.

It is a huge step from writing a statistical or graphical routine to implementing it in its final form. These modules would never have appeared without the careful design, interface programming, editorial support, and general project management of the SYSTAT team and others at SPSS. I wrote in the preface to Release 6.0 that I was excited about the future of SYSTAT at SPSS. I never imagined, however, how much would happen in a year. SPSS has expanded enormously this last year and has created a scientific division to develop and market scientific products. This has given SYSTAT more resources and has created more excitement for all of us at SPSS.

Leland Wilkinson
Sr. Vice President, SYSTAT Products
SPSS Inc.

Contents

Contents

Contents

Contents

Contents

Contents

Contents

Introducing SYSTAT 7.0

SYSTAT 7.0 provides a powerful statistical analysis system in a graphical environment, using descriptive menus and simple dialog boxes to do most of the work for you. Most tasks can be accomplished simply by pointing and clicking the mouse.

This chapter provides an overview of the windows, menus, dialog boxes, and online Help available in SYSTAT. For information on using SYSTAT commands, see Chapter 10.

Windows

Menus

Dialog Boxes

Getting Help

Windows

There are four types of windows in SYSTAT.

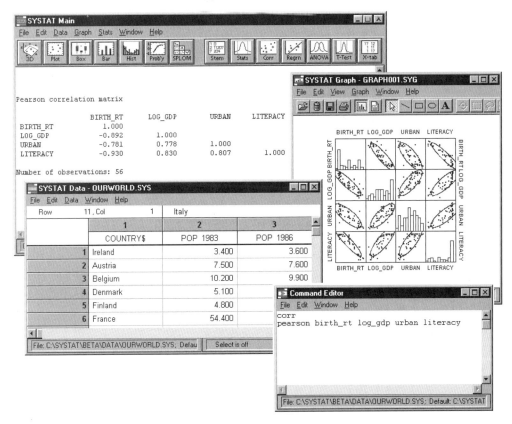

- Results from statistical analysis are displayed in the Main window.

- Data are entered, manipulated, and viewed in the Data window.

- Graphs are displayed and edited in the Graph window.

- Command files, statistical results, and text files can be viewed, edited, saved, and printed from the Command Editor.

Main
window

The results of your analysis are displayed in the Main window.

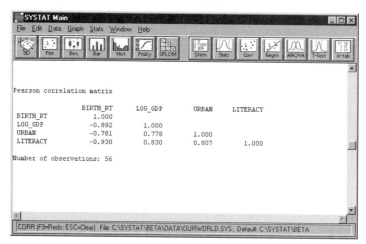

The Main window provides menus for running statistical analyses and producing graphs. It also contains a toolbar that provides quick access to many standard statistical techniques and graphs.

The Main window is also the place where you use SYSTAT's alternative command interface.

To use commands:

– From the **Edit** menu, select **Options**.

– In the **Options** dialog box, select **Command Prompt**.

Data window

The Data window displays your data in a row-by-column format.

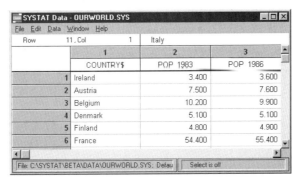

Each row is a case, and each column is a variable. You can type new data into an empty Data window, or you can edit and transform data.

— Use the Data window's **Edit** menu to cut, copy, delete, and paste rows, columns, and blocks of data.

— Use the Data window's **Data** menu to transform data and select subsets of cases.

See Chapter 5 for more information on the Data window.

Graph window

Output generated by **Graph** menu items and graphs automatically generated by statistical commands appear in the Graph window.

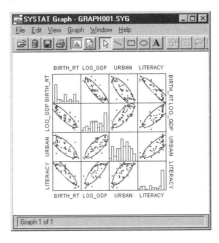

If you have more than one graph, use the scroll bar on the Graph window to move between graphs.

Use the Graph window toolbar and menus to:

- Insert annotations and other text

- Change font, color, and line attributes

- Identify individual points in scatterplots

- Rotate 3-D graphs with the Dynamic Explorer

- Tune tension for smoothers

- Select a subset of cases using the Lasso tool

See *SYSTAT: Graphics* for more information about the Graph window.

Command Editor

Use the Command Editor to create and edit command files and save commands generated during a session. You can also submit commands directly from the Command Editor.

See Chapter 10 for more information on the Command Editor.

Menus

Each SYSTAT window has its own menu bar that contains menus and selections appropriate to that window.

Main
window

The Main window contains menus for opening, saving and printing files, editing output, transforming data, running statistical analyses, and generating graphs.

File. Use the **File** menu to create new data and command files; open data files, including SYSTAT, Excel, Lotus, and dBASE files; save statistical output; print the contents of the Main window; and submit commands from the clipboard or from a command file.

Edit. Use the **Edit** menu to cut, copy, and paste statistical output and other text in the Main window; find and replace text strings in the window; clear text and output from the window; insert notes and titles into your output; change font characteristics (including color and size) for new output; and change SYSTAT options, including variable display order in dialog boxes, display of statistical *Quick Graphs*, and use of the command prompt in the Main window.

Data. Use the **Data** menu to transform data values; sort cases in the data file based on the values of one or more variables; transpose cases (rows) and variables (columns); merge data files; select subsets of cases and specify grouping variables that split the data file into two or more groups for analysis; weight data for analysis based on the value of a weight variable; and access SYSTAT's BASIC and Matrix programming procedures.

Graph. Use the **Graph** menu to create boxplots, histograms, scatterplots, 3-D data plots, function plots, and other graphical displays.

Stats. Use the **Stats** menu to run statistical procedures, including descriptive statistics, correlation, linear regression, analysis of variance, and many others.

Window. Use the **Window** menu to switch between the different SYSTAT windows or rearrange the display of windows.

Help. Use the **Help** menu to access SYSTAT's online Help system.

Data window

The Data window contains menus for opening, saving and printing files, editing data, and transforming data.

File. Use the **File** menu to create new data files; open data files, including SYSTAT, Excel, Lotus, and dBASE files; and print the contents of the Data window.

Edit. Use the **Edit** menu to cut, copy, and paste data into the Data window; find a specific case or variable; change font characteristics (including color and size) for data display; and change SYSTAT options, including variable display order in dialog boxes, display of statistical *Quick Graphs*, and use of the command prompt in the Main window.

Data. Use the **Data** menu to transform data values; sort cases in the data file based on the values of one or more variables; transpose cases (rows) and variables (columns); merge data files; select subsets of cases and specify grouping variables that split the data file into two or more groups for analysis; weight data for analysis based on the value of a weight variable; and access SYSTAT's BASIC and Matrix programming features.

Window. Use the **Window** menu to switch between the different SYSTAT windows or rearrange the display of windows.

Help. Use the **Help** menu to access SYSTAT's online Help system.

Graph window

The Graph window contains menus for opening, saving and printing, and editing graphs.

File. Use the **File** menu to open, save, and print graphs.

Edit. Use the **Edit** menu to copy graphs; change font characteristics, including color and size; change drawing attributes; and change SYSTAT options, including variable display order in dialog boxes, display of statistical *Quick Graphs*, and use of the command prompt in the Main window.

View. Use the **View** menu to move between graphs; switch between graph view and page view; access the Dynamic Explorer, which enables you to transform plot points and rotate 3-D graphs; and turn the display of the toolbar and rulers on and off.

Graph. Use the **Graph** menu to change the scale ranges on graph axes; control display of tick marks, change colors and fill patterns for graph elements; change style and size of plot symbols; and transpose axes.

Window. Use the **Window** menu to switch between the different SYSTAT windows or rearrange the display of windows.

Help. Use the **Help** menu to access SYSTAT's online Help system.

Command Editor

The Command Editor contains menus for opening and saving command files, submitting commands, and editing command files.

File. Use the **File** menu to open and save command files, submit commands, and print command files.

Edit. Use the **Edit** menu to edit command files; change font characteristics (including color and size) for command files; and change SYSTAT options, including variable display order in dialog boxes, display of statistical *Quick Graphs*, and use of the command prompt in the Main window.

Window. Use the **Window** menu to switch between the different SYSTAT windows or rearrange the display of windows.

Help. Use the **Help** menu to access SYSTAT's online Help system.

Dialog Boxes

Most menu selections in SYSTAT open dialog boxes. You use dialog boxes to select variables and options for analysis.

Each main dialog box for statistical commands and graphs has several basic components:

Source variable list. A list of variables in the working data file. Only variable types allowed by the selected command are displayed in the source list.

Target variable list(s). One or more lists indicating the variables you have chosen for the analysis, such as dependent and independent variable lists.

Command pushbuttons. Buttons that instruct SYSTAT to perform an action, such as run the procedure, display Help, or open a subdialog box to make additional specifications.

Various dialog box controls are shown below.

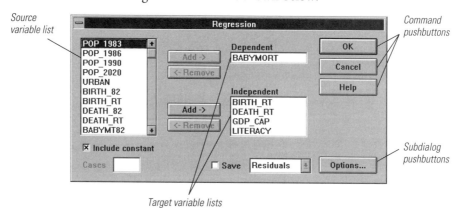

Source variable list

Command pushbuttons

Subdialog pushbuttons

Target variable lists

Subdialog boxes. Since many SYSTAT commands provide a great deal of flexibility, not all of the possible choices can be contained in a single dialog box. The main dialog box usually contains the minimum information required to run a command. Additional specifications are made in subdialog boxes.

In the main dialog box, pushbuttons with an ellipsis (...) after the name indicate that a subdialog box will be displayed.

Selecting variables. To select a single variable, you simply highlight it on the source variable list and click the right arrow button next to the target variable list box. If there is only one target variable list, you can double-click individual variables to move them from the source list to the target list.

You can also select multiple variables:

– To highlight multiple variables that are grouped together on the variable list, click and drag the mouse cursor over the variables you want. Alternatively, you can click the first one and then Shift-click the last one in the group.

– To highlight multiple variables that are not grouped together on the variable list, use the Ctrl-click method. Click the first variable, then Ctrl-click the next variable, and so on.

Getting Help

SYSTAT for Windows uses the standard Windows Help system to provide information you need to use SYSTAT and to understand the results. This chapter contains a brief description of the Help system and the kinds of help provided with SYSTAT for Windows.

The best way to find out more about the Help system is to use it. You can ask for help in any of these ways:

– Click on the **Help** button in a SYSTAT dialog box.

– Select **Contents** or **Search** from the **Help** menu in any SYSTAT window.

– For Help on commands from the command prompt, type HELP [command name].

Types of Help available

The SYSTAT Help system provides the following types of assistance:

Help for dialog boxes. Each SYSTAT dialog box has a **Help** button that takes you directly to a topic describing the use of that dialog box. This is the fastest way to learn how to use a dialog box.

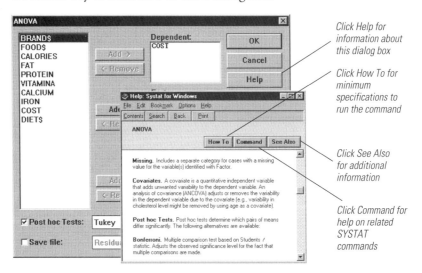

Help for SYSTAT commands. Help for SYSTAT commands is available in several ways:

- Click **Command** in a dialog box Help window for help on the related SYSTAT command.

- Click **Search** on the **Help** menu in any SYSTAT window and enter the name of the command.

- With the command prompt on in the main window, type HELP [command name].

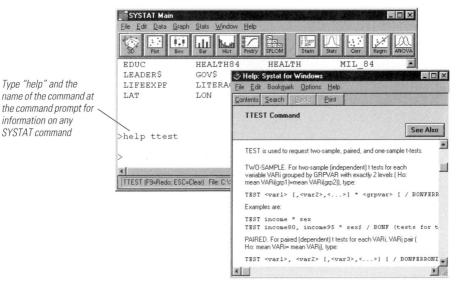

Type "help" and the name of the command at the command prompt for information on any SYSTAT command

Help menu. The **Contents** selection on the SYSTAT **Help** menu takes you to the table of contents of the Help system. Each topic listed there functions as a menu from which you can choose other topics. In this way, you can reach any topic in the Help system, although you may need to navigate through several menus on the way.

Search on the **Help** menu provides a searchable index of Help topics. Enter the first few letters of the term you want to find; then click the topic when it is displayed in the list.

A Quick Data Analysis Tour

This quick tour provides simple step-by-step instructions for performing basic analysis tasks in SYSTAT, including:

– Starting SYSTAT
– Entering data in the Data window
– Opening and saving data files
– Using menus and dialog boxes to create charts and run statistical analyses

A Quick Data Analysis Tour

Starting SYSTAT

To start SYSTAT for Windows:

Windows 3.1 and Windows NT:

- Double-click the SYSTAT icon in the **SYSTAT for Windows** program group.

Windows 95:

- Select Windows 95 **Start**→**Programs**→**SYSTAT for Windows**.

Entering Data

This section discusses how to enter data. If you prefer to start with data stored in a text file, see "Reading an ASCII Text File" on p. 22.

In the frozen food section of the grocery store, we recorded this information about seven dinners:

Brand$	Calories	Fat
Lean Cuisine	240	5
Weight Watchers	220	6
Healthy Choice	250	3
Stouffer	370	19
Gourmet	440	26
Tyson	330	14
Swanson	300	12

To enter these data into SYSTAT's Data window, save them in a SYSTAT file, and plot them, follow these steps:

- From the Main window, select **File➡New➡Data**.

This opens the Data window (or clears the contents of the Data window if it's already open).

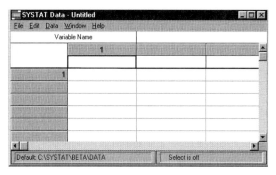

- Type names for the variables along the top row of the Data window, pressing Enter after each entry. Put a dollar sign ($) at the end of the first variable name to indicate that the variable contains character information. *Note*: Character values cannot exceed 12 characters.

- Click the top left data cell (under the name of the first variable) and enter the data. To move across rows, press Enter or Tab after each entry. To move down columns, press the down arrow.

The data file in the Data window should look something like this:

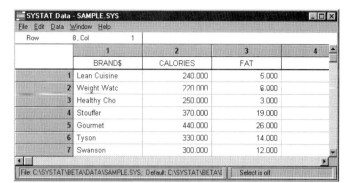

- When finished, select **File**➡**Save As** and type *SAMPLE* as the name for the data file. SYSTAT adds the suffix *.SYS (SAMPLE.SYS)*.

- Now go to the Main window and select **Graph**➡**Scatterplot**.

- In the **Scatterplot** dialog box, select *FAT* as the **X-variable** and *CALORIES* as the **Y-variable**.

- As an unnecessary embellishment, click **Appearance** in the **Plot** dialog box, select **Symbol and Label** from the drop-down list, click **Display case labels** in the **Case Labels** group of the subdialog box, and select *BRAND$* to label each plot point with the brand of the dinner.

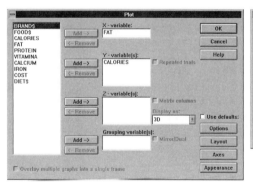
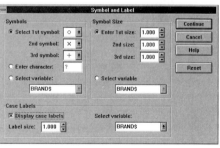

- Click **Continue** to return to the main dialog box, and click **OK** to run the command.

The plot is displayed in the Graph window.

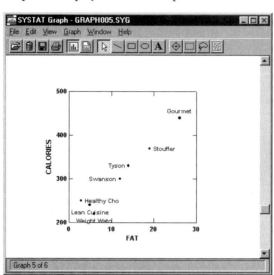

Notice that the three dinners from the "diet" shelf fall at the lower left corner and have fewer calories and less fat.

Using dialog boxes

Each time you use a dialog box to perform a step in an analysis, a command is generated. These "commands" are SYSTAT's instructions to perform the analysis. Instead of using dialog boxes to generate these commands, you can also turn on the command prompt in the Main window (use **Edit➧Options**) and type them yourself.

The commands from each SYSTAT session can be saved in a file, modified, and resubmitted later. See Chapter 10 for more information on saving commands.

Many users will never use commands instead of dialog boxes. We introduce them here briefly to show that commands succinctly document the steps in your analysis. It is not necessary that you understand commands, so you can skip the sections showing commands.

Command prompt

To turn the command prompt on or off:

- Select **Edit➠Options** in any window.

- In the **Options** dialog box, select **Command Prompt** in the **Display** group.

You can then type commands in the Main window at the prompt (>). When the command prompt is on, the commands corresponding to your dialog box choices are also displayed in the Main window.

For example, the following command was generated by the **Scatterplot** dialog box selections:

```
PLOT CALORIES*FAT / LABEL=BRAND$
```

As you make dialog box selections, SYSTAT generates and stores the corresponding commands. To recall previously run commands, press F9 in the Main window.

Reading an ASCII Text File

For the examples, we need more than seven cases and do not want you to enter more data, so this section shows you how SYSTAT reads raw (ASCII) data files created in a text editor or word processor. Each example shows the commands that you would see with the command prompt on.

For SYSTAT to read an ASCII file, it cannot contain any unusual ASCII characters. The file can contain no page breaks, control characters, column markers, and so on. SYSTAT can read alphanumeric characters, delimiters (spaces, commas, or tabs that separate consecutive values from each other), and carriage returns. See your word processor's documentation to find out how to save data as an ASCII text file.

Make sure that your text file satisfies the following criteria:

– Each case begins on a new line (to read ASCII files with two or more lines of data per case, use the BASIC procedure)
– Missing data are flagged with an appropriate code

Imagine that someone used his or her favorite text editor to enter 10 pieces of information (variables) about 28 frozen dinners:

BRAND$	Short names for brands
FOOD$	Words to identify each dinner as *chicken*, *pasta*, or *beef*
CALORIES	Calories per serving
FAT	Total fat in grams
PROTEIN	Protein in grams
VITAMINA	Vitamin A, percentage daily value
CALCIUM	Calcium, percentage daily value
IRON	Iron, percentage daily value
COST	Price per dinner in U.S. dollars
DIET$	*Yes*, the dinner was shelved with dinners touted as "diet" or low in calories; *no*, it was shelved with regular dinners

In a text editor, the data look similar to the following:

```
brand$  food$    calories fat protein vitamina calcium iron cost diet$
   1c   chicken    270     6    22        6       10     6  2.99  yes
   1c   chicken    240     5    19       30       10    10  2.99  yes
   1c   chicken    240     5    18        4       10     8  2.99  yes
   1c   pasta      260     8    15       20       30     8  2.15  yes
   1c   pasta      210     4     9       30       10     8  2.15  yes
```

```
ww   chicken   260    4   21    30    4   15   2.79   yes
ww   pasta     220    4   14    15    8   15   2.79   yes
ww   pasta     220    6   15     6   25   15   2.79   yes
hc   chicken   200    2   17     0    2    2   2.00   yes
hc   chicken   280    3   24    15    4   15   2.00   yes
ww   chicken   160    1   13    30    2    2   2.49   yes
hc   pasta     250    3   20     0    8    8   2.00   yes
ww   chicken   190    0   12    10    4    4   2.49   yes
st   beef      390   24   20     2    4   15   2.99   no
st   beef      370   19   24     2   20   15   2.99   no
st   chicken   320   10   27    10   15    8   2.69   no
st   chicken   330   16   18     2    2    4   2.99   no
gor  beef      290    8   18    15    4   10   1.75   no
gor  pasta     370   16   20    30   40    4   1.99   no
gor  pasta     440   26   20   100   35   10   1.75   no
gor  beef      300   34   22    15   10   20   1.75   no
ty   beef      330   14   24     8   10   10   3.00   no
ty   chicken   400    8   27    25    0   10   3.50   no
ty   chicken   340    7   31    70    0   15   3.50   no
ty   chicken   430   24   20    45    4    6   3.00   no
sw   chicken   550   25   22     0    6   15   2.25   no
sw   beef      330    9   25    10    2   25   2.85   no
sw   pasta     300   12   14     0   25   10   1.60   no
```

The first line contains names for the columns. SYSTAT will count these names (finding 10), and read 10 values for each case (dinner). We name this ASCII file *FOOD.DAT*.

Let's read the *FOOD.DAT* file and convert it to a SYSTAT file called *FOOD.SYS*.

- Select **File➡Open**.

- Double-click *DATA* in the **Directories** list to open the data directory.

- In the **Open File** dialog box, select **ASCII Text** from the drop-down list of file types, select *FOOD.DAT* from the list of files, and click **OK**.

The contents of the data file are displayed in the Data window.

- In the Data window, select **File➡Save As**.

- Type *FOOD* for the filename in the **Save** dialog box, and click **OK**.

Scatterplots provide a visual impression of the relation between two quantitative variables. Let's plot *CALORIES* versus *FAT* for this larger sample.

- In the Main window, select **Graph➡Scatterplot**.

- In the **Plot** dialog box, select *FAT* as the **X-variable** and *CALORIES* as the **Y-variable**.

- Click **OK** to run the command.

```
PLOT calories * fat
```

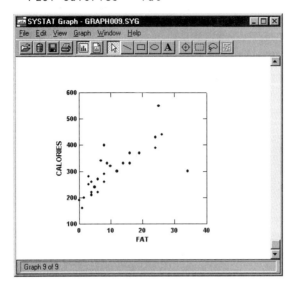

- Return to the **Scatterplot** dialog box.

- Click **Options** in the **Plot** dialog box, and select **Smoother** from the pop-up list.

- Select **LOWESS** in the **Smoother** dialog box.

- Click **Continue** to return to the main dialog box, and click **OK** to run the command.

The resulting line displays a "typical" calorie value for each value of *FAT* without fitting a mathematical equation to the complete sample.

```
PLOT calories * fat / SMOOTH=LOWESS
```

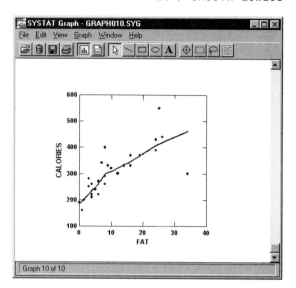

The smoother indicates, not surprisingly, that foods with a higher fat content tend to have more calories.

What foods and what brands have: the most calories? the fewest calories? the highest fat content? the lowest fat content?

- Return to the **Scatterplot** dialog box.

- Click **Appearance** in the **Plot** dialog box, select **Symbols and Labels** from the drop-down list, click **Display case labels** in the **Case Labels** group of the subdialog box, and select *BRAND$* to label each plot point with the brand of the dinner. Then repeat these steps for *FOOD$*.

```
PLOT calories * fat / SMOOTH=LOWESS  LABEL=brand$
PLOT calories * fat / SMOOTH=LOWESS  LABEL=food$
```

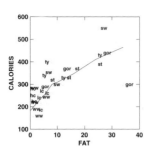 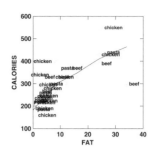

The top point in each plot is a chicken dinner made by *sw*—it must be fried chicken. Notice that the beef dinner by *gor* at the far right (close to the 300 calorie mark) contains considerably more fat than other dinners in the same calorie range.

Do diet dinners really have fewer calories and less fat than regular dinners? The dinners in the sample were selected from shelves where both regular and diet dinners were featured (*DIET$ no* and *yes*, respectively).

- Return to the **Scatterplot** dialog box.

- Select *DIET$* as the **Grouping variable**.

- Select **Overlay multiple graphs into a single frame**.

- Turn off **Display case labels** in the **Symbol and Label** subdialog box, and turn off **Smoothing** in the **Smoother** dialog box.

- Click **Options** in the **Plot** dialog box, and select **Plot Options** from the drop-down list.

- Select **Confidence kernel** and enter a *p* value of 0.75 for a 75% confidence interval.

- Click **Continue** to return to the main dialog box, and click **OK** to run the command.

```
PLOT calories * fat / GROUP=diet$  OVERLAY  KERNEL
```

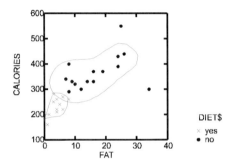

It is clear from the sample that the *DIET$ yes* dinners have fewer calories and less fat than the regular dinners.

Sorting and Listing the Cases

Complicated graphics and statistics may not always be what you need—
sometimes you can learn a lot simply by looking at numbers. This section
shows you how to sort the dinners by type of food (*FOOD$*), and within
the foods, by fat content.

- In the Main or Data window, select **Data⟶Sort**.

- In the **Sort** dialog box, select *FOOD$* and *FAT* as **Variables**, and then click **OK**.

- Select **Data⟶List Cases**.

- Select *FOOD$, FAT, CALORIES, PROTEIN*, and *BRAND$* as **Variables**.

- In the **Format** group, type 7 for **Character spaces** and type 0 for
  Decimal spaces.

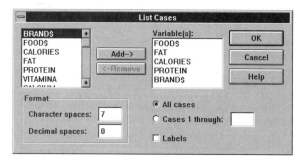

```
SORT food$ fat
LIST food$ fat calories protein brand$ / FORMAT=7,0
```

```
Case number FOOD$    FAT    CALORIE PROTEIN BRAND$
     1      beef       8     290      18 gor
     2      beef       9     330      25 sw
     3      beef      14     330      24 ty
     4      beef      19     370      24 st
     5      beef      24     390      20 st
     6      beef      34     300      22 gor
     7      chicken    0     190      12 ww
     8      chicken    1     160      13 ww
     9      chicken    2     200      17 hc
    10      chicken    3     280      24 hc
    11      chicken    4     260      21 ww
    12      chicken    5     240      19 lc
    13      chicken    5     240      18 lc
    14      chicken    6     270      22 lc
    15      chicken    7     340      31 ty
    16      chicken    8     400      27 ty
    17      chicken   10     320      27 st
    18      chicken   16     330      18 st
    19      chicken   24     430      20 ty
    20      chicken   25     550      22 sw
    21      pasta      3     250      20 hc
    22      pasta      4     210       9 lc
    23      pasta      4     220      14 ww
    24      pasta      6     220      15 ww
    25      pasta      8     260      15 lc
    26      pasta     12     300      14 sw
    27      pasta     16     370      20 gor
    28      pasta     26     440      20 gor
```

Within each type of food, the fat content varies markedly. The *diet* brands *ww*, *lc*, and *hc* are the first entries under *chicken* and *pasta*. If the data file were larger, it would be hard to see relationships if you had to scan pages and pages of listings (see the descriptors in the next section). Note that you can sort and list data in any procedure.

A Quick Description

As an early step in data screening, it is useful to summarize the values of grouping variables and to scan summary descriptors of quantitative variables.

Frequency counts and percentages

The **Crosstabs** procedure on the **Stats** menu features many **Print** options that allow you to customize exactly what reports appear in your output. For example, the **List** option reports the number of times (*count*) each category of a grouping variable occurs and also the percentage each count is of the total sample size. In our "grabbing" sampling strategy, we are interested in knowing what foods and how many of each brand and diet type we got.

- Select **Stats**▪➡**Crosstabs**▪➡**One-way**.

- In the **Options** group of the **One-way Frequency Tables** dialog box, select **List layout**.

- Select *FOOD$, BRAND$,* and *DIET$* for **Variables**.

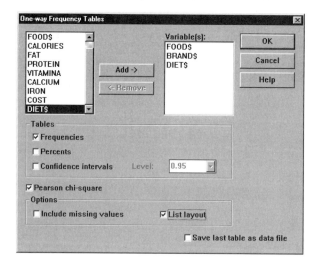

```
XTAB
   PRINT / LIST
   TAB food$ brand$ diet$
```

Count	Cum Count	Pct	Cum Pct	FOOD$
6	6	21.4	21.4	beef
14	20	50.0	71.4	chicken
8	28	28.6	100.0	pasta

Count	Cum Count	Pct	Cum Pct	BRAND$
4	4	14.3	14.3	gor
3	7	10.7	25.0	hc
5	12	17.9	42.9	lc
4	16	14.3	57.1	st
3	19	10.7	67.9	sw
4	23	14.3	82.1	ty
5	28	17.9	100.0	ww

Count	Cum Count	Pct	Cum Pct	DIET$
15	15	53.6	53.6	no
13	28	46.4	100.0	yes

For *FOOD$* (the name appears at the top right of the output), 14 of the 28 dinners in the sample (50% in the *Pct* column) are *chicken*, 21.4% are *beef*, and 28.6% are *pasta*. The number of dinners per *BRAND$* (middle panel) ranges from 3 to 5. There are 15 regular (*DIET$ no*) dinners and 13 diet (*DIET$ yes*) dinners.

The **List layout** option is also useful for summarizing counts that result from cross-classifying two factors. Let's look at combinations of *DIET$* and *BRAND$*.

- Select **Stats▶Crosstabs▶Two-way**.

- In the **Options** group of the **Two-way Tables** dialog box, select **List layout**.

- Select *DIET$* as the **Row variable** and *BRAND$* as the **Column variable**.

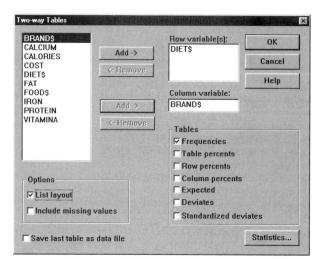

```
             Cum           Cum
  Count    Count   Pct     Pct  DIET$        BRAND$
      4        4  14.3    14.3  no           gor
      4        8  14.3    28.6  no           st
      3       11  10.7    39.3  no           sw
      4       15  14.3    53.6  no           ty
      3       18  10.7    64.3  yes          hc
      5       23  17.9    82.1  yes          lc
      5       28  17.9   100.0  yes          ww
```

There are 2 *DIET$* and 7 *BRAND$* categories—there should be 14 combinations, but only 7 are shown here. The brands for the diet dinners differ from those for the regular dinners. By examining the actual packages, we see that *st* and *lc* are made by the same company.

You may want to display frequencies for two factors as a two-way table. Let's turn off the **List layout** feature and look at *DIET$* by *FOOD$*.

- Select **Stats➡Crosstabs➡Two-way**.

- Select *DIET$* as the **Row variable** and *FOOD$* as the **Column variable**.

- Deselect **List layout** (click the check box to deselect it if it is currently selected).

```
PRINT
    TAB diet$ * food$
```

```
Frequencies
  DIET$ (rows) by FOOD$ (columns)

                beef   chicken    pasta    Total
           +----------------------------+
   no      |    6         6         3    |    15
           |                            |
   yes     |    0         8         5    |    13
           +----------------------------+
   Total        6        14         8        28
```

We failed to get any beef dinners in the *DIET$ yes* group.

Descriptive statistics

It is easy to request a panel of descriptive statistics. However, since we have not examined several of these distributions graphically, we should avoid reporting means and standard deviations (these statistics can be misleading when the shape of the distribution is highly skewed). It is helpful, however, to scan the sample size for each variable to see if values are missing. Also, minimum and maximum values can be useful for setting plot scales for subgroup displays.

- In the Main window, select **Stats**➧**Descriptive Statistics**➧**Basic Statistics**.

- In the **Descriptive Statistics** dialog box, select all of the variables in the source list for **Variables** (only numeric variables are available for this command), and click **OK** to calculate the default statistics.

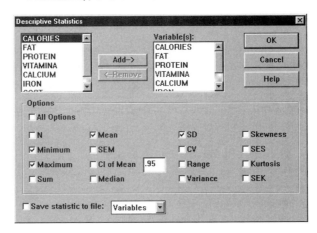

```
STATS
    STATISTICS
```

```
                     CALORIES        FAT      PROTEIN    VITAMINA     CALCIUM
    N of cases             28         28           28          28          28
    Minimum           160.000        0.0        9.000         0.0         0.0
    Maximum           550.000     34.000       31.000     100.000      40.000
    Mean              303.214     10.804       19.679      18.929      10.857
    Standard Dev       87.815      8.959        5.019      22.593      10.845

                         IRON       COST
    N of cases             28         28
    Minimum             2.000      1.600
    Maximum            25.000      3.500
    Mean               10.464      2.544
    Standard Dev        5.467      0.548
```

For each variable, SYSTAT gives the number of cases with nonmissing values, the largest and smallest values, and the mean and standard deviation. *CALORIES* for a single dinner range from 160 to 550 and average around 300 (303.214 to be exact). *VITAMINA* ranges from 0% to 100% with a mean of 18.9%. Since the mean is not close to the middle of the range, the distribution must be quite skewed or have a few extreme values.

Stats by group

You can use **By Groups** on the **Data** menu to stratify the analysis.

- In the Main or Data window, select **Data➧By Groups**.

- In the **By Groups** dialog box, select *DIET$* for **Variables**, and click **OK** to run the command.

- Return to the **Descriptive Statistics** dialog box.

- Select the following measures: **Minimum, Maximum, Mean, CI of Mean**, and **Median**.

```
BY diet$
ST / MEDIAN  MIN  MAX  MEAN  CI
```

```
The following results are for:
   DIET$       = yes

                  CALORIES      FAT    PROTEIN   VITAMINA   CALCIUM
N of cases          13          13        13        13        13
Minimum          160.000       0.0     9.000       0.0     2.000
Maximum          280.000     8.000    24.000    30.000    30.000
Median           240.000     4.000    17.000    15.000     8.000
Mean             230.769     3.885    16.846    15.077     9.769
95% CI Upper     251.770     5.225    19.467    22.233    14.910
95% CI Lower     209.769     2.544    14.225     7.921     4.629

                    IRON       COST
N of cases          13          13
Minimum            2.000     2.000
Maximum           15.000     2.990
Median             8.000     2.490
Mean               8.923     2.509
95% CI Upper      11.847     2.754
95% CI Lower       5.999     2.265


The following results are for:
   DIET$       = no

                  CALORIES      FAT    PROTEIN   VITAMINA   CALCIUM
N of cases          15          15        15        15        15
Minimum          290.000     7.000    14.000       0.0       0.0
Maximum          550.000    34.000    31.000   100.000    40.000
Median           340.000    16.000    22.000    10.000     6.000
Mean             366.000    16.800    22.133    22.267    11.800
95% CI Upper     404.127    21.353    24.519    38.302    18.865
95% CI Lower     327.873    12.247    19.748     6.231     4.735

                    IRON       COST
N of cases          15          15
Minimum            4.000     1.600
Maximum           25.000     3.500
Median            10.000     2.850
Mean              11.800     2.573
95% CI Upper      15.003     2.939
95% CI Lower       8.597     2.207
```

The median grams of protein for the 13 diet dinners is 17; the mean is 16.8. For the 15 regular dinners, these statistics are 22 and 22.1, respectively. Later we request a two-sample t test to see if this is a significant difference. A 95% confidence interval for the average cost of a diet dinner ranges from $2.27 to $2.75. The confidence interval for the average cost of the regular dinners is larger—$2.21 to $2.94.

The **By Groups** variable, *DIET$*, remains in effect for subsequent graphical displays and statistical analyses. To disengage it, return to the **By Groups** dialog box and select **Turn By Groups off**.

A First Look at Relations among Variables

What are the correlations among calories, fat content, protein, and cost?
We can use correlations to quantify the linear relations among these variables.

- In the Main window, select **Stats⟹Correlations**.

- In the **Correlations** dialog box, select **Continuous data** and select **Pearson** from the **Continuous data** drop-down list.

- Select *CALORIES, FAT, PROTEIN,* and *COST* for **Variables**.

- Click **Options** and select **Probabilities** and **Bonferroni** in the **Correlations Options** subdialog box. Because we study six correlations among four variables, we use Bonferroni adjusted probabilities to provide protection for multiple tests.

- Click **Continue** to return to the **Correlations** dialog box, and click **OK** to run the command.

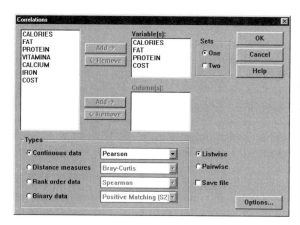
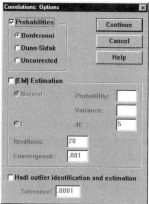

```
CORR
    PEARSON calories fat protein cost / BONF
```

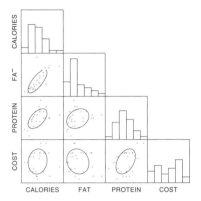

Quick Graphs. This is the *Quick Graph* that SYSTAT automatically generates when you request correlations. *Quick Graphs* are also available in procedures for cluster analysis, discriminant analysis, factor analysis, multidimensional scaling, nonlinear regression, and time series analysis. If you want to turn off a *Quick Graph*, use **Edit➠Options**.

The *Quick Graph* in this example is a scatterplot matrix (SPLOM). There is one bivariate scatterplot corresponding to each entry in the correlation matrix that follows. Univariate histograms for each variable are displayed along the diagonal, and 75% normal theory confidence ellipses within each plot.

The plot of *FAT* and *CALORIES* (top left) has the narrowest ellipse, and thus, the strongest correlation (that is, given that the configuration of the points is spread evenly, is not nonlinear, and has no anomalies). In the correlation matrix that follows, the correlation between *FAT* and *CALORIES* is 0.758.

```
Pearson correlation matrix

                CALORIES       FAT     PROTEIN        COST
CALORIES          1.000
FAT               0.758     1.000
PROTEIN           0.550     0.279       1.000
COST              0.099    -0.132       0.420       1.000

Bartlett Chi-square statistic:    38.865 DF=6 Prob= 0.000

Matrix of Bonferroni Probabilities

                CALORIES       FAT     PROTEIN        COST
CALORIES          0.0
FAT               0.000     0.0
PROTEIN           0.014     0.903       0.0
COST              1.000     1.000       0.156        0.0

Number of observations: 28
```

The p value (or Bonferroni adjusted probability) associated with 0.758 is printed as 0.000 (or less than 0.0005). As the scatterplot seemed to indicate, *FAT* and *CALORIES* are correlated. *PROTEIN* also has a significant correlation with *CALORIES* ($r = 0.55$, $p = 0.014$). We are unable to detect significant correlations between *COST* and *CALORIES*, *FAT*, and *PROTEIN*.

Subpopulations

The presence of subpopulations can mask or falsely enhance the size of a correlation. With **Correlations**, we could specify *DIET$* as a **By Groups** variable as we did previously. Instead, let's examine the data graphically and use 75% nonparametric kernel density contours to identify the diet *yes* and *no* groups. We will also look at univariate kernel density curves for the groups.

- Select **Graph➧Scatterplot Matrix**.

- Select *CALORIES*, *FAT*, *PROTEIN*, and *COST* as **Row variables** (they will also appear in the **Column variable** list).

- Select *DIET$* as the **Grouping variable**.

- Select **Only display bottom half of matrix and diagonal** and **Overlay multiple graphs into a single frame**.

- Click **Options** and select **Scatterplot Matrix Options** from the drop-down list.

- In the **Scatterplot Matrix Options** dialog box, select **Density displays in diagonal cells**, and select **Kernel Curve** from the drop-down list.

- Select **Confidence kernel** and enter a *p* value of 0.75.

- Click **Continue** to return to the main dialog box and then click **OK**.

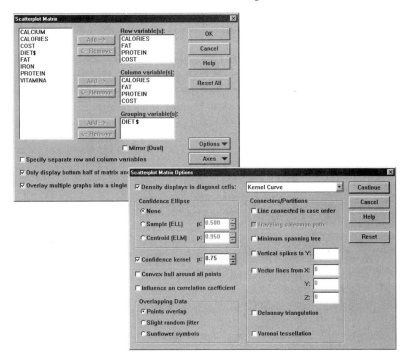

```
SPLOM calories fat protein cost / GROUP=diet$,
            OVERLAY  KERNEL=.75,
            HALF  DENSITY=KERNEL
```

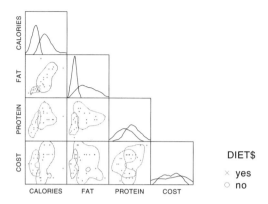

For *CALORIES* and *FAT*, look at the separation of the univariate densities on the diagonal of the display, while at the bottom right, notice that the price range (*COST*) for the diet dinners is within that for the regular dinners. *COST* is the *y* variable in the bottom row of plots. Within each group, *COST* appears to have little relation to *CALORIES* or *FAT*. It is possible that *COST* has a positive association with *PROTEIN* for the regular dinners (open circles in the *COST* versus *PROTEIN* plot).

Is there a relationship between cost and nutritive value as measured by the percentage daily value for vitamin A, calcium, and iron? Repeat the steps for the previous plot, but select *VITAMINA, CALCIUM, IRON,* and *COST* as **Row variables**.

```
SPLOM vitamina calcium iron cost / GROUP=diet$,
                     OVERLAY  KERNEL=.75,
                     HALF  DENSITY=KERNEL
```

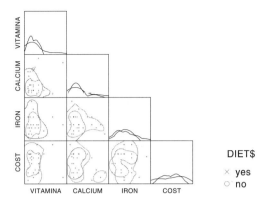

COST is the y variable for each plot on the bottom row. There is no strong relationship between cost and nutritive value (as measured by *VITAMINA*, *CALCIUM*, and *IRON*), except there is a small cluster of low-cost dinners with high calcium content. Later, we will find that these are *pasta* dinners.

3-D displays

In this section, we use 3-D displays for another look at calories, protein, and fat. In the display on the left, we label each dinner with its brand code; in the display on the right, we use the cost of the dinner to determine the size of the plot symbol.

To produce 3-D displays:

- In the Main window, select **Graph⟹Scatterplot**.

- In the **Scatterplot** dialog box, select *FAT* as the **X-variable**, *PROTEIN* as the **Y-variable**, and *CALORIES* as the **Z-variable**.

- Click **Axes**, and for each axis, select **Display grid lines**. Then click **Continue** to return to the main dialog box.

- Click **Options**, select **Plot Options** from the pop-up list, and select **Vertical spikes to Y** in the **Plot Options** subdialog box. Then click **Continue** to return to the main dialog box.

- To produce the plot on the left, click **Appearance** in the **Plot** dialog box, select **Symbols and Labels** from the drop-down list, click **Display case labels** in the **Case Labels** group of the subdialog box, and select *BRAND$* to label each plot point with the brand of the dinner.

- To produce the plot on the right, click **Appearance** in the **Plot** dialog box, select **Symbols and Labels** from the drop-down list, click **Select variable** in the **Symbol Size** group of the subdialog box, and select *COST* as the symbol size variable.

```
PLOT calories * protein * fat / LABEL=brand$,
              CSIZE=1.5  AX=BOOK  XGRID  YGRID  SPIKE

PLOT calories * protein * fat / AX=BOOK  XGRID,
              YGRID  SPIKE  SYM=1  SIZE=cost  FILL=6
```

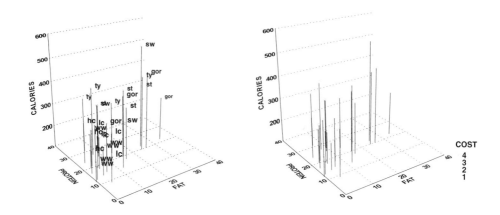

Notice the back corner of the left display—the tallest spike extends to *sw*, indicating the dinner with the most calories. On the floor of the display, we read that its fat content is between 20 and 30 grams and that its protein is a little over 20 grams. We see this same point in the display on the right—the size of its circle is not extreme, indicating a mid-range price. Notice the small circle toward the far right—this dinner costs much less than the *sw* dinner and has a higher fat content and a similar protein value. The most expensive dinners (that is, the larger circles) do not concentrate in a particular region.

A two-sample t test

One of the most common situations in statistical practice is that of comparing means for two groups. For example, does the average response for the treatment group differ from that for the control group? Ideally, the subjects should be randomly assigned to the groups.

For the food data, we are interested in possible differences in protein and calcium between the diet and regular dinners. Thus, the dinners are not randomly assigned to groups. In a real observational study, a researcher should carefully explore the data to ensure that other factors are not masking or enhancing a difference in means.

Do diet and regular dinners differ in protein and calcium content? In this example, we use the **t-test** procedure.

- In the Main window, select **Stats**➟**t-test**➟**Two Groups**.

- In the **Two-sample t-test** dialog box, select *PROTEIN* and *CALCIUM* for **Variables**, and select *DIET$* for the **Grouping variable**.

- Click **OK** to run the command.

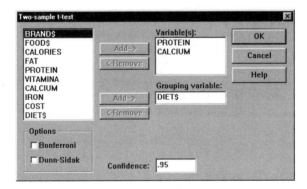

```
TTEST
    TEST protein calcium * diet$
```

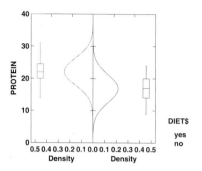
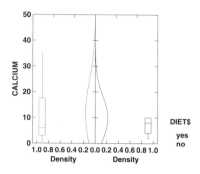

```
Two-sample t test on PROTEIN grouped by DIET$

   Group            N        Mean            SD
    no             15       22.133         4.307
    yes            13       16.846         4.337

      Separate Variance t =    3.228 DF =   25.4    Prob =      0.003
      Pooled Variance t =      3.229 DF =   26      Prob =      0.003

Two-sample t test on CALCIUM grouped by DIET$

   Group            N        Mean            SD
    no             15       11.800        12.757
    yes            13        9.769         8.506

      Separate Variance t =    0.501 DF =   24.5    Prob =      0.621
      Pooled Variance t =      0.487 DF =   26      Prob =      0.630
```

The **t-test** procedure produces two density plots as *Quick Graphs*. On the far left and right side of the density plot for each test variable are boxplots for each category of the grouping variable. The boxplot on the left side of each graph is for the *DIET$ no* group, and the boxplot on the right side of each graph is for the *DIET$ yes* group. The middle portion of each graph shows the actual distribution of data points, with a normal curve for comparison.

The results in the boxplots for *PROTEIN* are what we would like them to be. The median (horizontal line in each box) is in the center of the box, and the lengths of the boxes are similar. Also, the peaks of the normal curves, which represent the mean for a normal distribution, are very close to the median values. This indicates that the distributions are symmetric and have approximately the same spread (*variance*). This is not true for *CALCIUM*. These distributions are right-skewed and possibly should be transformed before analysis.

The mean values for *PROTEIN* are the same as those in the **By Groups** statistics—22.133 and 16.846. The standard deviations (*SD*) differ little

(4.307 and 4.337), confirming what we observed in the boxplots. This means that we can use the results of the *Pooled Variance t* test printed below the means. This test is usually the first one you see in introductory texts and assumes that the distributions have the same shape (that is, the variances do not differ). For *PROTEIN*, we conclude that the mean of 22.1 for the regular dinners does differ significantly from the mean of 16.8 for the diet dinners (t = 3.229, p value = 0.0003).

The *Separate Variance t* test does not require the assumption of equal variances. Considering the distributions for *CALCIUM* displayed in the boxplots and that the standard deviations for the groups are 12.757 and 8.506, we use the *Separate Variance t* test results. We are unable to report a difference in average *CALCIUM* values for the regular and diet dinners (t=0.501, p value=0.621).

Since the discussion of SYSTAT's procedures is very exploratory at this stage, you should not conclude that *CALCIUM* values are homogeneous. Always take the time to think about what possible subgroups might be influencing or obscuring results.

A one-way ANOVA

Does the cost of a dinner vary by brand? Let's try an analysis of variance (ANOVA) to determine whether the average price of frozen dinners varies by brand. After looking at the graphics earlier in this chapter, we assume that differences do exist, so we also request the Tukey HSD test for post hoc comparison of means. This test provides protection for testing many pairs of means simultaneously, allowing us to make statements about which brand's average cost differs significantly from another's.

Before we run the analysis of variance, we'll specify how the brands should be ordered in the output (results will be easier to follow if we order the brands from least to most expensive).

- In the Main or Data window, **Data➧Order**.

- In the **Order** dialog box, select *BRAND$* for **Variable**.

- Select **Enter sort** and type 'gor', 'hc', 'sw', 'lc', 'ww', 'st', 'ty'.

- Click **OK** to run the command.

- Select **Edit➧Options**.

- In the **Output Results** group of the **Options** dialog box, select **Long** from the **Length** drop-down list. (This will provide extended results for the analysis of variance.)

- Click **OK**.

To request an analysis of variance:

- In the Main window, select **Stats⟹Analysis of Variance (ANOVA)⟹ ANOVA**.

- In the **ANOVA** dialog box, select *COST* as the **Dependent** variable and *BRAND$* as the **Factors** variable.

- Select **Post hoc Tests**, and select **Tukey** as the test.

- Click **OK** to run the command.

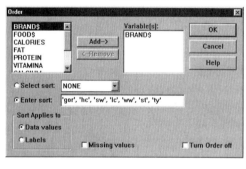
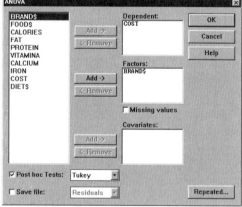

```
ANOVA
   PRINT=LONG
   CATEGORY brand$
   ORDER brand$ / SORT ='gor',
                'hc','sw','lc','ww','st','ty'
   DEPEND cost / TUKEY
   ESTIMATE
```

```
Categorical values encountered during processing are:
BRAND$ (7 levels)
   gor , hc , sw , lc , ww , st , ty

Dep Var: COST N: 28 Multiple R:  0.861 Squared multiple R:  0.742

                        Analysis of Variance

Source              Sum-of-Squares   DF  Mean-Square     F-Ratio       P

BRAND$                    6.017       6      1.003        10.042     0.000

Error                     2.097      21      0.100
-----------------------------------------------------------------------

Least squares means.
                             LS Mean          SE        N
   BRAND$      =gor           1.810         0.158        4
   BRAND$      =hc            2.000         0.182        3
   BRAND$      =sw            2.233         0.182        3
   BRAND$      =lc            2.654         0.141        5
   BRAND$      =ww            2.670         0.141        5
   BRAND$      =st            2.915         0.158        4
   BRAND$      =ty            3.250         0.158        4
```

We have interrupted the output here to point out that the means are ordered by increasing cost because of the **Order** feature. This feature also pertains to graphical displays.

- Select **Graph▹Bar**.

- Select *COST* as the **X-variable** and *BRAND$* as the **Y-variable**.

- Select **Options**, select **Error bars** from the drop-down list, and select **Standard error** in the **Error Bars** dialog box.

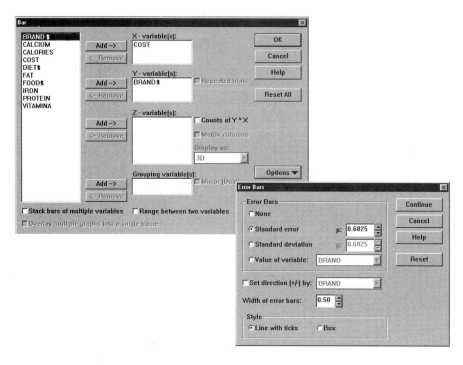

```
GRAPH
  ORDER brand$ /SORT='gor',
  'hc', 'sw', 'lc', 'ww', 'st', 'ty'
  BAR cost * brand$ /SERROR
```

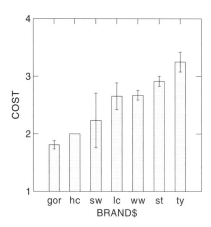

Tukey pairwise mean comparisons

We now continue with the output:

```
------------------------------------------------------------

COL/
ROW BRAND$
  1  gor
  2  hc
  3  sw
  4  lc
  5  ww
  6  st
  7  ty
Using least squares means.
Post Hoc test of COST
------------------------------------------------------------

Using model MSE of 0.100 with 21 DF.
Matrix of pairwise mean differences:

                1        2        3        4        5
    1         0.0
    2         0.190    0.0
    3         0.423    0.233    0.0
    4         0.844    0.654    0.421    0.0
    5         0.860    0.670    0.437    0.016    0.0
    6         1.105    0.915    0.682    0.261    0.245
    7         1.440    1.250    1.017    0.596    0.580

                6        7
    6         0.0
    7         0.335    0.0


Tukey HSD Multiple Comparisons.
Matrix of pairwise comparison probabilities:

                1        2        3        4        5
    1         1.000
    2         0.984    1.000
    3         0.590    0.968    1.000
    4         0.010    0.115    0.548    1.000
    5         0.009    0.100    0.506    1.000    1.000
    6         0.001    0.016    0.117    0.874    0.903
    7         0.000    0.001    0.006    0.120    0.138

                6        7
    6         1.000
    7         0.742    1.000

------------------------------------------------------------
```

The *F* ratio in the *Analysis of Variance* table at the beginning of the output indicates that there are one or more differences in average price among the seven brands (*F* = 10.042, *p* value < 0.0005).

Let's read the *Tukey* results that follow. SYSTAT first assigns a numeric code to each brand and follows this with the difference in cost for each pair of means. Differences between the *gor* brand and the others are reported in column 1 ($0.19 with *hc*, $0.42 with *sw*, and $1.44 with *ty*). The same layout is used in the last panel to report the probability associated with each difference. *Gor* is significantly less expensive than all brands except *hc* (2) and *sw* (3).

In column 2, notice that, on the average, the *hc* brand costs $0.92 less than the *st* brand and $1.25 less than the *ty* brand. From the probability table, these differences are significant with probabilities of 0.016 and

0.001, respectively. The only other significant difference is the last brand in column 3—the average price for the *sw* brand costs $1.02 less than the *ty* brand.

A two-way ANOVA with interaction

Do nutrients vary by type of food? Earlier in a scatterplot matrix, we observed a small cluster of dinners that had higher calcium values than the others. In the two-sample *t* test, we were unable to detect differences in average calcium values between the diet and regular dinners. Let's explore further here by using both food type and dinner type to define cells—that is, we request a two-way analysis of variance. Using the **List** feature in **Crosstabs**, we found that although our sample has *beef, chicken*, and *pasta* dinners, there were no *beef* dinners in the *DIET$ yes* group. (SYSTAT can analyze ANOVA48 designs with missing cells. See *SYSTAT: Statistics* for more information.)

Let's use **Select Cases** on the **Data** menu to omit the beef dinners, and then request an analysis of variance for a 2-by-2 design (*DIET$ yes* and *no* by *chicken* and *pasta*).

- In the Main or Data window, select **Data➠Select Cases**.

- In the **Select** dialog box, select *FOOD$* as the **Variable**.

- Select <> (not equal) from the drop-down list of operators.

- For **Variable or Function**, type 'beef' (include the quotation marks).

- Click **OK** to run the command.

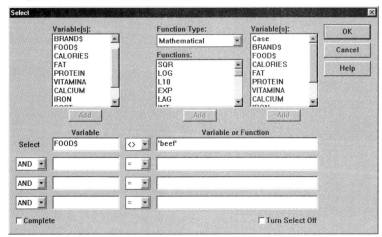

To get a bar chart of these cell means:

- Select **Graph➠Bar**.

- Select *CALCIUM* as the **Z-variable**, *DIET$* as the **Y-variable**, and *FOOD$* as the **X-variable**.

```
ANOVA
    SELECT food$ <> 'beet'
    BAR calcium * diet$ * food$
```

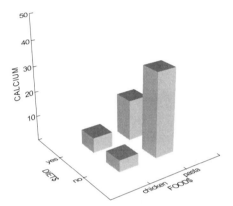

Suggestion. Try using the Dynamic Explorer to rotate this 3-D bar chart.

The boxplot in the two-sample *t* test example shows that the distributions of calcium for the *yes* and *no* groups are skewed and have unequal spreads. Let's use a power transformation of *CALCIUM* and look at the bar chart again.

- Return to the **Bar** dialog box.

- Click **Axes** and select **Z-Axis** from the list.

- Select **Power** in the **Transformations** group.

```
BAR calcium * diet$  * food$ / ZPOW
```

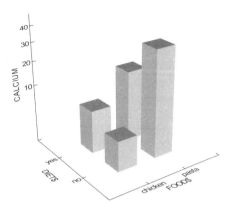

Before requesting the analysis of variance, we'll transform *CALCIUM*, taking the square root of each value.

- In the Main or Data window, select **Data➟Transform➟Let**.

- In the **Let** dialog box, select *CALCIUM* as the **Variable**, select **SQR** from the list of mathematical functions, and select *CALCIUM* from the variable list on the right to add it to the expression. The **Variable** or **Expression** box should now look like this: SQR(CALCIUM).

- Click **OK** to run the command.

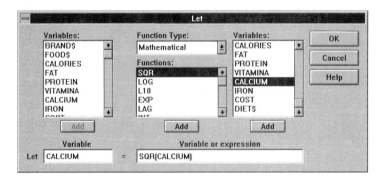

- Now request the analysis of variance, repeating the steps in the last example, except that here we use both *DIET$* and *FOOD$* as **Factor variables.**

```
ANOVA
   CATEGORY diet$ food$
   LET calcium = SQR(calcium)
   DEPEND calcium
   ESTIMATE
```

```
Categorical values encountered during processing are:
DIET$ (2 levels)
   no , yes
FOOD$ (2 levels)
   chicken , pasta

Dep Var: CALCIUM N: 22 Multiple R:  0.804 Squared multiple R:  0.647

                      Analysis of Variance
Source          Sum-of-Squares  DF  Mean-Square     F-Ratio      P

DIET$                    1.807   1        1.807       1.432   0.247
FOOD$                   39.298   1       39.298      31.136   0.000
DIET$*FOOD$              7.908   1        7.908       6.266   0.022

Error                   22.719  18        1.262
```

Since we have a significant *DIET$* by *FOOD$* interaction, we should be careful about interpreting main effects. The main effect for *DIET$* doesn't appear to be significant ($p = 0.247$)—but let's look at a scatterplot and see if that tells us anything more.

- Select **Graph➟Scatterplot.**

- Select *CALCIUM* for the **Y-variable** and *DIET$* for the **Grouping variable.** (SYSTAT will automatically use the case number as the X-variable.)

- Select **Overlay multiple graphs into a single frame.**

- Click **Appearance** and select **Symbol and Label** from the drop-down list.

- In the **Symbol and Label** dialog box, select **Display case labels** and select *FOOD$* as the case label variable.

- Click **Continue** to return to the main dialog box and then click **OK**.

```
PLOT calcium / OVERLAY GROUP=diet$ LABEL=food$
```

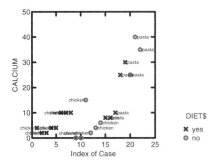

The scatterplot shows that all of the dinners with a *CALCIUM* value over 20 are pasta dinners (which is consistent with the significant main effect for *FOOD$*)—but it also shows that the highest values are also regular (*DIET$=no*) dinners. This suggests that further investigation might be warranted.

You can use SYSTAT's advanced hypothesis testing capability to request Bonferroni adjusted probabilities for tests of pairwise mean differences. (See *SYSTAT: Statistics*.)

Summary

The first step in any data analysis is to look at your data. SYSTAT provides a wide variety of graphs that can help you identify possible relationships between variables, spot outliers that may unduly affect results, and reveal patterns that may suggest data transformations for more meaningful analysis.

SYSTAT also provides a wide variety of statistical procedures for analyzing your data. We've covered some of the most common and basic statistical techniques in this chapter, but we've barely scratched the surface.

Data Files

Leland Wilkinson, Laszlo Engelman, and Michael Pechnyo

You can create a new SYSTAT data file by entering data in the Data window or by importing data saved in another application. SYSTAT can open data files saved in the following formats:

- SYSTAT, FASTAT, and MYSTAT (*.SYS*)
- SPSS (*.SAV*)
- Excel (*.XLS*)
- Lotus 1-2-3 (*.WKS*, *.WK1*)
- dBASE (*.DBF*)
- DIF files (*.DIF*)
- ASCII text (*.DAT*, *.TXT*)

You can select **File**➡**Open** to open a file saved in any of the above formats, and you can select **File**➡**Save** to save data in any of these formats (except SPSS). With commands, the USE and SAVE commands open and save SYSTAT data files. To open and save files in other formats, use IMPORT and EXPORT.

Select **Data**➡**Merge** to merge files side by side, combining variables from the two files. Select **Data**➡**Append** to merge files end to end, adding more cases for the same variables.

Select **Data**➡**Transpose** to transpose the cases and variables of a file, changing rows to columns and vice versa.

To create a new data file by entering data in the Data window, see Chapter 5.

Opening and Saving Data Files

The Data window
Opening data files
Saving data files

Merging, Appending, and Transposing Data Files

Merging files side by side (adding variables)
Merging files end to end (adding cases)
Transposing files

Data Files

Opening and Saving Data Files

A SYSTAT data file includes not only the data, but the name and type of each variable. You can create a new SYSTAT data file by entering data in the Data window or by importing data from another application.

SYSTAT can open data files saved in the following formats:

- SYSTAT, FASTAT, and MYSTAT (*.SYS)
- SPSS (*.SAV)
- Excel (*.XLS)
- Lotus 1-2-3 (*.WKS, *.WK1)
- dBASE (*.DBF)
- DIF files (*.DIF)
- ASCII text (*.DAT, *.TXT)

 For information on creating and editing data files in the Data window, see Chapter 5.

The Data window

The active data file is displayed in the Data window, where you can also enter and edit data, run transformations, and select subsets of cases.

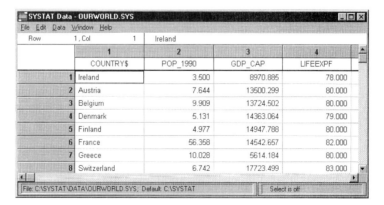

- To view the active data file in the Data window, select
  Window➠**Data** or type EDIT at the command prompt.

- To open an empty Data window in which you can start entering new
  data, select **File**➠**New**➠**Data**, or type NEW at the command prompt.

- To automatically display the Data window every time you open a data
  file, select **Edit**➠**Options** and select the **Open data in Data Editor**
  option.

☞   To display the command prompt in the Main window, select
  Edit➠**Options** and select **Command Prompt**.

Opening data files

To open a SYSTAT, SPSS, spreadsheet, database, or ASCII data file,
select **File**➠**Open** in the Main window.

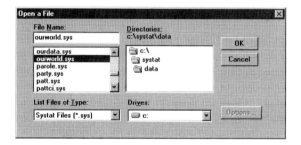

SYSTAT data files (*.*SYS*) are listed by default. To open a file of a different
type, select its type from the drop-down list under **List Files of Type**.

Note: *SYSTAT lists files with the default extension for each file type (for example,*
       *.XLS for Excel). To open a file with a different extension, select the file type
       and then type the full name, including the nonstandard extension. For
       *example, to open an Excel file named GIZMO.BAK, select **Excel (*.xls)** and*
       *type **gizmo.bak** (or ***.bak**).*

If you are opening a text, spreadsheet, or database file from another application, click **Options** to open the **Import Options** dialog box.

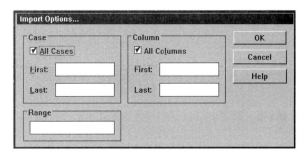

You can import all cases and columns, or you can import a range by entering the number of the first and last case or column (for example, cases 50 through 100). For spreadsheet data, you can import a range of cells. Use the same method for specifying ranges as you would in the spreadsheet application.

Note: *SYSTAT does its best to import data based on the options you specify. However, depending on the type of data, not all options apply. For example, you cannot import a range of cells when importing dBASE files.*

Using commands

You can open an existing SYSTAT data file with the **USE** command:

    USE *filename*

For all other types of files, including spreadsheet, database, and ASCII text files, use **IMPORT**:

    IMPORT *filename*/TYPE=*filetype* ROWS=*m .. n,*
                    COLUMNS=*n* RANGE=*rangename,*

where *filename* is the name of the input data file that was written by one of the specified applications, and *filetype* is the type of file you are importing.

File = *filename*   Specify the name of the file you are importing. We recommend that you specify the entire path name of the file. In this version of SYSTAT, you no longer have to enclose filenames in quotation marks.

Type = *filetype*   Specify the type of file. Options include SPSS, EXCEL, EXCEL2, EXCEL4, LOTUS, LOTUS2, DBASE2, DBASE3, DBASE4, DIF, MAP, and ASCII.

Columns = *n*   With spreadsheet files, you can specify the number of columns to read.

Range = *rangename*   Import only the range given by *rangename* (for spreadsheet files). The default is the entire file.

Rows = *m .. n*   Choose which rows (cases) to import. The default is all rows.

It is recommended that you specify a file to save before using IMPORT:

```
SAVE newtest
 IMPORT test / TYPE=ASCII
```

Note: *For information on importing and working with .MAP files, see SYSTAT: Graphics.*

Importing ASCII text files

An ASCII text file is created in a word processor or text editor and contains text and numbers with no special characters or formatting. Before you try to read in an ASCII file, check the following:

- Each case is written as one line.
- The variable names are written at the top of the file and are separated by spaces and/or a comma.
- The values of the variables are separated by one or more spaces (blanks) and/or a comma.
- Missing numerical data are flagged by a period (.) and missing character data are marked by a space enclosed within quotation marks (" ").

For example, suppose that you have the following data in a text file named *TEST.DAT*. Note that the file contains variable names and follows the SYSTAT convention of adding a dollar sign to the names of string variables.

```
NAME$           SEX$      AGE
Johnson         male      35
'Bob Smith'     male      43
Williamson      female    54
```

To open this file, select **File➠Open**, select **ASCII Text (*.txt)** for the file type, and specify *TEST.DAT* as the file to open, as shown below.

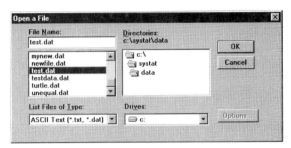

With commands:

```
SAVE newtest
IMPORT test / TYPE=ASCII
```

Reading variable names

If the first line of data contains only labels (character strings), SYSTAT uses them as the SYSTAT variable names. If a variable name ends with a dollar sign ($), SYSTAT reads the variable as a string variable, even if it contains numeric data. If a variable name does not end with $, SYSTAT determines the variable's type from the first data value. If there are no variable names in the source file and if the first row contains numeric information, SYSTAT creates the variable names *VAR(1)*, *VAR(2)*, ..., *VAR(N)*.

Blank cells. SYSTAT considers blank cells to be numeric. Therefore, if any blank cells are in the first row in the spreadsheet file, they are considered to be missing numeric values. This means that the first row is interpreted as data rather than variable names.

Long variable names. Long variable names are truncated. Also, any characters other than letters and digits are removed from the name. The truncation is done before those names are processed into SYSTAT variable names. Therefore, any information at the end of long variable names is lost. SYSTAT numbers variable names that would be identical when truncated.

Subscripted variables. Variable names followed explicitly by subscripts (*i*), where *i* ranges from 1 to *n*, are subscripted when converted. String variable names can also be subscripted. The usual restriction for subscripted variable names applies—that is, the total length of the variable name, including the letter(s) for the name, the dollar sign ($), and the parentheses, cannot exceed 12 characters. See Chapter 5 for more information.

Reading dBASE files

When specifying a range of rows or records for import, deleted records are included in the count. This is consistent with the way dBASE goes to records by record number. For dBASE III and IV, SYSTAT changes logical fields to character fields. The character used for the dBASE logical value is retained. Also, SYSTAT skips memo fields. A warning message is given when this occurs.

Date fields are converted into numeric values. For example, if your dBASE file contained a value for November 2, 1987, it would be stored as 19871102. SYSTAT converts this to $0.19871102E + 8$.

Importing spreadsheet files (Excel and Lotus)

You can specify a named range of cells to read from the spreadsheet. Leading blank rows and columns are skipped. You can import worksheets only if they are saved in row and column order. (Lotus uses this form by default. It can, however, read files stored in other orders.) Numeric results of formulas are imported; a warning is given to show that the data may not be accurate (if numbers were changed and the spreadsheet was saved before recalculating, the values saved may not reflect the changes that were made). To import selected columns, specify the column numbers, not variable names or alphabetic headers.

Data Interchange Format (DIF) files

Logical values in a DIF file have the values 0 and 1 to represent false or true, and are stored as 0 or 1.

Saving data files

To save a new data file, or to save an existing data file under a new name, select **File➠Save As**.

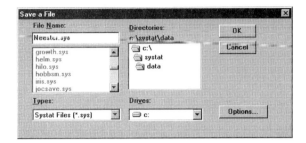

Specify a directory and filename. Filenames can be up to eight characters long, plus a three-letter extension, and they can contain letters or numbers. Use underscores for spaces. Filenames cannot include periods, aside from the period that separates the filename from the extension.

When saving SYSTAT data files, you can click **Options** to specify a matrix type. Available types include rectangular, SSCP, covariance, correlation, dissimilarity, and similarity.

To save or export the data in a different format, such as a spreadsheet or database file, select the desired format under **Save File as Type**. See "Exporting data" below for more information on exporting data files.

Note: *When you save a file and do not specify an extension, SYSTAT automatically adds the default extension for that file type (for example, *.SYS for SYSTAT data files).*

To save an updated version of an existing data file under the existing name (for example, after running a transformation), use **File➠Save Data**.

Using commands

You can save a SYSTAT data file with the SAVE command:

```
SAVE filename
RUN
```

To save data in a different format, such as Excel or dBASE, use EXPORT:

```
EXPORT filename (varlist) / TYPE=filetype  ROWS=m .. n
```

where *filename* is the name of the exported data file you are creating. (SYSTAT automatically assigns the appropriate extension to the filename depending on the specified file type.) For example,

```
EXPORT lotusfil / TYPE=lotus2
```

The following options are available:

File = *filename*   Specify the name of the file you are exporting. It is recommended that you specify the entire path name.

Type = *filetype*   Specify the *filetype* of the file to export. Options include EXCEL, EXCEL2, EXCEL4, LOTUS, LOTUS2, DBASE2, DBASE3, DBASE4, DIF, and ASCII.

Exporting data

SYSTAT can export files in the following formats:

ASCII. Data are written in rectangular format, like a spreadsheet, in plain text rather than binary.

dBASE. Because dBASE requires fixed-format numeric fields, EXPORT first checks to find the best format to use for the numbers. The fixed format also limits the size of the values that dBASE accepts. If a number is larger than the field size allowed, SYSTAT writes the largest value that fits in that field. Missing values are inserted as blanks. Dollar signs ($) are illegal characters in dBASE variable names and are replaced by underscores (_).

Excel and Lotus. SYSTAT writes missing values as blanks, string values without trailing blanks, and variable names exactly as they appear in the SYSTAT file.

Data Interchange Format (DIF). Missing values are written as SYSTAT missing values. String values are written without trailing blanks.

Single or double precision

You can save SYSTAT data files in single or double precision. Double precision is the default and tells SYSTAT to save numeric values using 8 bytes per value, retaining up to 15 significant decimal digits. Single precision stores values in 4 bytes, which ensures approximately 7 significant digits. SYSTAT stores all character values in 12-byte strings. If you want to save in single precision, select **Single** in **Edit➠Options**, or specify the **SINGLE** option with the **SAVE** command:

```
SAVE filename / SINGLE
```

File comments

You can store a comment in your data file. SYSTAT displays the comment every time you use the file in order to document your data files—for example, include the source of the data, the date they were entered, the particulars of the variables, etc. The comment can be as many lines as you want. If your command is too long to fit on one line, use commas to continue onto subsequent lines. If you use commands, enclose each line in single or double quotation marks:

```
SAVE filename /,
       'Edited by Joe on Jan. 10', 'Data from Dr. Jones'
```

Merging, Appending, and Transposing Data Files

This section describes how to manipulate files, including merging files side by side, merging files end to end, transposing rows to columns, and unpacking repeated measures on a single record into one record per measure.

There are two ways to merge files: *horizontally* (side by side, joining different variables for the same cases) and *vertically* (end to end, adding more cases for the same variables). **Data➠Merge** performs horizontal concatenization:

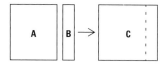

With commands:

```
SAVE c
MERGE a b
```

Data➠Append performs vertical concatenization:

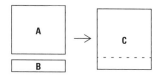

With commands:

```
SAVE c
APPEND a b
```

You can merge or append only two files at one time. If you have more than two files, merge them successively, two at a time, until they are all part of one file.

Merging files side by side (adding variables)

Use **Data➤Merge** to join two SYSTAT files horizontally (side by side). SYSTAT joins the cases from the two files in order, matching the first case from each file, the second case from each file, and so on, until the last case.

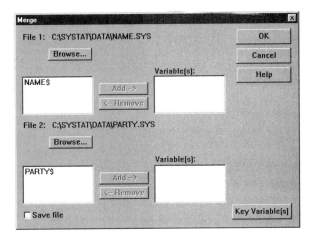

Click **Browse** to specify each of the files to be merged. If one file has more observations than the other, SYSTAT assigns missing values to the variables from the shorter file for all of the unmatched observations. If the same variable name appears in both files, SYSTAT uses the values from the second file, thus overwriting the values for the same variable in the first file.

Optionally, you can select the variables from each file to be included in the merged data file. If no variables are selected, all variables from both files are included. You can also select a key variable as described below.

The command syntax is

```
MERGE filename1 (varlist1) filename2 (varlist2) /,
       keyvar list
```

where *varlist1* and *varlist2* are optional—use them to select a subset of the variables in any order you want. The list of key variables is also optional.

Selecting a subset of the variables

You can subset and reorder variables when you merge:

```
MERGE moe(X Y Z) joe(C A B)
MERGE moe(Z) joe
MERGE moe joe(A B)
```

The first example merges two files, extracting variables X, Y, and Z from MOE and variables C, A, and B from JOE. The second selects variable Z from MOE and all of the variables in JOE. The third selects all of the variables from MOE and A and B from JOE.

Merging by key variables

You can merge files using a key (index) variable (or several key variables). In a drug study, for example, you might have demographic data for the patients in one file and laboratory test results in another file. If both files contain the patients' last names (ID) you could use the patients' names (or ID's) as the key variable to link each patient's demographics with his or her test results.

You must sort both files on the key variable(s) before merging. SYSTAT matches the cases that have the same values for the key variable(s) and joins them in a case in the new file. If there are values for the key variable(s) in one file and not in the other, the merged file records missing values for the variable whose file did not have values. In the following example, we start with files A and B and create file C:

```
SAVE c
MERGE a b / key
```

File A

Key	X
1	10
2	20

File B

Key	Y
1	100
3	300

File C

Key	X	Y
1	10	100
2	20	.
3	.	300

Generating replicates of a record	One key variable can have many occurrences of a value that appears only once in the other file. For example, you may need to join information about a mother to the data records for each of her children. For this, SYSTAT replicates the values from the *MOMS* file. For example, using the *FAMILY ID* as the *key*,

File KIDS			File MOMS			File PAIRS		
FAMILY	**X**		**FAMILY**	**Y**		**FAMILY**	**X**	**Y**
1	10		1	100		1	1	100
1	1		2	140			0	
1	12					1	1	100
2	6						1	
2	9					1	1	100
							2	
						2	6	140
						2	9	140

3.1
A simple side-by-side merge

This example demonstrates merging two files. One file, *NAME*, contains the names of men who have been presidential candidates in the variable *NAME$*. The second file, *PARTY*, contains their party affiliations in the variable *PARTY$*:

NAME data file:	**NAME$**	*PARTY data file:*	**PARTY$**
	Eisenhower		Republican
	Stevenson		Democrat
	Kennedy		Democrat
	Goldwater		Republican
	Johnson		Democrat
	Humphrey		Democrat
	McGovern		Democrat
	Nixon		Republican
	Ford		Republican
	Carter		Democrat
	Reagan		Republican
	Bush		Republican
	Clinton		Democrat

A one-to-one correspondence exists between the cases in the two files. The first case from the *NAME* file corresponds with the first case in the *PARTY* file. To merge these files, select **Data▥▶Merge** and specify *NAME* and *PARTY* as the files to merge.

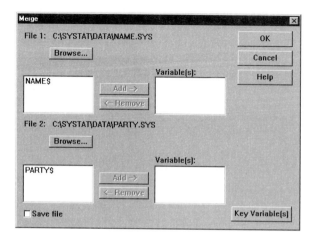

Since no variables are selected, all variables from both files are included in the merged data file. With commands:

```
SAVE candidat
MERGE name party
```

3.2
Merging with
a key variable

This example merges the files *CANDIDAT* and *ELECTION* by the variable *NAME$*. *CANDIDAT* was created in the example above. The data in the *ELECTION* file are shown below.

NAME$	LOSER$	YEAR
Eisenhower	Stevenson	1952
Eisenhower	Stevenson	1956
Kennedy	Nixon	1960
Johnson	Goldwater	1964
Nixon	Humphrey	1968
Nixon	McGovern	1972
Carter	Ford	1976
Reagan	Carter	1980
Reagan	Mondale	1984
Bush	Dukakis	1988
Clinton	Bush	1992

Both data files included in the merge must first be sorted by the key variable *NAME$*. You can do this using **Data➠Sort** or the SORT command:

```
USE candidat
SAVE candsort
SORT name$

USE election
SAVE elecsort
SORT name$
```

To merge the two files, select **Data➠Merge**, specify the *sorted* data files *CANDSORT* and *ELECSORT* as the files to merge, and select **Key Variable** to specify *NAME$* as the key variable. With commands:

```
SAVE mergfile
MERGE elecsort candsort / name$
```

Now list the cases in the file:

```
Case number NAME$        LOSER$        YEAR         PARTY$
     1      Bush         Dukakis       1988       Republican
     2      Carter       Ford          1976       Democrat
     3      Clinton      Bush          1992       Democrat
     4      Eisenhower   Stevenson     1952       Republican
     5      Eisenhower   Stevenson     1956       Republican
     6      Ford                        .         Republican
     7      Goldwater                   .         Republican
     8      Humphrey                    .         Democrat
     9      Johnson      Goldwater     1964       Democrat
    10      Kennedy      Nixon         1960       Democrat
    11      McGovern                    .         Democrat
    12      Nixon        Humphrey      1968       Republican
    13      Nixon        McGovern      1972       Republican
    14      Reagan       Carter        1980       Republican
    15      Reagan       Mondale       1984       Republican
    16      Stevenson                   .         Democrat
```

The missing values occur where entries in the candidate file have no matching value for *NAME$* in the election data file (for example, Ford, Goldwater, Humphrey, etc., did not win). The election file has three names that have more than one entry: Eisenhower, Nixon, and Reagan. In these cases, SYSTAT replicates the corresponding values from the candidate file.

Note: *If you select a subset of variables while merging, you need not include the key variable(s) in both subsets (of course, they must be in both files). The following, for example, is valid:*
MERGE indoor(time,loc,co2) outdoor(nox)/time,loc

Merging files end to end (adding cases)

Use **Data➡Append** to join two files vertically. SYSTAT places cases from the second file you name below those from the first.

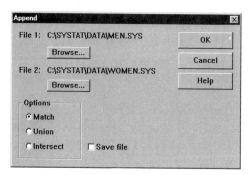

Click **Browse** to select the each of the files to be appended. If the two files do not contain the same variables in the same order, you can select **Union** to include all variables or **Intersect** to include only those variables appearing in both files. For example, if *filename1* has variables *A*, *B*, and *D* and *filename2* has variables *A*, *B*, and *C*:

- **Match** displays an error message because the two files do not contain the same variables in the same order.
- **Union** writes a new file with variables *A*, *B*, *C*, and *D*. Values of *C* are missing value codes for *filename1*, and values of *D* are missing value codes for *filename2*.
- **Intersection** includes only variables *A* and *B* in the new file.

With commands:

```
APPEND filename1 filename2 / MATCH or UNION or,
                             INTERSECTION
```

To save the appended files permanently, use **SAVE** before **APPEND**. For example,

```
SAVE finance
APPEND sales updates

SAVE people
APPEND males females
```

3.3
A simple
end-to-end
merge

Following are two SYSTAT files, named *MEN* and *WOMEN*:

MEN			WOMEN	
SEX$	**AGE**		**SEX$**	**AGE**
Male	18		Female	23
Male	35		Female	40
Male	24		Female	40
Male	20		Female	31

To append them end to end, select **Data⟶Append** and select the two files to be appended. With commands:

```
SAVE sexes
APPEND women men
```

SYSTAT places the cases from *WOMEN* before those from *MEN* because *WOMEN* are listed first in the APPEND command.

Case	SEX$	AGE
1	Female	23
2	Female	40
3	Female	26
4	Female	31
5	Male	18
6	Male	35
7	Male	24
8	Male	20

Transposing files

Use **Data⟶Transpose** to transpose the cases and variables of a file, changing rows to columns and vice versa.

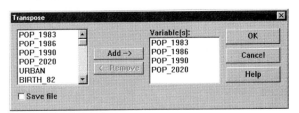

You can select variables to include in the transposed data file. If no variables are selected, all numeric variables are included. You cannot transpose string variables, except for a variable named *LABEL$*—its values are used to label the variables in the transposed file. Any other string variables are dropped from the transposed data file.

When there is no *LABEL$* variable, the names for the columns in the new transposed file are *COL(01–N)*, where *n* is the number of cases in the original matrix.

With commands:

```
USE file1
SAVE file2
TRANSPOSE varlist
```

Varlist is optional and may include only *LABEL$* and numeric variables.

Transposing a symmetric matrix (for example, correlations) is unnecessary, since the transpose of a symmetric matrix is the original matrix.

 Matrix can transpose large files depending on memory space available. For more information, see Chapter 12.

4

Saving and Printing Output and Graphics

SYSTAT allows you to save and print your results using the **File** menu. Using these options, you can:

– Save data and output in text files.

– Save charts in a number of graphics formats.

– Print data, output, and charts.

– Save output from selected statistical procedures in SYSTAT data files.

In addition, you can use **Edit➡Options** or the OUTPUT command to automatically direct subsequent output to a specified file or to the printer.

You can open your saved output and graphs in word processors and other applications. Virtually any application can handle text output, and SYSTAT offers a number of graph formats that are compatible with most Windows applications.

Often, the easiest way to transfer results to other applications is by copying and pasting using the Windows clipboard. This works for charts as well as text, although results vary depending on the type of data and the target application.

Saving Output and Graphs

Saving output in the Main window
Directing output to a file or printer
Saving results from statistical analyses
Saving graphs

Printing Data, Output, and Charts

Setting up the printer
Exporting results to other applications

Saving Output and Graphs

In any SYSTAT window, select **File➠Save** to open a dialog box that allows you to save the contents of the current window. SYSTAT saves data and output in text files, and saves charts in a number of graphics formats. You can also save output from selected statistical procedures in SYSTAT data files.

You can use **Edit➠Options** or the OUTPUT command to automatically direct subsequent output to a specified file or to the printer.

Note: To display the command prompt, select **Edit ➠ Options** and select **Command Prompt**.

Saving output in the Main window

SYSTAT displays statistical output in the Main window. Select **File➠Save As** to save the contents of the window in a text file.

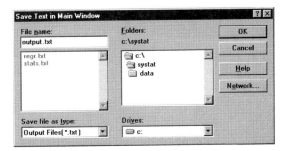

Specify a directory and filename for the output file. You can edit the saved output file in any word processor or similar application.

Note: If the command prompt is displayed, commands are displayed in the Main window along with the results and are also saved in the output file.

Directing output to a file or printer

You can use **Edit➡Options** or the OUTPUT command to automatically direct your output to a text file or to the printer.

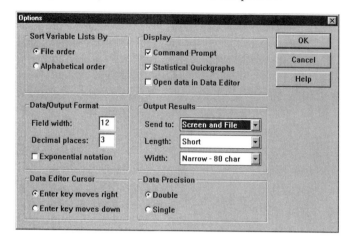

In the **Output Results** group, select **Screen and File** to send subsequent output to a text file, or select **Screen and Printer** to send output directly to the printer.

Note: *The **Screen and Printer** option is intended for printing to a local printer only. If you are printing to a network printer, the output will not print until you close the output file by typing **OUTPUT** * or quitting SYSTAT.*

With commands:

```
OUTPUT <filename> | VIDEO or * | PRINTER or @ |
                    [ /COMMANDS, ERRORS, WARNINGS ]
```

For example, the commands below send a listing of cases, including commands, to the text file *MYFILE.DAT*. The OUTPUT * command at the end closes the text file so that subsequent output is sent to the screen only.

```
USE ourworld.sys
OUTPUT myfile /COMMANDS
LIST country$ health
OUTPUT *
```

Saving output and data in BASIC

In BASIC, you can use the PRINT command to list cases without case numbers and variable names, or you can use the PUT command to save the contents of the current data file to a text file. See the examples in Chapter 11 for more information.

> *Note:* *You can use **Edit ➡ Options** or the PAGE, FORMAT, and NOTES commands to annotate and control the appearance of your output. See Chapter 9 for more information.*

Saving results from statistical analyses

Many procedures include an option (**Save** or **Save File**) that saves the results of the analysis in a SYSTAT data file. The contents of the file depend on the analysis. For example:

– **Correlations** can save Pearson and Spearman correlations.
– **Factor Analysis** can save factor scores, residuals, and a number of other statistics.
– **Linear Regression** can save residuals and diagnostics for each case.
– **Basic Statistics** can save selected statistics for each level of one or more grouping variables.
– **Crosstabs** can save the count in each cell for later use as table input.

Check each procedure to see what is saved.

Saving graphs

SYSTAT displays graphs in a Graph window. To save the current graph, select **File ➡ Save As** and specify a filename.

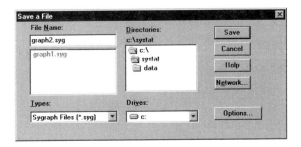

By default, the file is saved as a Sygraph file (*.*SYG*). You can select a different file type from the drop-down list. Available formats include:

- SYGRAPH, SYSTAT's native chart format (*.*SYG*)

- Windows bitmap (*.*BMP*)

- Windows metafile (*.*WMF*)

- Encapsulated postscript (*.*EPS*)

- Tagged image file format (*.*TIF*)

- Macintosh PICT (*.*PCT*)

- Computer graphics metafile (*.*CGM*)

- JPEG

- GIF

Depending on the graphic format, you can select from a number of options when saving the file. See the online Help for details.

Printing Data, Output, and Charts

In any SYSTAT window, select **File**➠**Print** to open the **Print** dialog box, which enables you to print your data, output, charts, and command files.

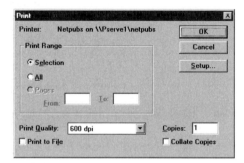

For data, output, and command files, you can choose to print the current selection, the entire contents of the window, or a specified page range. If you are printing a graph, you can print all graphs or just the current one.

You can specify the print quality in dots per inch (DPI). (Generally, you want to specify the maximum DPI for your printer.) If you select more than one copy, some printers allow you to collate the output.

Note: *While SYSTAT allows you to print your data directly from the Data window, you have more control over the appearance of the output if you first list the data in the Main window, and then print or save from there. See Chapter 7 and Chapter 11 for examples.*

Sending output to the printer automatically

You can use **Edit**➠**Options** or the OUTPUT command to send output to the printer automatically. See "Directing output to a file or printer" on p. 78.

Setting up the printer

You can control various printer settings, such as page size and orientation. The available options vary for different printers. To open the **Print Setup** dialog box, select **File➠Print Setup**.

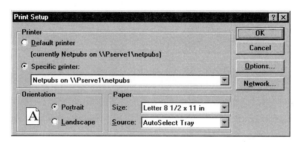

If more than one printer is installed on your system or network, you can choose which one to print to. You can also specify paper size and orientation—portrait (tall) or landscape (wide).

Note: *The orientation selected in the Print Setup dialog box determines the orientation of the Page view in the Graph window.*

Exporting results to other applications

You can open your saved output and charts in word processors and other applications. In SYSTAT, save the file in a format that the other application can handle; then open or import the file in the other application. Virtually any application can handle text output, and SYSTAT offers a number of graph formats that are compatible with most Windows applications. See the target application's documentation for specifics.

For example, you can save a SYSTAT graph as a Windows metafile (*.WMF*), then insert or import the metafile into most Windows word processor. (In Microsoft Word 6, select **Insert➠Picture.**)

Exporting results using the clipboard

Often, the easiest way to transfer results to other applications is by copying and pasting using the Windows clipboard. This works for charts as well as text, although results vary depending on the target application.

- In SYSTAT, select the output or chart.
- Select **Edit**➠**Copy**.
- In the other application, click the cursor where you want the output to appear.
- Select **Edit**➠**Paste**.

If you have problems with **Paste**, try using **Edit**➠**Paste Special** in the target application. With **Paste Special**, you can specify whether you want to paste the clipboard contents as text or a Windows metafile (graphic). (Note that **Paste Special** is not available in all applications.)

Note: *In order for columns to line up properly, you must highlight text output after you paste it and apply a fixed-pitch font (for example, Courier or Courier New). Or, use **Paste Special** to paste the text as a metafile graphic.*

Entering and Editing Data

5

Leland Wilkinson, Laszlo Engelman, and Mark Bjerknes

You use the Data window to enter, edit, and save data. Entering data is a straightforward process: simply type the variable names and then type the data.

You must enter a variable name at the top of a column before you can enter any data values in that column. To enter non-numeric (string) data, you must first type a variable name that ends with a dollar sign ($); this defines the variable as a string variable.

You can edit data to correct errors, change variable names, or add, delete, or move variables or cases. SYSTAT provides a number of tools to help you edit your data. You can locate specific variables, find cases that meet specific conditions, or specify an ID variable to identify each case in the Data window.

In addition to the usual rectangular, case-by-variable organization, SYSTAT accommodates two other data structures: tabulated form and matrix input

You can transform, manipulate, and define your data in a number of other ways:

- To open an existing data file, including data files saved in other applications, see Chapter 3.
- To transform existing variables and derive new variables, see Chapter 6.
- To define labels that group cases, order the resulting groups, and are displayed in output, see Chapter 8.
- To combine two data files to create a new data file, or transpose cases and variables in a data file, see Chapter 3.

Entering and Editing Data

The Data Window

Data file structure

Entering Data

Editing Data

Moving around in the Data window

Correcting data and changing variable names

Adding variables or cases

Dropping variables

Deleting cases

Cutting and pasting variables or cases

Finding data

Case ID

Deriving new variables

Cell display format

Other Data Structures

The Data Window

You use the Data window to enter, edit, and save data. You can also run transformations and view the results, select subsets of cases, and transpose, append, and merge data files as described in this and the following chapters.

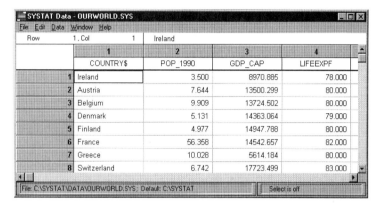

- To view the Data window, use **Window**➠**Data** or type EDIT at the command prompt.

- To open an empty Data window where you can start entering new data, use **File**➠**New**➠**Data**, or type NEW at the command prompt.

- To open an existing data file, use **File**➠**Open**. See Chapter 3 for more information.

- To automatically display the Data window every time you open a data file, use **Edit**➠**Options** and select the **Open data in Data Editor** option.

 To display the command prompt in the Main window, use **Edit**➠**Options** and select **Command Prompt**.

Note: *The Data window does not have all of the functionality of a typical "spreadsheet" such as Excel or Lotus 1-2-3. For example, you cannot store formulas in individual cells. In addition, rows are always cases, and columns are always variables.*

Data file structure

SYSTAT uses data organized in rows and columns. The rows are *cases* and the columns are *variables*. A case contains information for one unit of analysis, such as a person, an animal, a business, or a jet engine. Variables are the information collected for each case, such as age, body weight, profits, or fuel consumption.

For example, the data from the file *OURWORLD.SYS* is shown. Each row (case) has data for one of 15 countries, and the columns (variables) include the name of the country, population in 1990, gross domestic product per capita, years of life expectancy estimates for females, literacy, type of country, and the number of McDonald's restaurants.

1	2	3	4	5 6	7
Austria	7.644	13500.299	80	98 Europe	30.0
Belgium	9.909	13724.502	80	98 Europe	12.0
Denmark	5.131	14363.064	79	99 Europe	16.0
Finland	4.977	14947.788	80	100 Europe	9.0
France	56.358	14542.657	82	99 Europe	193.0
Greece	10.028	5614.184	80	95 Europe	1.0
Ireland	3.500	8970.885	78	99 Europe	14.0
Switzerland	6.742	17723.499	83	99 Europe	25.0
Spain	39.269	10153.121	82	97 Europe	42.0
UK	57.366	14259.401	79	99 Europe	400.0
Italy	57.664	13930.604	81	93 Europe	14.0
Sweden	8.526	15563.332	81	99 Europe	56.0
Portugal	10.354	6963.158	78	83 Europe	2.0
Netherlands	14.936	13785.455	81	99 Europe	69.0
WGermany	62.168	15211.956	81	99 Europe	391.0

When data are arranged in rows and columns like these data, and then stored in a file, we call the file a *cases-by-variables* or *rectangular* data file.

Variable names

You must assign a name to every variable. Variables names are used to specify analysis and to label output. Variable names can contain up to eight letters or numbers and must begin with a letter. For example, the variables shown above from the *OURWORLD* data file have the following names:

Col.	Variable Name	Description
1	*COUNTRY$*	Name of country
2	*POP_1990*	Population in 1990 in millions
3	*GDP_CAP*	Gross domestic product per capita (in U.S. dollars)
4	*LIFEEXPF*	Life expectancy of females (in years)
5	*LITERACY*	Percentage of the population who can read
6	*GROUP$*	Words to indicate type of country
7	*MCDONALD*	Number of McDonald's restaurants

– Names of character or string variables *must* end with a dollar sign (although the dollar sign does not count as one of the eight letters).

– The underscore character (_) is used to indicate a space within a name.

Variable names, unlike character values, are not case sensitive. If you type "govern," SYSTAT automatically uses "*GOVERN.*"

Numeric versus string variables

SYSTAT accepts numbers and characters as data. The variable *LIFEEXPF* is a *numeric* variable: it contains numbers (72, 75, ...) that represent years of life. *GROUP$* is a *character* variable: it contains alphanumeric characters that identify types of countries.

Numeric variables. Numeric variables can have up to 15 digits. Use a minus sign for negative numbers. SYSTAT will analyze numbers like these:

```
   1234.5678901      150      0.675843      -1.8394
```

You may also use exponential notation for very large or very small numbers. For example, for 1.5E4 and 1.5E–4:

$$1.5E4 \qquad = 1.5 \times 10^4 = 15000$$
$$1.5E\text{-}4 \qquad = 1.5 \times 10^{-4} = .00015$$

Character (string) variables. Character or string variables contain text information. A character value may be up to 12 characters long and contain any common typewriter characters. Some valid values are:

```
male      New York      $)#($&%^/#@
female    Chicago       !@#$%^&*)?($
```

When storing values of string variables, SYSTAT differentiates upper and lower case—"europe" is not the same as "EUROPE" nor "Europe." If you include numbers within character values, SYSTAT treats them as text. You cannot do numerical analyses on them.

Subscripted variables

You can use subscripted variables when you want to have an easy way to specify a subset of variables. For example, if you have ten questions, you could simply name them *Q(1)*, *Q(2)*, ..., *Q(10)* (or, for character variables, *Q$(1)*, *Q$(2)*, and so on).

You can then refer to the range of variables using subscript notation, such as:

```
STATS Q(1 .. 10)
```

to get descriptive statistics for the responses to all ten questions. SYSTAT will perform an analyses on all the variables from *Q(1)* to *Q(10)* regardless of the order in which they appear in the file.

Subscripted names can be used for numeric or character variables as long as the total length of the variable name does not exceed 12 characters, including the parentheses and the dollar signs for character variables.

Grouping variables

A **grouping variable** contains a value that identifies group membership for each case. The values of these variables are used to separate the cases into groups (or cells) in subsequent analyses and graphs. In the *OURWORLD* data file, *GROUP$* is a character grouping variable, and *GROUP* is a numeric grouping variable: "1" for "Europe", "2" for "Islamic", and "3" for "New World." A numeric grouping variable named *SEX* might contain the number "1" for males and "2" for females. A character grouping variable *SEX$* could have the values "Male" and "Female."

Missing data

You may not have a value for a particular variable—a subject does not have a middle name, or a state failed to report their total sales. In the Data window, missing numeric values are indicated by a period; missing string values are represented by an empty cell.

Arithmetic involving missing values propagates missing values. If you add, subtract, multiply, or divide when data are missing, the result is missing. If you sort your cases using a variable with missing values, the cases with values missing on the sort variable are listed first. If you specify conditions and a value is missing, SYSTAT sets the result to missing. For example, if you specify:

```
IF agè > 21 THEN LET age$='Adult'
```

and *AGE* is missing, the value of the new variable *AGE$* is set to missing.

To perform an analyses on only those cases with no values missing, use:

```
SELECT COMPLETE
```

prior to the analysis.

Note: *If you are entering data in an ASCII text file, enter a period (.) to flag the position where a numeric value is missing. Where character data are missing in an ASCII text file, enter a blank space surrounded by single or double quotation marks.*

Maximum file size

There is no limit to the number of variables or cases your data file can contain. However, the amount of memory available on your system may impose a practical limit.

Entering Data

Entering data in the Data window is a straightforward process: simply type the variable names, following the rules for variable names described above, and then type the data. After typing each value, press Enter. You can enter data by case or by variable.

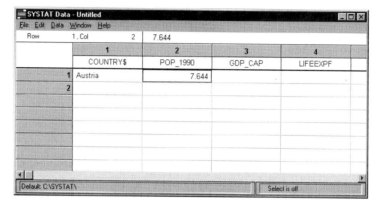

- You must enter a variable name at the top of a column before you can enter any data values in that column.

- The active cell is highlighted with a heavy border. The value of the active cell is displayed in the cell editor at the top of the Data window.

- To enter non-numeric (string) data, you must first type a variable name that ends with a dollar sign ($), to define the variable as a string variable.

Note: *Data values are not recorded until you press Enter or select another cell. To clear the Data window, making it ready for new data, use* **File➧ New➧ Data** *or type* NEW *at the command prompt.*

Entering non-numeric data

You must create a string variable before you can enter non-numeric character data such as names. You do this by adding a dollar sign ($) at the end of the variable name, for example *GROUP$*.

> **Note:** *Once you have entered a variable name, you cannot change its type from character to numeric or vice versa. If you forget to put a dollar sign at the end of a character variable name, you must delete the incorrect variable and type the correct name as a new variable.*

Entering data by case or by variable

You can enter data by case (one row at a time) or by variable (one column at a time). Select **Edit➠Options** to specify whether the cursor moves across (for case entry) or down (for variable entry) when you press Enter.

Saving data

To save your data in a SYSTAT data file, select **File➠Save** or, at the command prompt, type:

`SAVE filename`

See Chapter 3 for more information on saving data files.

Editing Data

You can edit data to correct errors, change variable names, or add, delete, or move variables or cases. SYSTAT provides a number of tools to help you edit your data. You can locate specific variables, find cases that meet specific conditions, or specify an ID variable to identify each case in the Data window.

Note: *Any changes you make to the data file are not permanent unless you save the data file.*

Moving around in the Data window

You can use either the mouse or the keyboard to move around in the Data window and to select cells, cases, or variables.

– Click the mouse in any cell to select the cell. The value of the cell is displayed in the cell editor at the top of the Data window.

– Use the scroll bars on the bottom and right side of the window to scroll through the data to see more cases and variables. Click the scroll arrows to move one case or variable at a time, or drag the icon to move to a new location in the data.

With the keyboard, you can move in all directions using the arrow keys. You can also move right and left using Tab and Shift-Tab, and move up and down using Enter and Shift-Enter (depending on how the Enter key is configured in the **Edit➠Options** dialog box).

Press	To move
Tab or right arrow	Right (one cell)
Shift-Tab or left arrow	Left
Enter or down arrow	Down
Shift-Enter or up arrow	Up
Ctrl-Home	First cell (top left)
Ctrl-End	Last cell (bottom right)
Home	Start of row
End	End of row
Page Up	Up one page
Page Down	Down one page
Ctrl-Page Down	Right one page
Ctrl-Page Up	Left one page

Note: *Use **Edit➡ Options** to specify whether the cursor moves across (for case entry) or down (for variable entry) when you press Enter.*

Selecting data

You can select cells using either the mouse or the keyboard.

- Click on the number at the top or left side of any row or column to select the row or column.

- Drag the mouse to select a range of adjacent cells, variables, or cases, or hold down the Shift key as you click on adjacent rows or columns.

- To select a range using the keyboard, hold down the Shift key and use the arrow keys to extend the selection. You can also use Shift with some shortcut key combinations; for example, Shift-End selects all the cells to the end of the current row, and Ctrl-Shift-End extends the selection to the bottom right corner.

Correcting data and changing variable names

You can easily change data values and variable names in the Data window. Simply select the cell, edit the value, and press Enter. When you select a cell, the current value is displayed in the cell editor at the top of the Data window. To replace (type over) the current value, just type the new value. To edit the current value—for example, if the cell contains a very large number and you just want to change one digit—press F2 or click an insertion point in the value in the cell editor.

Note: *You can change variable names, but you cannot change a variable's type from numeric to character or vice versa. If you want to change GROUP to a string variable, you must create a new variable GROUP$ and drop GROUP.*

Adding variables or cases

You can add new variables and/or cases to a file in the same way you entered the original data.

- To add a new variable, click the cursor in the variable name row at the top of the Data window, scroll past the last existing variable name, and type a name for the new variable.

– To add new cases, move the cursor to the first empty row and type the new data.

– To add a new variable between two existing variables, first create the variable at the end of the data file, then copy the new variable to the clipboard and paste it into the desired position. See "Cutting and pasting variables or cases" on p. 97 for details.

– To add variables or cases from *another* file, use **Data▸Merge** or **Data▸Append**. See Chapter 3 for more information.

Dropping variables

To delete one or more variables, select the variables in the Data window as described above and use **Edit▸Delete**, or with commands:

```
DROP varlist
```

You can specify several variables, a range of variables, or a range of subscripted variables:

```
DROP accident tchrsal wine
DROP quest(1..7), age
```

Note: *The difference between **Edit▸Delete** and **Edit▸Cut** is that **Delete** simply deletes the selected data, while **Cut** copies the data to the clipboard so that it can be pasted to a new location. **Copy** works like **Cut**, except that it also leaves the data in its original location.*

Deleting cases

Using the mouse, you can delete cases just like you delete variables. Select them and use **Edit▸Delete** (or the Delete key). With commands:

```
DELETE n1, n2, …
```

where *n1* and *n2* are case numbers. Here are some valid DELETE commands:

```
DELETE 3
DELETE 3 .. 10
DELETE 3,5 .. 8,10
```

SYSTAT removes the specified cases, moving subsequent cases up to fill their places. Be aware that SYSTAT renumbers the cases after they have been deleted. It is often helpful to create an ID variable that numbers each case to make it easier to track them through various file manipulations.

If you want to delete cases based on conditions, use an IF *condition* THEN DELETE statement in BASIC. See Chapter 11 for more information.

Cutting and pasting variables or cases

You can rearrange variables by using **Edit**➧**Cut** and **Edit**➧**Paste**, or the CUT and PASTE commands.

For example, to move one or more adjacent variables to a different position in the data file:

- Select the variables you want to move using either the keyboard or mouse (as described above).
- Select **Edit**➧**Cut** to delete the variables from their current location and copy them to the clipboard.
- Select the column where you want to paste the variables and select **Edit**➧**Paste**. The variables are pasted to the left of the selected column.

You can also use **Edit**➧**Copy** to copy variables to the clipboard without deleting them from their original location. However, if you try to paste the same variables to another location in the same data file, SYSTAT prompts you to specify new names for the pasted variables (since two variables in the same data file cannot have the same name).

Note: You can use **Copy** and **Paste** to copy just about any type of data, and even to copy data from one application to another, within the limits of common sense. In the Data window, that means that pasted data must be of the appropriate type and "shape." You cannot paste a string value into a numeric variable, or copy a range of cells and paste them into a single cell.

Using commands

You can also cut and paste variables using commands. First you *cut* the variable you would like to move by typing:

```
CUT var1 or varlist
```

The variable(s) then disappear from the Data window. Then you *paste* the variable(s) by specifying the name of the variable it should follow:

    PASTE var2

Think of the **PASTE** command as **PASTE BEFORE** as in **CUT** *var1* and **PASTE** it back into the Data window before *var2*.

You can cut a block of adjacent variables using commands. For example, *POP-1983, POP_1986, POP_1990,* and *POP_2020* are four consecutive columns in the *OURWORLD* file. We could specify:

    CUT POP_1983 .. POP_2020

and then

    PASTE URBAN

to position the four variables to the left of the *URBAN* column.

Finding data

You can find cases or variables that meet specific conditions.

Finding cases that satisfy conditions

You can use **Edit➡Find Case** or the **FIND** command to search your file for cases meeting specific conditions.

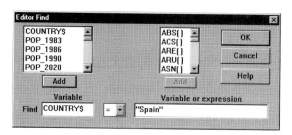

Paste or type the name of the variable that you want to search, and specify the condition. Note that string values must be enclosed in single or double quotes. The *condition* can contain the arithmetic operators, functions, and relational and logical operators discussed in Chapter 6.

With commands, type **FIND** followed by the condition:

    FIND country$ = 'Spain'
    FIND sex$ = 'Male' AND age > 21

After a case is found, you can then type FIND alone, and SYSTAT will search again for the next case that satisfies the condition.

Finding variables

When using a large data file with many variables, it sometimes takes a long time to scroll over to view a certain variable. You can use **Edit➠Find Variable** or the FIND command to quickly move the cursor to a specific variable.

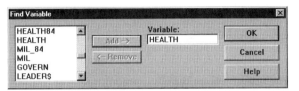

With commands:

```
FIND var
```

Case ID

You can specify an ID variable to be displayed on the left side of the Data window using **Data➠ID Variable** or the IDVAR command. The value of the specified variable is displayed instead of the case number on the left side of the Data window.

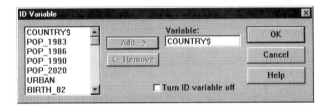

To return to displaying the case number, select **Turn ID variable off**.

With commands, use the IDVAR command:

```
IDVAR var
```

To return to displaying case number, type IDVAR without an argument.

Deriving new variables

You can use **Data➠Transform** to transform variables or create new variables from existing ones. For example:

```
LET total = quiz1 + quiz2 + final
LET lg_wt = LOG (weight)
IF age < 13 THEN LET age$ = 'child'
```

When deriving new variables, you can see the result in the last Data window column at the far right. For more information, see Chapter 6.

Cell display format

You can specify the number of characters and the number of decimal places displayed for each value in the Data window, or you can display tiny numbers in exponential notation (instead of zeros). See Chapter 9 for more information.

Other Data Structures

In addition to the usual rectangular, case-by-variable organization, SYSTAT accommodates two other data structures: tabulated form and matrix input.

Data in
tabulated form

Use **Data**➠**Frequency** or the FREQ command to identify that the data are counts. That is, cases with the same values are entered as a single case with a count.

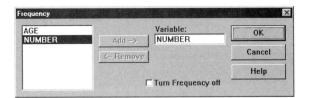

For example, Morrison's data from a breast cancer study of 764 women are shown below. Instead of 764 cases, the data file contains 72 records for cells defined by the factors: 1) survival, 2) age group, 3) diagnostic center, and 4) tumor status.

	SURVIVE$	AGE	CENTER$	TUMOR$	NUMBER
1.	Alive	50	Boston	MaxBengn	0
2.	Alive	50	Boston	MaxMalig	4
3.	Alive	50	Boston	MinBengn	24
4.	Alive	50	Boston	MinMalig	11
5.	Dead	50	Boston	MaxBengn	0
6.	Dead	50	Boston	MaxMalig	6
7.	Dead	50	Boston	MinBengn	7
8.	Dead	50	Boston	MinMalig	6
9.	Alive	50	Glamorgn	MaxBengn	1
10.	Alive	50	Glamorgn	MaxMalig	8
		⋮			
31.	Dead	60	Boston	MinBengn	20
32.	Dead	60	Boston	MinMalig	8
33.	Alive	60	Glamorgn	MaxBengn	4
34.	Alive	60	Glamorgn	MaxMalig	10
35.	Alive	60	Glamorgn	MinBengn	39
36.	Alive	60	Glamorgn	MinMalig	27
37.	Dead	60	Glamorgn	MaxBengn	0
38.	Dead	60	Glamorgn	MaxMalig	3
39.	Dead	60	Glamorgn	MaxBengn	12
40.	Dead	60	Glamorgn	MinMalig	14
		⋮			
63.	Dead	70	Glamorgn	MinBengn	7
64.	Dead	70	Glamorgn	MinMalig	3
65.	Alive	70	Tokyo	MaxBengn	1

	SURVIVE$	AGE	CENTER$	TUMOR$	NUMBER
66.	Alive	70	Tokyo	MaxMalig	5
67.	Alive	70	Tokyo	MinBengn	6
68.	Alive	70	Tokyo	MinMalig	1
69.	Dead	70	Tokyo	MaxBengn	0
70.	Dead	70	Tokyo	MaxMalig	1
71.	Dead	70	Tokyo	MaxBengn	3
72.	Dead	70	Tokyo	MinMalig	2

NUMBER is the count of women in each cell. Use **Data➠Frequency** to identify the variable *NUMBER* as the count variable as shown above. With commands:

```
FREQ = number
```

Matrix input

You can enter a triangular matrix such as a correlation matrix. As usual, variable names go in the top row. Next, type the correlations. Since correlation matrices are symmetric, only type the lower diagonal portion, as shown.

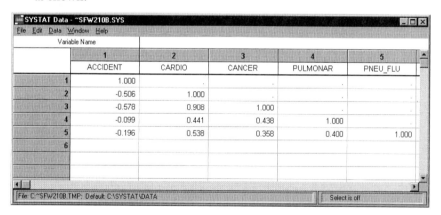

Select **File➠Save As** to save the data, and click **Options** to specify the type of matrix. Available types include rectangular (the usual file of cases and variables), SSCP, covariance, correlation, dissimilarity, and similarity. With commands, use the TYPE command before saving the data:

```
TYPE = RECT | SSCP | COVA | CORR | DISS | SIMI
```

For example:

```
TYPE = CORR
SAVE myfile
RUN
```

6

Re-expressing and Transforming Data

Leland Wilkinson and Laszlo Engelman

Often, the data as recorded are not sufficient for a complete analysis. For example, you may need to re-express values to improve symmetry, derive new variables such as a total score or a ratio of two variables, select a subset of the cases, etc. To execute these tasks, you specify statements of this form:

```
LET variable = expression
IF condition THEN LET assignment
SELECT condition1 AND condition2 OR ...
```

SYSTAT provides dozens of functions for use in these statements. For example, you could use the **SQR** function to take the square root of each subject's income and store the result as *SQR_INC*:

```
LET sqr_inc = SQR(income)
```

If you prefer menus, use **Data➡Transform** to specify **LET** and **IF...THEN LET** statements. If you use commands, simply type each statement, one per line, in the procedure you are currently running. The same statements are available in SYSTAT BASIC when more complex programming tasks are needed.

In this chapter, we introduce you to the functions and operators that you can use to construct transformations. In Chapter 11, we describe the BASIC procedure that has commands for more complex data manipulation tasks.

Re-expressing and Transforming Data

Overview

The word *transformations* describes a powerful set of functions, arithmetic operators, and other statements that operate on data values. Following is a brief overview of the tasks you can do with transformations.

Derive new variables. If you have two quiz scores and a final exam score for each student, you can use the arithmetic operators + and * to compute their TOTAL score:

```
LET total = quiz1 + quiz2 + 2*final
```

Re-express data. Transformed values may meet assumptions required for statistical analyses better than the original data. For example, often the distribution of the logarithm of body weight is more symmetric than that of untransformed weights. To re-express weight in log base 10 units, use the L10 function:

```
LET lg_wt = L10(weight)
```

Compute summary variables. For each case, SYSTAT's multivariable functions compute results across variables. For example, use the AVG function to compute the average of the scores S1 to S6 for each subject:

```
LET average = AVG(s1,s2,s3,s4,s5,s6)
```

Assign new values conditionally. For example, using the variable *TEMP* (winter temperature), derive a new variable *TEMP$* containing a character descriptor:

```
IF temp < 32 THEN LET temp$ = 'Cold'
```

Execute global edits. Use relational operators (<, >, and =) and logical operators (AND and OR) in conditional transformations. For example, the statement

```
IF (age > 20 AND income < 7000 AND job$ = 'No'),
    THEN LET relief$ = 'Yes'
```

stores the word *Yes* in the variable named *RELIEF$* for every subject over 20 years old who reports an income less than $7,000 and is unemployed.

Select cases. Use relational operators to restrict your analysis to subjects satisfying certain conditions. For example,

```
SELECT age >= 21
```

omits all subjects under 21.

Rank or standardize the values of a variable. Rank replaces the values of a variable with their rank from smallest to largest. Standardize replaces the values of a variable with their z scores or score on a 0,1 scale.

Manipulate character variables. Use SYSTAT's character functions to manipulate character values, including changing case, extracting characters or text strings, converting characters to numbers, etc.

Format and transform dates and times. For example, write the fifth of February, 1995, as Feb 5, 1995, 2/5/95, or 5-2-95; or, you could compute the time between events in, say, days or even seconds.

Generate random numbers. SYSTAT has functions to generate values from uniform, normal, t, F, chi-square, exponential, gamma, beta, logistic, Studentized range, Weibull, binomial, and Poisson distributions. In addition, density, cumulative, and inverse cumulative functions are available for each.

Uniform random numbers, for example, are useful in cross-validation studies for selecting random subsamples of cases. To randomly assign values of 0 and 1 to a new variable, *WEIGHT*, in which approximately 50% of the values are 1's, use the uniform random number (URN) generator:

```
LET weight = 0
IF URN < .5 THEN LET weight = 1
```

or, more simply:

```
LET weight = URN < .5
```

You can use the normal cumulative function, ZCF, and its inverse, ZIF, in place of a table of normal probabilities. That is, use ZCF to find the area under the normal curve to the left of a given z score, and use ZIF to find the z score given an area.

Where and how. You can transform values:

- Using **Transform**, **Standardize**, **Rank**, and **Select Cases** on the **Data** menu, which is available from both the Main window and the Data window
- Within commands for current statistical analyses or graphical displays
- In the BASIC programming procedure

For more complex data transformations, use the full power of the SYSTAT BASIC transformation language—including IF...THEN...ELSE statements, FOR...NEXT loops, DIMENSION statements, and GOTO commands. See Chapter 11 for more information.

Transformation Statements

In the examples in the overview, two specifications were used:

    LET *variable* = *expression*

and

    IF *condition* THEN LET *assignment*

The LET or IF...THEN LET statements can be specified by typing commands within any SYSTAT procedure or by using **Data⟶Transform**, which provides access to the **Let** and **If...Then...Let** dialog boxes.

The **Let** and **If...Then...Let** dialog boxes are shown here:

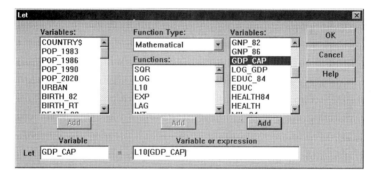

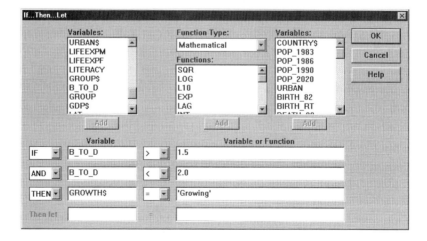

Functions are categorized as Mathematical, Multivariable, Group and Interval, Date and Time, Character, and Distribution. See "Operators and Functions" on p. 115 for descriptions of the functions.

You can use the dialog boxes, or you can specify transformation commands in any of SYSTAT's statistical or graphical procedures. Just type your transformation statements before the HOT command for that procedure. For example, to transform GNP per capita to log base 10 units for an **ANOVA** procedure:

```
ANOVA
   USE ourworld
   LET gdp_cap = L10(gdp_cap)
   DEPEND gnp_cap
   ESTIMATE
```

The results of transformations are not automatically saved in a file. To save results using menus, select **File➞Save**. With commands, type

```
SAVE filename
```

after **ESTIMATE** and then type **RUN**.

Note: *Beginning in SYSTAT Version 6, transformations can be performed in any statistical or graphical procedure.*

LET and IF...THEN LET

The LET *variable=expression* statement assigns values given by the expression to the variable. You can use any mathematically valid combination of variables, numbers, functions, and operators in the expression. Some valid LET statements are:

```
LET change = week2 - week1
LET logit  = 1 / (1 + EXP(a+b*x))
LET trendy = income > 40000 AND car$ = 'BMW'
```

If the expression contains any character values, they must be enclosed in single or double quotation marks. Recall that character values are case sensitive.

You can join a number of simple expressions with logical AND and/or OR to form complex relational expressions. For example,

```
income > 40000 AND car$ = 'BMW'
```

For more information, see "Logical operators" on p. 116.

Changing an existing variable. If *variable* (the variable following LET) already exists in the file, its values are replaced by the value of *expression* for each case. For example, LET X = 2 replaces all values in X with 2.

Making a new variable. If *variable* does not exist, a new variable with that name is added in the first column at the right side of the data matrix. For example, LET B = A adds a variable named *B* as a new column, and its values are the same as those in *A*. If a variable in the expression does not exist, you get an error message.

Relations, operators, and functions. You can use any of the relations, operators, and functions discussed in "Operators and Functions" on p. 115. Be sure to place the arguments of functions inside parentheses—for example, LOG(weight), SQR(income).

An example. The *OURWORLD* data file has *B_TO_D*, a derived measure of the potential for population growth for countries. We computed this variable by dividing the birth rate by the death rate for each country:

```
LET b_to_d = birth_rt / death_rt
```

The new variable looks like this (select **Window➧Data** to display the Data window if it is not visible):

		1	2	3	4
		COUNTRY$	BIRTH RT	DEATH RT	B TO D
10		UK	14.000	11.000	1.273
11		Italy	10.000	9.000	1.111
12		Sweden	13.000	11.000	1.182
13		Portugal	12.000	10.000	1.200
14		Netherlands	13.000	8.000	1.625
15		WGermany	11.000	11.000	1.000
16		Norway	14.000	11.000	1.273
17		Poland	14.000	9.000	1.556
18		Hungary	12.000	13.000	0.923
19		EGermany	12.000	12.000	1.000
20		Czechoslov	14.000	11.000	1.273
21		Gambia	48.000	18.000	2.667
22		Iraq	46.000	7.000	6.571
23		Pakistan	43.000	14.000	3.071
24		Bangladesh	42.000	14.000	3.000

SYSTAT Data - OURWORLD.SYS
File Edit Data Window Help
Row   17 , Col   40

File: C:\PROGRA~1\SYSTAT\DATA\OURWORLD.SYS; Default C:\PROGRA~1\SY   Select is off

The United Kingdom has a birth-to-death ratio of 1.273 (14 births for every 11 deaths), while Iraq has a ratio of 6.571 (46 births for every 7 deaths). When you create a new variable, SYSTAT adds it to the right side of your data file. Above, we used **Edit➡Cut** and **Edit➡Paste** to reorder the variables.

IF...THEN LET statements

IF *condition* THEN LET *assignment* statements let you conditionally define variables. For all cases where the condition is true, SYSTAT executes the assignment. The following are valid statements:

```
IF age > 80 THEN LET age$ = 'Elderly'
IF X = 99   THEN LET x = .
IF SEX$ = 'Male' AND age > 30 THEN LET group = 1
IF a=-9 AND (b<10 OR b>20) THEN LET c = LOG(d)*SQR(e)
```

In the second statement, the value of variable *X* becomes a period (SYSTAT's symbol to mark missing data) for all cases where SYSTAT finds the value 99. In the third statement, males over 30 years old are assigned to group 1. In the last statement, for the condition

```
a=-9 AND (b<10 OR b>20)
```

to be true, the value of variable *A* must be a specific value (–9) *and* the value of *B* must be extreme (less than 10 *or* greater than 20). If a case satisfies these conditions, the logarithm of the value of variable *D* is multiplied by the square root of the value of variable *E*. The result is stored in variable *C*.

An example. Let's use the new birth-to-death ratio to make a character variable that identifies countries as "shrinking" or "exploding." Use **Transform➡Data➡If Then Let**. With commands:

```
IF b_to_d < 1.0 THEN LET growth$ = 'Shrinking'
IF b_to_d > 2.0 THEN LET growth$ = 'Exploding'
```

```
IF b_to_d > 1.5 AND,
   b_to_d < 2.0 THEN LET growth$ = 'Growing'
```

	COUNTRY$	B TO D	GROWTH$	POP 19
17	Poland	1.556	Growing	
18	Hungary	0.923	Shrinking	
19	EGermany	1.000		
20	Czechoslov	1.273		
21	Gambia	2.667	Exploding	
22	Iraq	6.571	Exploding	
23	Pakistan	3.071	Exploding	
24	Bangladesh	3.000	Exploding	

By scrolling through the data, we see *Shrinking* for Hungary. Poland is *Growing*, while Gambia, Iraq, Pakistan, and Bangladesh are *Exploding*. The value of *GROWTH$* is blank (that is, missing) for countries that failed to satisfy any of the conditions (East Germany, Czechoslovakia).

Built-in variables

Built-in variables allow you to index aspects of files:

CASE   Case (observation) number
COMPLETE   No missing values

Generating a case number

For example, if your cases are ordered by time, create a new variable named *TIME* containing the case sequence numbers:

```
LET time = CASE
```

Shortcuts

There are several shortcuts you can use to minimize typing for transformation statements.

Specifying contiguous variables

As a shortcut when selecting adjacent variables in a file, type the first and last variable names and use a double period (..) to include all variables in between:

```
LET total = SUM(score1, score2, score3, score4)
LET total = SUM(score1 .. score4)
```

This shortcut can also be used with the @ sign shortcut, which allows you to use the @ sign as a placeholder for multiple variable names (see "Multiple transformations: The @ sign" below):

```
LET (blue .. getgoing) = @ <> 0
```

When using subscripts (such as *Q(1)*, *Q(2)*, etc.), variables that are *not* contiguous can be specified using the double-period shortcut. For example,

```
SELECT Q(1 .. 10)
```

selects the variables *Q(1)* to *Q(10)*, regardless of their order in the data file.

Multiple transformations: The @ sign

To transform several variables, you can specify a LET statement for each:

```
LET gdp_cap = L10(gdp_cap)
LET     mil = L10(mil)
LET  gnp_86 = L10(gnp_86)
```

Or, you can use the @ sign to specify the same transformations in one statement:

```
LET (gdp_cap, mil, gnp_86) = L10(@)
```

The syntax for multiple transformations is

```
LET (var1, var2, var3,…) = expression with @ sign
```

The variable names *must* be separated by commas and enclosed within parentheses ( ). The @ sign is a placeholder for the variable names. The *function* can be any function or expression listed in this chapter.

This @ shortcut notation can also be used with relational operators:

```
LET (blue,depress,cry,sad,no_eat,getgoing) = @ <> 0
```

This dichotomizes the values of six variables into 0 and 1.0. When the value of a variable is *not* 0, the statement on the right is *true*, so the result is 1.0. If the value *is* 0, the statement is *false*, so the result is 0.0.

Clearing transformations

When you transform variables, the results of the transformation replace the values of variables (if they were not renamed) and remain for the current session. To return to the original values of the variables, select or type:

```
LET / CLEAR
```

This removes the assignments of all LET and IF...THEN LET statements, while other data-related commands (for example, LABEL, IDVAR, etc.) remain in effect.

Operators and Functions

The functions and operators discussed in this section can be used:

– In any LET, IF...THEN LET, or SELECT expression
  In some FIND expressions (depending on data type)
– In the BASIC procedure
– In the calculator

Functions are categorized as Mathematical, Multivariable, Group and Interval, Date and Time, Character, and Distribution.

Arithmetic operators

You can use the following arithmetic operators:

+	Addition	*	Multiplication
–	Subtraction or negative sign	/	Division
** *or* ^	Exponentiation		

Some examples are:

```
quiz1 + quiz2
y - 2
year*year
birth_rt / death_rt
x^2
```

These could be used, for example, as follows:

```
LET total = quiz1 + quiz2
IF (city$ = 'LA') THEN LET code=y-2
```

SYSTAT sets the resulting values of inadmissible operations (for example, division by 0) to missing.

Relational operators

Relational operators are used in relational expressions to compare either two numeric or two character expressions.

= *or* ==	Equal to	<> *or* ><	Not equal to
<	Less than	>	Greater than
<= *or* =<	Less than or equal to		
>= *or* =>	Greater than or equal to		

Some examples are:

```
score1 < score2
state$ = 'NY'
age > 21
x <> .
age <= 65
income >= 3000
```

These could be used, for example, as follows:

```
IF (state$ == 'NY') THEN LET region = 1
```

Logical operators

The logical operators AND and OR connect two relational expressions, and NOT negates a logical expression. These operators yield results that are either *true* or *false*.

AND	*or*	&	Boolean "and"
OR	*or*	|	Boolean "or"
NOT	*or*	!	Boolean "negative"

This expression selects people of workforce age—those older than 17 *and* younger than or equal to 65:

```
age > 17 AND age <= 65
```

Note that even if you are testing for different conditions on the same variable, you must specify a complete relational expression for each condition.

Correct: `age > 17 AND age <= 65`
Incorrect: `age > 17 AND <= 65`

Here, we select people who are not of workforce age—those younger than or equal to age 17 *or* older than age 65:

```
age <= 17 OR age > 65
```

The logical operator NOT reverses the value of an entire expression. To select people who are not of workforce age, we could also specify:

```
NOT (age > 17 AND age <= 65)
```

If the result of an expression is *true*, it is assigned a value of 1; if it is *false*, it is assigned a value of 0. NOT sets any nonzero value (true) to 0, and any 0 value (false) to 1 (true).

Note: *SYSTAT follows the standard for programming languages and returns 0 for false and 1 for true. Microsoft BASIC is nonstandard and returns 0 for false and −1 for true.*

Logical AND. To demonstrate how a result is determined, let's examine:

```
LET trendy = income > 40000  AND  car$=='BMW'
```

For any case where the subject's income is over $40,000 *and* the subject's car is a BMW, the result of the expression is true and the value of *TRENDY* is 1. If the subject has a lower income *or* a different car, the result is false and *TRENDY* is assigned 0. If the subject fails to report income or car model, the value of *TRENDY* is set to missing. In summary, when AND is used:

Condition 1		Condition 2		Result	Value
True	AND	True	*yields*	True	1
True	AND	False	*yields*	False	0
False	AND	True	*yields*	False	0
False	AND	False	*yields*	False	0
True	AND	Missing	*yields*	Missing	.
Missing	AND	True	*yields*	Missing	.
False	AND	Missing	*yields*	False	0
Missing	AND	False	*yields*	False	0

Logical OR. If the logical operator OR is used instead of AND, for example,

```
LET TRENDY=INCOME > 40000  OR  CAR$=='BMW'
```

only one of the conditions has to be true for the result to be true (1).

Condition 1		Condition 2		Result	Value
True	OR	True	*yields*	True	1
True	OR	False	*yields*	True	1
False	OR	True	*yields*	True	1
False	OR	False	*yields*	False	0
True	OR	Missing	*yields*	True	1
Missing	OR	True	*yields*	True	1
False	OR	Missing	*yields*	Missing	.
Missing	OR	False	*yields*	Missing	.

Order of expression evaluation

Expressions are evaluated from left to right according to the precedence of operators. That is, operators with higher precedence are evaluated before those with lower. Order of precedence from highest to lowest runs as follows:

1.	Expressions enclosed in parentheses	( )
2.	Exponentiation	^ *or* **
3.	Negation	-
4.	Multiplication and division	*, /
5.	Addition and subtraction	+, -
6.	Comparison	=, <>, <, >, <=, >=
7.	Logical negation	NOT
8.	Logical comparison	AND
9.	Logical comparison	OR

Because of this order of precedence, the expressions

$$A + B*C \quad \text{and} \quad A + (B*C)$$

are the same, but differ from

$$(A + B)*C$$

Multiplication (*) has a higher precedence than addition (+) and is therefore performed first. If A=1, B=2, and C=3, the above expressions evaluate as follows:

$$A + B*C \quad = \quad 1 + 2*3 = 1 + 6 = 7$$
$$A + (B*C) \quad = \quad 1 + (2*3) = 1 + 6 = 7$$
$$(A + B)*C \quad = \quad (1 + 2)*3 = 3*3 = 9$$

The only exception to the "left to right" rule is with exponentiation. The exponentiation a^b^c is evaluated "right to left"; that is, a^b^c means a^(b^c).

Mathematical functions

These functions modify the variable, number, or expression you place inside the parentheses.

Function	Result
SQR (*a*)	Square root of a [a ≥ 0]
LOG (*a*)	Natural logarithm of a [a > 0]
L10 (*a*)	Logarithm base 10 [a > 0]
EXP (*a*)	Exponential function e^a
LAG (*var,n*)	Lag variable by shifting values down *n* rows; if *n* is omitted, default=1.0
INT (*a*)	Integer part of a
LGM (*a*)	Log gamma: $LGM(n) = LOG(\Gamma(n)) = LOG((n-1)!)$
SGN (*a*)	−1 if a < 0, 0 if a = 0, and 1 if a > 0
ABS (*a*)	Absolute value lal
SIN (*a*)	Sine of a (in radians)
COS (*a*)	Cosine of a (in radians)
TAN (*a*)	Tangent of a (in radians)
ASN (*a*)	Arcsine of a (which yields radian results)
ACS (*a*)	Arccosine of a (which yields radian results)
TNH (*a*)	Hyperbolic tangent of a
ATN (*a*)	Arctangent of a (which yields radian results)
ATH (*a*)	Arc hyperbolic tangent of a (Fisher's *z*) (which yields radian results)
AT2 (*a,b*)	Arc tangent with sine (a) and cosine (b) argument
MOD (*a,b*)	The remainder of a/b

Some examples are:

```
LOG(weight)
SQR(3)
INT(cardio+cancer)
SIN(COS(TAN(3*Y)))
```

These could be used, for example, as follows:

```
LET lg_weight = LOG(weight)
```

Arguments of trigonometric functions must be in radians, not degrees. LOG is the natural logarithm and L10 is the base 10 logarithm. You can obtain logs in other bases by dividing the natural log by the log of the base; for example, for $Log_2 A$, use LOG(A)/LOG(2). SYSTAT sets the resulting values of inadmissible operations (for example, square roots of negative numbers) to missing.

6.1
Creating lagged variables

The LAG function shifts values down *n* rows, replacing the first *n* values with a missing value:

```
LAG (var, n)
```

If *n* is omitted, the default is 1. Some examples are:

```
LET y=LAG(x)
LET z=LOG(LAG(x))
```

The first case of a lagged variable is set to missing.

Multivariable functions

The functions described below operate on values of variables within a case. With these functions, you can:

– Compute summary descriptive statistics across values of selected variables
– Search selected variables for specific numeric or character values
– Compute the slope of the line-of-best-fit through points with equally spaced *x* values or values that you specify
– Compute the area under a curve created by connecting equally spaced points or points with spacing that you specify

Function	Result
MIS($y1,y2,...$)	Number of missing values
NUM($y1,y2,...$)	Number of values that are not missing (number of usable values)
AVG($y1,y2,...$)	mean of nonmissing values
STD($y1,y2,...$)	Standard deviation of nonmissing values
MIN($y1,y2,...$)	Smallest among nonmissing values (minimum value)
MAX($y1,y2,...$)	Largest among nonmissing values (maximum value)
SUM($y1,y2,...$)	Sum of nonmissing values
SLE($y1,y2,...$)	Coefficient *b* of the regression line $y = a + bx$, where *x*'s are equally spaced
SLU($x1,y1,x2,y2,...$)	Coefficient *b* of the regression line $y = a + bx$
ARE($y1,y2,...$)	Area under the values of (x_i,y_i), where *x*'s are assumed to be equally spaced
ARU($x1,y1,x2,y2,...$)	Area under *y* by the trapezoidal rule

Function	Result
COD(*number,var1,var2,...*)	The index (using integers 1, 2, 3, ...) when *number* matches a value in *var1* through *varp*, respectively; 0 otherwise
COD('*charval*',*var1$,var2$,...*)	The index (using integers 1, 2, 3, ...) of *var1$, var2$*, ... when *charval* matches the value of the respective variable, 0 otherwise
INC(*number,var1,var2,...*)	A 1 (true) if *number* matches a value in *var1, var2, ...*, or *varn*; 0 (false) otherwise
INC('*charval*',*var1$,var2$,...*)	A 1 (true) when *charval* matches a value in *var1$, var2$, ..., or varn$*; 0 (false) otherwise

- Arguments are not restricted to variable names—they can be explicit values or other functions—and they can contain arithmetic operators (for example, (INDEX–1)).

- Either commas or spaces can be used to separate arguments unless an ambiguity arises. For example, when using AVG to compute the mean,

  AVG(10 313 -29 236 19)   differs from   AVG(10,313,-29,236,19)

  For the first result, four numbers are averaged (the second is 313–29). For the second result, five numbers are used (the third is –29).

- Use a double period (..) as a shortcut notation to shorten a list of contiguous variables—that is, for Q1, Q2, ..., Q20, use Q1 .. Q20.

6.2 Finding the number of missing values

Use the MIS function to report the number of missing values. For example, if you have survey results, use MIS to find the number of questions each respondent did not answer. We use the *TESTSCOR* data file:

SUBJECT$	Q1	Q2	Q3	Q4	Q5	Q6	Q7	Q8	Q9	Q10	NUM_MISS
N. Smith	1	3	5	1	2	.	3	.	5	1	2
G. Henry	.	2	.	1	3	4	.	3	2	4	3
C. Bauer	3	1	4	8	9	1	5	.	2	2	1
R. McMahon	2	5	.	1	3	4	2	.	.	5	3
S. Collins	1	2	.	5	2	.	3	1	2	2	2
L. Ryan	5	4	1	2	.	.	3	.	5	1	3
E. Clark	3	2	1	2	3	3	.	4	5	1	1
T. Price	5	3	4	4	.	2	.	.	1	3	3

and create a new variable, *NUM_MISS*, containing the number of questions each respondent did not answer:

```
LET num_miss = MIS(q1 .. q10)
```

Instead of typing sequential variable names (*Q1, Q2, Q3, Q4*, etc.), use a double period (..) to include all variables in between (*Q1 .. Q10*). If you save the data, *NUM_MISS* is the last variable.

6.3
Summary
statistics

Using four scores (S1 through S4) as data for each subject, we use the NUM, SUM, MIN, and STD functions to compute:

— *NUM_SCRS* (how many scores are present)
— *TOTAL* (the sum of their scores)
— *SMALLEST* (their minimum score)
— *SD* (the standard deviation of the scores)

We specify:

```
LET num_scrs = NUM (s1,s2,s3,s4)
LET total    = SUM (s1,s2,s3,s4)
LET smallest = MIN (s1,s2,s3,s4)
LET sd       = STD (s1,s2,s3,s4)
```

Following are the original data with results for three subjects:

Original Data					Derived Values			
NAME$	**S1**	**S2**	**S3**	**S4**	**NUM_SCRS**	**TOTAL**	**SMALLEST**	**SD**
Smith	7	6	.	3	3	16	3	2.082
Jones	8	4	6	5	4	23	4	1.708
Wilson	2	5	3	7	4	17	2	2.217

6.4
Slope of the
line-of-best-fit

For each case, the SLE and SLU functions compute the slope of the line-of-best-fit across two or more responses. Consider these four responses (R_i) across four time points (T_i):

	T1	**R1**	**T2**	**R2**	**T3**	**R3**	**T4**	**R4**
Case 1	2	10	4	20	8	40	16	80
Case 2	2	1	4	20	8	15	16	2
		⋮						⋮

The SLE function produces the slope if you assume that the times are equally spaced. To incorporate the actual spacing (2, 4, 8, 16), use the SLU function. The resulting slopes can then be used as data in statistical procedures or graphical displays—for example, to test if the average slope for a control group differs from that for the treatment group. Below, for example, are the responses for case 1 plotted at equally spaced times and at the actual times:

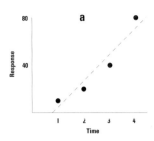 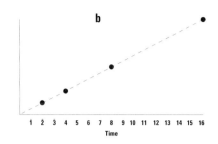

To request the slope for equally spaced time points, **a**, or the slope using the actual times, **b**, specify

```
LET slope_a = SLE(r1 r2 r3 r4)
LET slope_b = SLU(t1 r1  t2 r2  t3 r3  t4 r4)
```

You can get the same results for *SLOPE_B* by inserting the times directly:

```
LET slope_b = SLU (2 r1  4 r2  8 r3  16 r4)
```

For a view of how the results are stored, see Example 6.5.

6.5 Computing the area under a curve

For each case, the **ARE** and **ARU** functions compute the area under the polygon formed by connecting values of variables you specify. Consider the data for case 2 above:

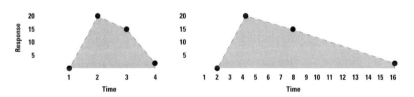

Let's use the **ARE** and **ARU** functions:

```
LET area_1  = ARE (r1  r2  r3  r4)
LET area_2  = ARU (t1 r1  t2 r2  t3 r3  t4 r4)
                   or
LET area_2  = ARU ( 2 r1  4 r2  8 r3  16 r4)
```

The results for Example 6.4 and Example 6.5 with the input data are:

	T1	R1	T2	R2	T3	R3	T4	R4	SLOPE_A	SLOPE_B	AREA_1	AREA_2
Case 1	2	10	4	20	8	40	16	80	23	5	105	630
Case 2	2	1	4	20	8	15	16	2	-.2	-.44	36.5	159
	⋮										⋮	

6.6 Matching specific values

The INC and COD functions can be used with character or numeric variables to find specified values. Within each case, the INC and COD functions search the values of selected variables for a value that matches the value you specify. When a match is found:

— *INC* returns a 1 (true).
— *COD* returns the index or order of the variable with the match (1 if the value is found in the first variable listed, 2 if it is found in the second, etc.).

If no match is found, both *INC* and *COD* return 0.

As an example, suppose respondents in a survey were asked about their favorite bath soaps:

— Is Ivory soap among the first, second, or third choices?
— What is the preference order of Ivory?

Character data. The data and results for three cases are:

						Results	
NAME$	**CHOICE_1$**	**CHOICE_2$**	**CHOICE_3$**	**CHOICE_4$**	**PREFRNCE$**	**ORDER**	**PREF**
Smith	Ivory	Dial	Camay	Safeguard	yes	1	1
Jones	Palmolive	Irish Spring	Camay	Ivory	no	0	0
Wilson	Zest	Ivory	Camay	Palmolive	yes	2	1

To create the new variables *PREFRNCE$* and *ORDER*, we use the INC and COD functions:

```
LET prefrnce$ = 'no'
   IF INC('Ivory', choice_1$, choice_2$, choice_3$),
         THEN LET prefrnce$ = 'yes'
   LET order = COD('Ivory', choice_1$, choice_2$,
                     choice_3$)
```

A more direct use of the INC function is

```
LET pref = INC('Ivory', choice_1$, choice_2$,
                  choice_3$)
```

A *PREF* value of 1 indicates that Ivory is among the first three choices, and a value of 0 indicates that Ivory is not one of the first three choices.

Numeric data. For the same scenario, the data might be numeric brand codes:

1	Camay	3	Dove	5	Ivory	7	Safeguard
2	Dial	4	Irish Spring	6	Palmolive	8	Zest

The data and results are:

					Results	
NAME$	CHOICE_1	CHOICE_2	CHOICE_3	CHOICE_4	PREFRNCE$	ORDER
Smith	5	2	1	7	yes	1
Jones	6	4	1	5	no	0
Wilson	8	5	1	6	yes	2

The commands to obtain *PREFRNCE$* and *ORDER* are:

```
LET prefrnce$ = 'no'
IF INC(5,choice_1,choice_2,choice_3),
     THEN LET prefrnce$ = 'yes'
LET order = COD(5,choice_1,choice_2,choice_3,
                choice_4)
```

Remember to use **SAVE** *filename* if you want to save the new variables.

Group and interval functions

The COD function is used to recode values of a grouping variable. The INC function compares each value of a numeric or character variable with a list of values you specify. If a match is found, SYSTAT returns a 1; if not, SYSTAT returns a 0. The CUT function lets you define intervals on a quantitative (continuous) variable or divide the values of a character variable alphabetically.

Function	Result
COD(*var,num1,num2,...*)	Values of *var* are replaced: *num1* becomes 1, *num2* becomes 2, etc.
COD(*var$,'text1','text2',...*)	Values of *var$* are replaced: *text1* becomes 1, *text2* becomes 2, etc.
INC(*var,num1,num2,...*)	A 1 (true) if the value in *var* matches one of the numbers *num1, num2, ...*; 0 (false) otherwise.
INC(*var$,'text1','text2',...*)	A 1 (true) if the value in *var$* matches a value in *text1, text2, ...*; 0 (false) otherwise.
CUT(*var,num1,num2,...*)	Use to define intervals along a continuous variable. Values in *var* less than or equal to *num1* get value 1. Values greater than *num1* and less than or equal to *num2* get value 2, etc.

Function	Result
CUT(var$,'text1','text2',…)	Use to group variables alphabetically. Values in var$ less than text1 (alphabetically), including text1, get value 1. Values between text1 and text2, including text2, get value 2, etc.

☞ For more information about defining group codes and intervals, see Chapter 8.

6.7 Recoding grouping variables: COD

COD can be used to recode values of either a numeric *or* a character grouping variable. For example, you may have a numeric variable named *JOB*, which has about 30 or 40 occupation codes, and you want to isolate a subset of those cases. The statement

```
LET newjob = COD(job,63,47,85)
```

assigns values to the variable *NEWJOB* based on values of the *numeric* variable *JOB*. The values of *JOB* and the corresponding values of *NEWJOB* are:

JOB	NEWJOB
63	1
47	2
85	3
all else	.

where the period (.) is SYSTAT's symbol for missing data. The statement

```
LET newjob = COD(job$,'truck driver','bus driver',
                 'cab driver')
```

assigns values to the variable *NEWJOB* based on values of the *character* variable *JOB$*. The values of *JOB$* and the corresponding values of *NEWJOB* are:

JOB$	NEWJOB
truck driver	1
bus driver	2
cab driver	3
all else	(missing)

For character variables, SYSTAT's symbol for missing data is a space.

6.8 Finding a match: INC

The INC function compares each value of a numeric or character variable with a list of values you specify. If a match is found, SYSTAT returns a 1; if not, SYSTAT returns a 0. Valid INC statements are:

```
LET driver = INC(job,63,47,85)
LET driver = INC(job$, 'truck driver','bus driver',
                 'cab driver')
```

In the first example, if *JOB* contains a 63, 47, or 85, *DRIVER* will contain a 1. All other values of *JOB* receive a 0.

In the second example, if *JOB$* contains "truck driver," "bus driver," or "cab driver," the new variable *DRIVER* will contain a 1. All other values for *JOB$* receive a 0 for *DRIVER*.

6.9
Defining intervals on a continuous variable: CUT

CUT can be used to define intervals on a continuous *numeric* variable. For example, if your file contains a variable *AGE* with the age in years of each subject, you could define 12, 19, and 64 as cutpoints to separate subjects into the four age groups shown on this number line:

Each cutpoint is the upper limit of an interval. Notice that to create four age groups, you specify three cutpoints. Each interval includes its upper limit. The first interval extends from $-\infty$ up to and including 12 ($-\infty$, 12). The second interval contains any number greater than (but not equal to 12) and less than or equal to 19 (12, 19). The third interval includes values greater than 19 and less than or equal to 64 (19, 64). The fourth interval includes all values greater than 64 (64, $+\infty$).

The function that does this is:

```
LET age_grp = CUT(age,12,19,64)
```

It assigns the number 1 to the children, 2 to the teens, 3 to the adults, and 4 to the seniors.

You can use the **LABEL** command to assign names to the intervals:

```
LABEL age_grp / 1=child, 2=teen, 3=adult, 4=senior
```

6.10 Defining cutpoints alphabetically: CUT

CUT also divides *character* variables alphabetically into intervals. Suppose the variable *NAME$* contains the following values:

Richards, Carson, Young, Stern, Parker, Buck, Smith, Martin, Howe

The CUT function

```
LET group = CUT(name$, 'Howe', 'Richards')
```

assigns codes alphabetically to the variable *GROUP*:

NAME$	GROUP
Richards	2
Carson	1
Young	3
Stern	3
Parker	2
Buck	1
Smith	3
Martin	2
Howe	1

The new variable *GROUP* contains a 1 for Howe and the names preceding Howe alphabetically, a 2 if the name falls between Howe and Richards (including Richards), and a 3 if it follows Richards.

Date and time functions

SYSTAT has functions that format and transform dates and times. SYSTAT can:

- Give the current date or time in the format you specify.
- Transform date or time character values to numeric values.
- Transform numeric date and time values to character values with a specified format.
- Return the day of the century (DOC) that corresponds to a given year, month, and day. Use DOC to compute time between events.
- Return the day of the week corresponding to a given day of the century.

Use the following functions to change the format of dates and times, to convert numbers to dates and times, and vice versa.

Function	Action
NOW$('format')	The current time and/or date in *format* you specify.
VAL(var$,'format', field)	Extract numbers from dates or times with character values in *var$*. *Format* is the format of the dates or times in *var$*. *Field* is the number of the *format* element you want to extract (for example, for *format* mm/dd/yy, 1 corresponds to month, 2 to day, and 3 to year).
STR$(var,'format')	Write numeric dates or time values stored in *var* as characters using *format*.
DOC(var$,'format')	Return day of century from a character variable containing a date in the specified *format*.
DOC(yvar,mvar,dvar)	Return day of century from year, month, and day variables (specify the arguments in this order).
DOW$(docvar)	Return day of week (Monday, Tuesday, ...) from numeric day of century *docvar*.
DAT(n,'format')	Return day or time from a numeric day of century *n* in specified format of either Y (year), M (month), D (day), h (hour), m (minute), or s (second)—specify only one.

In these date and time functions, SYSTAT uses the following built-in symbols:

D	Day	s	Second	.	Decimal point
M	Month	m	Minute	#	A number before or after a decimal
Y	Year	h	Hour		

Note that hours, minutes, and seconds are assumed to be coded as fractions of days. Also, the number of *m*'s indicates how month is reported:

mm	1 through 12
mmm	Jan, Feb, Mar, Apr, May, ..., Dec
mmmmmmmm	January, February, March, April, May, ..., December

Note: *For this version of SYSTAT, you must limit your format to 12 characters.*

Current time and date: NOW$

The NOW$ function gives the current date or time. You can use NOW$ in the calculator or as part of a transformation statement. For example, if on November 2, 1994, you type

    CALC NOW$('mm/dd/yy')

SYSTAT informs you that it is

    '11/02/94'

If you type

```
CALC NOW$('mmm dd, yyyy')
```

the result is

```
'Nov 2, 1994'
```

Following are the same NOW$ functions used in LET statements:

```
LET TIME$  = NOW$('hh:mm:ss')
LET DATE1$ = NOW$('mm/dd/yy')
LET DATE2$ = NOW$('mmm dd, yyyy')
```

Converting times and dates to numbers: VAL

The VAL function converts date or time character values to numeric values. You must specify the format of the character variable and indicate which field you want to save as a numeric variable. For example,

```
LET month = VAL(date$,'mm/dd/yy',1)
```

- In this command, *DATE$* is the name of the character variable holding the dates.
- mm/dd/yy tells SYSTAT that the first two characters of each *DATE$* value represent the month. This is followed by a slash, two characters representing the day of the month, another slash, and two characters representing the year. For example, a value of *DATE$* could be 03/24/81.
- The last parameter tells SYSTAT which field to read into the new variable. The 1 in this example represents the month field. So, for the date 03/24/81, SYSTAT reads the value 3 and stores it in the numeric variable *MONTH*.

Converting times or dates to characters: STR$

The STR$ function transforms a numeric date or time to a character value using a format you specify:

```
LET newvar$ = STR$(oldvar,'format')
```

SYSTAT interprets the values as days.

The LET statement

```
LET date$ = STR$(dayofcnt,'mm/dd/yy')
```

transforms the following day-of-the-century values in *DAYOFCNT* to the character dates in *DATE$*:

DAYOFCNT	DATE$
1	1/ 1/ 0
366	1/ 1/ 1
15316	12/ 7/41
30000	2/19/82

Day of the century: DOC

The DOC function gives the day of the century corresponding to a particular year, month, and day. The syntax of the DOC function is

```
DOC(year, month, day)
DOC(yvar, mvar, dvar) or DOC(var$,'format')
```

where *year* is either a year value or a variable containing year values, *month* is a month value or a variable containing month values, and *day* is a day of the month value or a variable containing the day of the month. A year value can be a complete year (for example, 1964) or just the last two digits (64). A month value must be the number of the month (for example, 12) rather than the name of the month (December).

Day of the week: DOW$

The DOW$ function gives the day of the week corresponding to a given day of the century. The syntax of the DOW$ function is

```
DOW$(dayofcnt)
```

where *dayofcnt* is either a day-of-the-century value or a variable containing the day-of-the-century value.

You can imbed the DOC function in the DOW$ function to find the day of the week corresponding to a particular date. For example, to find out on which day of the week October 5, 1910, fell, type:

```
CALC DOW$(DOC(1910,10,5))
```

SYSTAT responds:

```
'Wednesday'
```

Character functions

SYSTAT has the following functions for manipulating character values:

UPR$	Change to caps	IND	Find the position of a character
LOW$	Change to lower case	SND$	Soundex encoding
CAP$	Initial caps	CAT$	Join character strings
CNT$	Center	MID$	Extract characters
RGT$	Right-justify	SUB$	Replace *text1* with *text2*
LFT$	Left-justify	PUT$	Replace characters
SQZ$	Remove imbedded blanks	RPD$	Right pad with character string
SQZ$	Remove text	LPD$	Left pad with character string
VAL	Convert character numbers to numeric values	ASC$	ASCII characters
STR$	Convert numbers to character values	ICH	ASCII codes
LAB$	Extract values specified by LABEL		

These functions can:

- Convert the values of a character variable to all upper case or all lower case, or capitalize only the first letter and make the rest of the letters lower case
- Center, or left- or right-justify character values
- Delete blanks or specified text from character values
- Find the position of a particular character in each value of a character variable
- Convert numbers to character values or character variables containing numbers to numeric variables
- Extract text strings from or insert text strings into character values
- Use Soundex coding to create four-digit, alphanumeric codes based on the sound of the word rather than its spelling
- Concatenate the values of two character variables into a single variable
- Find the ASCII code corresponding to a character or find the character corresponding to the ASCII code

Note: *In this version of SYSTAT, results of operations on character variables are limited to 12 characters.*

6.11
Changing
case

The UPR$, LOW$, and CAP$ functions allow you to change the case of character values.

Function	Result
UPR$(*var$*)	Change the values of *var$* to all capitals.
LOW$(*var$*)	Change the values of *var$* to all lower case.
CAP$(*var$*)	Capitalize the first letter of each *var$* value. Make the remaining letters of each value lower case.

The following examples use the *NATIONS* data file with 16 cases:

COUNTRY$

Austria	New Guinea
Burkina Faso	New Zealand
Costa Rica	Norway
France	Portugal
Ireland	Sierra Leone
Italy	UK
Ivory Coast	USA
Netherlands	Yugoslavia

Let's use the UPR$, LOW$, and CAP$ functions to display the country names in four ways:

– As entered in the file
– In capital letters
– In lowercase letters
– With initial capital letters

To list these variables, we use picture format, where the < specifies that the values of the character variable are left justified (for a description of picture format, see Chapter 7):

```
USE nations
LET country2$ = UPR$(country$)
LET country3$ = LOW$(country$)
LET country4$ = CAP$(country3$)

LIST country$ .. country4$ / FORMAT =,
'<<<<<<<<<<<<      <<<<<<<<<<<<      <<<<<<<<<<<<      <<<<<<<<<<<<'
```

```
COUNTRY$          COUNTRY2$          COUNTRY3$          COUNTRY4$
-----------       -----------        -----------        -----------
Austria           AUSTRIA            austria            Austria
Burkina Faso      BURKINA FASO       burkina faso       Burkina Faso
Costa Rica        COSTA RICA         costa rica         Costa Rica
France            FRANCE             france             France
Ireland           IRELAND            ireland            Ireland
Italy             ITALY              italy              Italy
Ivory Coast       IVORY COAST        ivory coast        Ivory Coast
Netherlands       NETHERLANDS        netherlands        Netherlands
New Guinea        NEW GUINEA         new guinea         New Guinea
New Zealand       NEW ZEALAND        new zealand        New Zealand
Norway            NORWAY             norway             Norway
Portugal          PORTUGAL           portugal           Portugal
Sierra Leone      SIERRA LEONE       sierra leone       Sierra Leone
UK                UK                 uk                 Uk
USA               USA                usa                Usa
Yugoslavia        YUGOSLAVIA         yugoslavia         Yugoslavia
```

6.12 Justifying character values

The CNT$, RGT$, and LFT$ functions center and justify character values.

Function	Result
CNT$(*var$*,*n*) *or* CNT$(*var$*)	Center values of variable *var$*, where *n* is width of character field. If you do not specify *n*, SYSTAT assumes a width of 72.
CNT$('*text*')	Center *text* in a 72-character field.
RGT$(*var$*,*n*) RGT$(*var$*)	Right-justify values of variable *var$*, where *n* is width of character field. If you do not specify *n*, SYSTAT assumes a width of 72.
RGT$('*text*')	Right-justify *text* in a 72-character field.
LFT$(*var$*)	Left-justify values of *var$*.
LFT$('*text*')	Left-justify *text*.

SYSTAT assumes that each character field is 72 characters wide, which centers text on the screen or page. Internally, transformations use 72 characters, but a character variable stores only 12 characters. Therefore, for character variables, you need to set *n* to 12. For example, the following commands:

```
USE nations
LET country2$ = CNT$(country$,12)
LET country3$ = RGT$(country$,12)
LET country4$ = SQZ$(country3$)
```

produce three new variables with values centered, right justified, and without spaces. To list these variables, we use picture format, where $ specifies that the values of the character variables are printed as they are stored.

```
   LIST country$ .. country4$ / FORMAT =,
'$$$$$$$$$$$$   $$$$$$$$$$$$   $$$$$$$$$$$$   $$$$$$$$$$$$'
```

```
COUNTRY$        COUNTRY2$       COUNTRY3$       COUNTRY4$
-----------     -----------     -----------     -----------
Austria         Austria         Austria         Austria
Burkina Faso    Burkina Faso    Burkina Faso    BurkinaFaso
Costa Rica      Costa Rica      Costa Rica      CostaRica
France          France          France          France
Ireland         Ireland         Ireland         Ireland
Italy           Italy           Italy           Italy
Ivory Coast     Ivory Coast     Ivory Coast     IvoryCoast
Netherlands     Netherlands     Netherlands     Netherlands
New Guinea      New Guinea      New Guinea      NewGuinea
New Zealand     New Zealand     New Zealand     NewZealand
Norway          Norway          Norway          Norway
Portugal        Portugal        Portugal        Portugal
Sierra Leone    Sierra Leone    Sierra Leone    SierraLeone
UK              UK              UK              UK
USA             USA             USA             USA
Yugoslavia      Yugoslavia      Yugoslavia      Yugoslavia
```

Note that we also used the **SQZ$** function to remove the blanks from some of the names. **SQZ$** is discussed below.

6.13 Deleting blanks or other characters

Use **SQZ$** to delete blanks, commas, apostrophes, or other characters from character values.

Function	Result
SQZ$(*var$*)	Remove all imbedded blanks
SQZ$(*var$*,'*text*')	Remove *text* from the values of *var$*

For example, if you had numbers entered as character values (235,235), you could use **SQZ$** to remove the commas and then convert the character values to numeric values:

```
LET chrvar2$ = SQZ$(chrvar$, ",")
LET numvar = VAL(chrvar2$)
```

These commands convert the character value 235,235, originally stored in *CHRVAR$*, to the number 235235 and store it in *NUMVAR*.

Some examples of **SQZ$** are:

SQZ$(city$) By default blanks are removed. New York becomes NewYork.

SQZ$(name$,'n') Remove all *n*'s.

SQZ$(name$,',') Remove all commas.

SQZ$(airport$,"'") Remove all apostrophes, as in O'Hare.

Locating a character in a string

The IND function locates a particular character in each value of a character variable.

Function	Result
IND(*var$*,'*char*')	The position of the first occurrence of *char* in each value of *var$*

For example, the following LET statement:

```
LET position = IND(team$,'e')
```

finds the character position of the letter *e* in each team name. The *POSITION* values that SYSTAT returns for a given value of *TEAM$* are:

TEAM$	POSITION
Mets	2
Yankees	5
Blue Jays	4
Cubs	0

Note that SYSTAT returns the position of the first *e* in Yankees.

Converting numbers to characters and vice versa

Although SYSTAT allows you to type numbers as values of character variables, the numbers are considered characters and cannot be used in calculations. You can use the VAL function to convert the values into numbers. Conversely, you can use the STR$ function to convert numbers to characters.

Function	Result
VAL(*var$*)	Convert numbers stored in the character variable *var$* to numeric values that can be used in calculations
STR$(*var*)	Convert numeric values of *var* to character values

Suppose you entered years as numbers but want to use the values to label points in a plot. First, convert the numbers to characters and store them in the variable *YEAR$*:

```
LET year$ = STR$(year)
```

Then specify *YEAR$* as the label. For example,

```
PLOT yvar*xvar / LABEL=year$
```

Now suppose, conversely, that you enter the year as characters and then want to do calculations. Use the VAL function to convert the character values to numbers:

```
LET year = VAL(year$)
```

Extracting and inserting characters

SYSTAT has several functions for manipulating character strings.

Function	Result
MID$(var$,p,j)	Extract a string of j characters from each value of var$, beginning with the pth character
SUB$(var$,'text1','text2')	Replace text1 with text2
PUT$(var$,'text',p,j)	Beginning at the pth character of var$, replace the next j characters with the first j characters of text
RPD$(var$,'char')	Right pad the values of var$ with char
LPD$(var$,'char')	Left pad the values of var$ with char

The following commands illustrate the mechanics of the MID$, PUT$, RPD$, and LPD$ functions. These functions operate on the values of the variable *CHARDATA$* shown on the left in the table below.

```
USE chardata
LET last4$    = MID$(chardata$, 9, 4)
LET insert_x$ = SUB$(chardata$,'efgh','XXXX')
LET insert_y$ = PUT$(chardata$, 'YYYY', 5, 4)
LET rtpad_x$  = RPD$(chardata$, 'X')
LET lftpad_y$ = LPD$(chardata$, 'Y')
LIST chardata$ last4$ insert_x$ insert_y$ rtpad_x$,
     lftpad_y$ / FORMAT='<<<<<<<<<<<<  >>>>>>>>>>>,
<<<<<<<<<<<<  <<<<<<<<<<<<  <<<<<<<<<<<<  >>>>>>>>>>>'
```

The results for each value of *CHARDATA$* are:

```
CHARDATA$     LAST4$        INSERT_X$     INSERT_Y$     RTPAD_X$      LFTPAD_Y$
------------  ------------  ------------  ------------  ------------  ------------
abcdefghijkl        ijkl    abcdXXXXi     abcdYYYYijkl  abcdefghijkl  abcdefghijkl
abc  fghijkl        ijkl    abc  fghi     abc YYYYijkl  abc  fghijkl  abc  fghijkl
cdefghijkl            kl    cdXXXXijk     cdefYYYYkl    cdefghijklXX  YYcdefghijkl
abcdefgh                    abcdXXXX      abcdYYYY      abcdefghXXXX  YYYYabcdefgh
123.456.78            78    123.456.7     123.YYYY78    123.456.78XX  YY123.456.78
```

Remembering that values of character variables can contain up to 12 characters, we make the following observations for the first case:

- *LAST4$* contains the last four characters (*ijkl*) of the string *abcdefghijkl*. SYSTAT starts at the ninth character (*i*) and extracts four characters.
- For *INSERT_X$*, SYSTAT replaces the string *efgh* with *XXXX*.
- To create *INSERT_Y$*, SYSTAT starts at the fifth character (*e*) of *abcdefghijkl* and replaces four characters with *YYYY*.
- Since the value *abcdefghijkl* contains the maximum number of characters, it is not altered by the RPD$ function. Notice that for shorter values of *CHARDATA$*, SYSTAT adds X's to the right side of the value.

— Since the value *abcdefghijkl* contains the maximum number of characters, it is not altered by the LPD$ function. Notice that for shorter values of *CHARDATA$*, SYSTAT adds Y's to the left side of the value.

6.14 Converting numbers from European to American notation

You can use SYSTAT's character functions to convert numbers from European notation to American notation. When writing numbers, Europeans use commas where Americans use periods (decimal points) and vice versa. In SYSTAT, numbers in European notation must be stored as character values. However, you can use the SUB$, SQZ$, and VAL functions to convert European numbers to American numbers stored as numeric values.

Suppose the variable *EUR_NUM$* contains numbers in European notation. To convert these number to American notation, you could type:

```
LET no_prd$ = SQZ$(eur_num$,'.')
LET am_num$ = SUB$(no_prd$,',','.')
LET am_num  = VAL(am_num$)
```

Now list the data:

```
LIST eur_num$ no_prd$ am_num$ am_num / FORMAT=,
'<<<<<<<<<<<<   <<<<<<<<<<<<   <<<<<<<<<<<   ######.###'
```

EUR_NUM$	NO_PRD$	AM_NUM$	AM_NUM
365.452,137	365452,137	365452.137	365452.137
256,4	256,4	256.4	256.400
8957	8957	8957	8957.000
2.734.102,56	2734102,56	2734102.56	2734102.560

Note: *You can also use the DECIMAL command to change the character that SYSTAT uses to show the decimal point in output. For example, type DECIMAL ',' to use a comma as the decimal indicator in output.*

6.15
Extracting
first names

Suppose your file contains a variable FULLNAME$ with both the first and last names of each subject:

FULLNAME$

Scout Finch
Jane Eyre
Tom Sawyer
Billy Budd

You can extract the first name of each subject and store the result in the variable *FIRST$*. There are two ways to create *FIRST$*.

**Using MID$**. You can use IND and MID$ together to create FIRST$:

```
LET index  = IND(fullname$,' ')
LET first$ = MID$(fullname$,1,INDEX-1)
```

The first **LET** statement finds the position of the blank between the first and last name and stores the position in the variable *INDEX*. The second LET statement starts with the first character of *FULLNAME$*, extracts *INDEX*–1 characters, and stores the resulting string in the variable *FIRST$*. So, for the first case, *Scout Finch*, *INDEX* gets the value 6, since the blank is the sixth character. Then the MID$ function extracts the first five (*INDEX*–1) characters (*Scout*) of *FULLNAME$*, and stores the string in *FIRST$*.

Note that you can create *FIRST$* with only one **LET** statement by imbedding the IND function in the MID$ function as follows:

```
LET first$ = MID$(fullname$,1,IND(fullname$,' ')-1)
```

**Using PUT$**. Alternatively, you can create *FIRST$* by using the PUT$ function to replace the letters in each last name with blanks:

```
LET index  = IND(fullname$,' ')
LET first$ = PUT$(fullname$,' ',INDEX,13-INDEX)
```

So, for the first case, *INDEX* gets the value 6 as before. Then the PUT$ function starts with the sixth character and replaces the next seven (13–*INDEX*) characters with blanks. The result, *Scout*, is stored in the variable *FIRST$*.

As with the MID$ function, you can save a step by imbedding the IND function in the PUT$ function:

```
LET first$ = PUT$(fullname$,' ', IND(fullname$,' '),
               13-IND(fullname$,' '))
```

6.16 Concatenating character strings

Use the **CAT$** function to join the values of two variables into a single variable.

Function	Result
CAT$(*var1$*,*var2$*)	Join contents of *var1$* with *var2$*, eliminating trailing blanks

Note: *For this version of SYSTAT, the result can be at most 12 characters long.*

Suppose a file called *MYDATA* contains the following data:

AGE$	SEX$
Adult	Female
Child	Male
Adult	Male
Teen	Female
Child	Female
Child	Male
Adult	Female
Child	Female
Teen	Male

You can use **CAT$** to combine these values into a new variable named *SEX_AGE$*. To make the new values easier to read, separate the *SEX* and *AGE$* values with a blank. You can do this by first appending an underscore to the beginning of the *AGE$* value, concatenating the *SEX$* and *AGE$* variables, and using the **SUB$** function to replace the underscores with blanks:

```
USE mydata
LET age$ = CAT$('_',age$)
LET sex_age$ = CAT$(sex$,age$)
LET sex_age$ = SUB$(sex_age$,'_',' ')
```

Now sort the values by *SEX_AGE$* and list the results:

```
SORT sex_age$
LIST sex$ age$ sex_age$ / FORMAT='  <<<<<<  <<<<<< ,
<<<<<<<<<<<< '
```

```
SEX$    AGE$    SEX_AGE$
------  ------  ------------
Female  _Adult  Female Adult
Female  _Adult  Female Adult
Female  _Child  Female Child
Female  _Child  Female Child
Female  _Teen   Female Teen
Male    _Adult  Male Adult
Male    _Child  Male Child
Male    _Child  Male Child
Male    _Teen   Male Teen
```

The results are as expected. To save the data, type **SAVE** *filename*. Now we can use *SEX_AGE$* as a grouping variable and request plots, statistics, or other statistical analyses separately for the six groups.

6.17
ASCII codes

The **ICH** function gives the ASCII code for a character. The **ASC$** function returns the character corresponding to a given ASCII code.

Function	Result
`ICH( 'char' )`	ASCII code corresponding to the character *char*
`ICH( var$ )`	ASCII code corresponding to the value in *var$*
`ASC$( int )`	ASCII character corresponding to the integer *int*
`ASC$( var )`	ASCII character corresponding to the value in *var*

The following table shows some characters and their ASCII codes:

Character	ASCII code
A	65
a	97
3	51
?	63
#	35
}	125
Å	143
å	134

So, for example, **ICH**('3')=51 and **ASC$**(35)=#.

To obtain an ASCII table, specify:

```
BASIC
    FOR I = 1 to 256
    LET a$ = ASC$(I)
    PRINT I, A$,
    RUN
```

6.18
Using Soundex
to code names

The Soundex encoding function (**SND$**) allows you to create an alphanumeric code of a word based on how the word sounds rather than its spelling. The **SND$** function can be used to create a new variable to select similarly spelled duplicate records.

Function	Result
`SND$( var$ )`	An alphanumeric SOUNDEX code of *var$*

The **SND$** function uses a formula to replace letters with numbers in an *Xnnn* format, where *X* is the letter with which the word begins and *nnn* is up to three numbers indicating the "sound" of the rest of the word.

Soundex ignores vowels (*A*, *E*, *I*, *O*, *U*) and the consonants *H*, *W*, and *Y*. It then codes for the remaining letters:

B, F, P, V	→**1**		L	→**4**
C, G, J, K, Q, S, X, Z	→**2**		M, N	→**5**
D, T	→**3**		R	→**6**

If the same code occurs consecutively, the second occurrence is skipped. Some names with their Soundex codes are:

Berry	B6
Wilson	W425
Anderson	A536
Johnson	J525
Smith	S53
Carlson	C642

For a quick way to see the Soundex code of a name, use SYSTAT's calculator:

```
CALC SND$('Smith')
```

It returns:

```
S53
```

Let's say you want to check for duplicate records in a large file like this one named *SOUNDEX*, but you wonder about alternative spellings. First create a variable containing the Soundex code for the *LASTNAM$* variable:

```
LET CODE = SND$(lastnam$)
```

Then sort the file by this new variable:

		LASTNAM$	**INCOME**	**AGE**	**SEX$**	**CODE$**
CASE	1	Barrett	376.300	22.000	F	B630
CASE	2	Barrott	872.100	34.000	F	B630
CASE	3	Howell	987.200	36.000	F	H400
CASE	4	MacCarthy	765.100	45.000	M	M263
CASE	5	MacLoud	987.300	40.000	F	M243
CASE	6	McCarthy	765.000	24.000	M	M263
CASE	7	McCarty	367.100	38.000	F	M263
CASE	8	McLoud	987.300	40.000	F	M243
CASE	9	McLeod	542.300	32.000	M	M243
CASE	10	Stephens	683.200	30.000	F	S315
CASE	11	Stevens	743.200	55.000	M	S315
CASE	12	Wilkenson	999.300	48.000	F	W425
CASE	13	Wilkinson	235.100	48.000	M	W425

By viewing the file, you could then easily pick out duplicate records. If you are looking for a specific duplicate record, instead of creating the

CODE variable, you can use **Select** to select all records with alternative spellings of the same name:

```
SELECT SND$('stephens') = SND$(lastnam$)
```

Since the Soundex code for both names (Stephens and Stevens) is S315, all three cases are selected. Now, we just list the selected cases to compare *AGE*, *SEX*, and *INCOME* to be sure that we have unique records, or a duplicate spelling of the same record.

```
LASTNAM$   INCOME   AGE   SEX$
Stephens    683.2   30.0     F
Stevens     743.2   55.0     M
```

You will discover that the records for Stephens and Stevens are unique.

Note: *Soundex uses the first letter of the word to begin the code, so words such as Carson and Karson have different codes—C625 and K625. Also, Soundex is not useful for languages other than English.*

Distribution functions

For 13 distributions, SYSTAT provides cumulative, density, inverse, and random variate functions.

Distribution	Cumulative	Density	Inverse	Random data
Uniform	UCF *(x,low,hi)*	UDF *(x,low,hi)*	UIF *(α,low,hi)*	URN *(low,hi)*
Normal (0,1)	ZCF *(z,loc,sc)*	ZDF *(z,loc,sc)*	ZIF *(α,loc,sc)*	ZRN *(loc,sc)*
t	TCF *(t,df)*	TDF *(t,df)*	TIF *(α,df)*	TRN *(df)*
F	FCF *(F,df1,df2)*	FDF *(F,df1,df2)*	FIF *(α,df1,df2)*	FRN *(df1,df2)*
Chi-square	XCF *(χ2,df)*	XDF *(χ2,df)*	XIF *(α,df)*	XRN *(df)*
Gamma	GCF *(γ,p)*	GDF *(γ,p)*	GIF *(α,p)*	GRN *(p)*
Beta	BCF *(β,p,q)*	BDF *(β,p,q)*	BIF *(α,p,q)*	BRN *(p,q)*
Exponential (0,1)	ECF *(x,loc,sc)*	EDF *(x,loc,sc)*	EIF *(α,loc,sc)*	ERN *(loc,sc)*
Logistic (0,1)	LCF *(x,loc,sc)*	LDF *(x,loc,sc)*	LIF *(α,loc,sc)*	LRN *(loc,sc)*
Studentized	SCF *(x,k,df)*	SDF *(x,k,df)*	SIF *(α,k,df)*	SRN *(k,df)*
Weibull	WCF *(x,p,q)*	WDF *(x,p,q)*	WIF *(α,p,q)*	WRN *(p,q)*
Binomial	NCF *(x,n,p)*	NDF *(x,n,p)*	NIF *(α,n,p)*	NRN *(n,p)*
Poisson	PCF *(x,p)*	PDF *(x,p)*	PIF *(α,p)*	PRN *(p)*

*where **low** is the smallest value and **hi** is the largest; **loc** is the center of location and **sc** is the scale value. Default values are displayed in the* Distribution *column. If* **low**, **hi**, **loc**, *or* **sc** *is omitted, its default value is assumed.*

Cumulative distribution functions compute the probability that a random value from the specified distribution falls below or is equal to the given value. The result of the **density functions** is the height at x of the ordinate under the density curve of the specified distribution. **Inverse distribution functions** take a specified alpha (a probability value between 0 and 1) and return the critical value below which lies that proportion of the specified distribution. **Random variate functions** generate pseudo-random variates from the specified distribution.

By default, *Uniform* refers to a distribution uniformly distributed from 0 to 1 (specify *low* and *hi* to change these values). *Normal* refers to the standard normal distribution N(0,1) with mean 0 and standard deviation 1 (specify a different mean as *loc* and standard deviation as *sc*.) *Exponential* has parameter 1 (you can also use *loc* and *sc*). *Logistic* is the standard L(0,1) (you can also use *loc* and *sc*). All of the others require you to specify their parameters. These parameters can be noninteger.

The algorithms for all functions are chosen to favor numerical accuracy over speed. Some functions may take time to evaluate for some choices of parameters.

Use the cumulative distribution functions to obtain probabilities associated with observed sample statistics. For many applications, to obtain significance levels, you must find the upper tail probabilities; for example,

```
LET p = 1 - FCF(4.14,3,7)
```

Use the inverse distributions to determine critical values and to construct confidence intervals. They are also handy for power calculations.

You can use transformations for the random variate functions to produce random deviates of the desired distributions. To produce a random normal deviate with the required mean and standard deviation, use one like:

```
LET normal = mean + stddev*ZRN   or
LET norm = ZRN(10,2)
```

To produce a uniform deviate between *A* and *B*, use an expression like:

```
LET unifrmab = a + (b-a)*URN   or
LET unifrmab = URN(a,b)
```

To get an extreme value variate with location **ALPHA** and scale **BETA**, use:

```
LET extreme = alpha - beta*LOG(ERN)
```

To get a gamma variate with shape **ALPHA** and scale **BETA**, use:

```
LET gamma = beta*GRN(alpha)
```

If **ALPHA** is an integer, the above expression returns an Erlang variate.

Random number generators

The algorithm for uniform variates generates the numbers by a triple modulo method. Each uniform variate is constructed from three multiplicative congruential generators with prime modulus. The initial seeds for each generator are 13579, 12345, and 131 (Wichman and Hill, 1982). You can modify the last seed of this generator by using **RSEED**:

```
RSEED = seed
```

where *seed* is any positive integer.

6.19 Generating a new file of random data

You can generate a new file with random numbers using the Data window or the BASIC procedure.

For example, to fill 200 cases for a variable *A* with normal random data, select **File⟶New⟶Data** to open the Data window with an empty worksheet, and create a variable named *A*. Then select **Edit⟶Fill Worksheet** and specify the desired number of rows. Finally, use **Data⟶Transform** to fill the variable with random values:

```
LET a=ZRN
```

With commands, first specify **NEW** and then use **REPEAT** to specify the number of cases you want:

```
BASIC
  NEW
  REPEAT=200
  LET a=ZRN
  SAVE filename
  RUN
```

Ranking and Standardizing Variables

You can use **Rank** and **Standardize** on the **Data** menu to transform the values of a variable to their rank order or to standardized scores (*z* scores or a 0,1 scale). If you are using commands, these transformations can be executed in any procedure.

Ranks

To replace the values of one or more variables with their rank values, select **Data**➠**Rank** or use the RANK command. Rank changes the values of only the variables(s) you select. All other variables are copied to the new file unchanged.

The **rank** is the case number a value has if the data are sorted by that variable. For example, the smallest value is rank 1, and the largest value in a sample of 15 cases is 15. Ties are averaged. This example shows how ties are handled:

Value	Rank
1	1
2	2
3	3.5
3	3.5
10	5
11	6

Save file specifies an output file for the results. Otherwise, the transformed data are stored in a temporary file.

With commands, simply type RANK followed by the variable(s) you want to rank as shown below. If no variable is specified, all numeric variables are ranked.

```
RANK age, income
```

If you want to have both the ranks and the original values in one file, use LET to make a copy of the variable before ranking:

```
LET age2 = age
```

Standardized scores

You can standardize one or more variables with **Data**➠**Standardize** or the STANDARDIZE command. Standardize replaces the values of each specified variable with its sample standard score (*z* score) or range standardized scores.

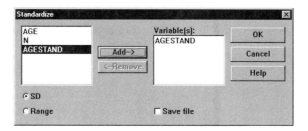

SD
: Replace values of each variable you specify with its sample standard score (*z* score). For each variable, SYSTAT subtracts the variable's sample mean from each value and then divides the difference by the sample standard deviation. The standardized values have mean 0 and standard deviation 1.

Range
: Subtract the smallest data value of each variable from each value and divide by its range; thus, the new scale starts at 0 and ends at 1.0.

$$\frac{value - minimum}{maximum - minimum}$$

The results are stored in a different file. If you want both standardized scores and values of the original variable, use LET to make a copy of the variable before standardizing. The default is SD.

Examples are:

```
STANDARDIZE
STANDARDIZE question(1) .. question(5)
```
or
```
STANDARDIZE / RANGE
STANDARDIZE question(1) .. question(5) / RANGE
```

6.20
Standardizing age

This example uses the *CHILDREN* data set:

SEX$	AGE	N
Female	5	1
Female	6	4
Female	5	5
Female	3	8
Female	5	10
Female	5	13
Female	6	14
Male	6	2
Male	4	3
Male	6	6
Male	8	7
Male	6	9
Male	4	11
Male	5	12

We create and list a variable *AGESTAND* that contains the standardized values of *AGE*.

```
USE children
SORT sex$
LET agestand=age
STANDARDIZE agestand
LIST age agestand
```

SYSTAT responds:

```
Case number          AGE      AGESTAND
         1         5.000       -0.237
         2         5.000       -0.237
         3         6.000        0.593
         4         5.000       -0.237
         5         3.000       -1.898
         6         5.000       -0.237
         7         6.000        0.593
         8         6.000        0.593
         9         4.000       -1.068
        10         6.000        0.593
        11         8.000        2.254
        12         6.000        0.593
        13         4.000       -1.068
        14         5.000       -0.237
```

AGESTAND now has standardize age values with mean 0 and standard deviation 1. Remember that standardizing does not change the shape of the distribution. If the data are highly skewed or bimodal before standardizing, they will be so after. Standardizing simply moves the location and rescales the spread of your values.

The Calculator

SYSTAT's calculator is available with every statistical analysis or graphical display. Use it just as you would any hand calculator to:

- Balance your checkbook
- Get the current date and time
- Take the antilog of an output result (for example, EXP(1.826))
- Compute your own test statistic for comparing a smaller model (S) nested within a larger model (L)—use the residual sum of squares from the two models:

$$F = \frac{(SS_S - SS_L)/(df_S - df_L)}{SS_S/df_L}$$

- Find the probability associated with the resulting F statistic
- Try out a transformation statement to check if your formula is correct—for example, compute percentage change:

$$\frac{after - before}{before} \bullet 100$$

The calculator does not know the values of any variables in your current file—it uses only the numbers you enter in it. All of the functions and operators described in this chapter are available in SYSTAT's calculator.

Today's date and time

If you type:

```
CALC NOW$ ('mmm dd, hhhh:mm')
```

SYSTAT responds:

```
'Jan 21,    16:10
```

Finding the antilog

To exponentiate the value 1.826 (that is, to compute $e^{1.826}$), type:

```
    CALC EXP(1.826)
```

and the result:

```
6.209
```

Computing an F statistic

In Example 8.4 in Chapter 8, we use the *LONGLEY* data to fit a multiple regression model with six independent variables. In Example 8.5, we use forward stepping to select a subset of three predictors. The residual sum of squares for the six-variable model is 836,424.056 with 9 *df*, for the three-variable model, 1,323,360.743 with 12 *df*. Let's construct an *F* statistic to compare the two models (that is, to test $H_0: \beta_4 = \beta_5 = \beta_6 = 0$):

CALC ((1323360.743 - 836424.056)/3) / (836424.056/9)

The calculator returns an *F* of 1.746.

Finding the p value associated with F. This expression requests the *p* value for $F = 1.746$ with numerator $df = 3$ and denominator $df = 9$:

CALC 1 - FCF(1.746, 3, 9)

The calculator returns the probability 0.227. The inclusion of the extra three variables does not significantly improve the fit of the model.

List, Sort, and Select

Laszlo Engelman

This chapter describes how to:

– Display data values or results from analyses

– Sort the cases in ascending or descending order

– Select a subset of cases based on conditions:

```
SELECT sex$ = 'Male' AND age > 21
```

Overview

Listing Data

Sorting Cases

Selecting a Subset of Cases

Overview

This chapter describes these items on the **Data** menu:

List Cases List all or selected variables in a data file.

Sort Sort the cases in a file according to values of one or more numeric or string variables.

Select Cases Specify a condition to select a subset of cases for analysis. For example, using *AGE>21* restricts subsequent analyses to adults, omitting any case where the value of *AGE* is 21 or less.

LIST, SORT and SELECT are available in any procedure. With commands:

```
LIST varlist
SORT varlist
SELECT condition1 AND condition2 OR ...
```

Listing Data

Often during the steps of an analysis, you need to stop to view data values. For example, you may want to see values of specific variables side by side for a few selected cases, check that transformations or recoding worked as intended, or scan other data values for cases with extreme residuals.

You can list values of cases for one or more variables using **Data⇒List Cases** or the LIST command. Variables are displayed in the order they are selected. If no variables are selected, all variables are listed.

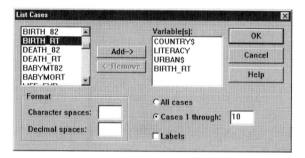

You can list all cases, or the first *n* cases up to a number you specify.

Format. Specify the number of character spaces and the number of decimal places to print for numeric variables.

Label. Display defined category labels instead of values. (Select **Data⇒ Label** to define category labels.)

With commands:

```
USE filename
LIST varlist / FORMAT=m,n or 'picture format',
              N=n  LABEL
```

You can use **Data⇒ID Variable** to select a numeric or string variable whose values are listed before other values for each case.

When you want to list more than five variables across the panel, select **Edit⇒Options** and specify **Wide-132 char** under **Output Results**. This allows you to print up to eight variables (plus a case number or label) on each line.

Using commands, you can specify the width and justification for each column. See "Picture format" on p. 157.

7.1
Listing all variables and cases

To list all values in the *MINWRLD* data file, select **Data➞List Cases** and click **OK**. Since no variables are selected, all variables are listed.

With commands:

```
USE miniwrld
LIST
```

The first three cases of *MINIWRLD* are shown below:

```
Case number COUNTRY$       POP_1990     URBAN         BIRTH_RT     BABYMORT
Case number GDP_CAP        EDUC         HEALTH        MIL          GOV$
Case number LIFEEXPM       LIFEEXPF     LITERACY      GROUP$       B_TO_D
          1 France           56.358       73.000        14.000        6.000
          1  14542.657      648.069      728.249       432.780 Democracy
          1     73.000       82.000       99.000 Europe            1.556
          2 Greece           10.028       65.000        11.000       10.000
          2   5614.184      115.000      158.700       260.400 Democracy
          2     75.000       80.000       95.000 Europe            1.222
          3 Switzerland       6.742       58.000        12.000        5.000
          3  17723.499      853.538     1209.077       330.769 Democracy
          3     75.000       83.000       99.000 Europe            1.333
```

The individual cases are too long to fit on one line (80 characters), so each case spreads across three lines. (You can use **Edit➞Options** to specify a wider output format if needed.)

You can also display separate panels for selected variables:

```
LIST country$ .. babymort
LIST gdp_cap .. gov$
```

7.2
Listing 10 cases for selected variables

Here we list only cases 1 through 10 of the variables *COUNTRY$, LITERACY, URBAN*, and *BIRTH_RT* in the *MINIWRLD* file. With commands:

```
USE miniwrld
LIST country$ literacy urban birth_rt / N=10
```

```
Case number COUNTRY$       LITERACY      URBAN       BIRTH_RT
          1 France             99.0       73.0         14.0
          2 Greece             95.0       65.0         11.0
          3 Switzerland        99.0       58.0         12.0
          4 Spain              97.0       91.0         11.0
```

```
 5    UK           99.0    76.0    14.0
 6    Hungary      99.0    54.0    12.0
 7    Iraq         55.0    68.0    46.0
 8    Pakistan     26.0    28.0    43.0
 9    Ethiopia     55.2    14.0    45.0
10    Afghanistan  12.0    16.0    44.0
```

7.3 Specifying an ID variable

You can use **Data▸ID Variable** before using **List cases** to select a string variable, *COUNTRY$*, to list before other values for each case. We also use **format** to specify one decimal space in each field. With commands:

```
USE miniwrld
IDVAR=country$
LIST literacy urban birth_rt / N=10, /FORMAT = 1
```

```
* Case ID * LITERAC URBAN  BIRTH_R
France        99.0    73.0   14.0
Greece        95.0    65.0   11.0
Switzerland   99.0    58.0   12.0
Spain         97.0    91.0   11.0
UK            99.0    76.0   14.0
Hungary       99.0    54.0   12.0
Iraq          55.0    68.0   46.0
Pakistan      26.0    28.0   43.0
Ethiopia      55.2    14.0   45.0
Afghanistan   12.0    16.0   44.0
```

7.4 Incorporating group labels

You can use **Data▸Value Label** in conjunction with **Label** to add group labels to your listing. For example:

```
USE survey2
LABEL marital / 1='Never', 2='Married', 3='Divorced',
                4='Separated'
LABEL educatn / 1,2='Dropout', 3='HS grad',
                4,5='College', 6,7='Degree +'
LIST marital educatn age sex / N=12  LABEL
```

```
Case number MARITAL     EDUCATN   AGE        SEX
     1      Divorced    College   58.000     1.000
     2      Married     HS grad   45.000     2.000
     3      Divorced    HS grad   50.000     2.000
     4      Separated   HS grad   33.000     2.000
     5      Married     HS grad   24.000     1.000
     6      Married     Dropout   58.000     2.000
     7      Never       HS grad   22.000     1.000
     8      Married     Dropout   30.000     1.000
     9      Married     HS grad   57.000     2.000
    10      Married     Dropout   39.000     1.000
    11      Married     HS grad   23.000     2.000
    12      Separated   Dropout   55.000     2.000
```

Picture format

You can use picture format, available on the FORMAT option of the LIST command, to display your data. You use symbols to tell SYSTAT exactly how to format your listing. This gives you greater control over the appearance of your output. Here are some of the things you can do with picture format:

– Specify the number of characters or digits in each field.
– Specify the number of spaces between variables.
– For numeric data, you can specify the number of digits to display after the decimal point for each variable individually.
– Choose whether to left- or right-justify the values within a field.
– Insert characters, such as vertical bars (| |), to separate columns.

The syntax for the picture format option is:

```
LIST varlist / FORMAT = 'symbol strings'
```

Note that you must enclose your symbol strings in quotation marks. Use a #, >, <, or $ for each digit or character. Numeric variables are always right-justified. For string variables, the symbol you use determines whether it is left- or right-justified:

symbol		symbol	
blank	Separate fields	Y	Years
>	Right-justify	M	Months
<	Left-justify	D	Days
$	Do not justify	h	Hours
.	Decimal point	m	Minutes
		s	Seconds
#	Numeric digit		

If you include any other symbol (such as a vertical bar) in the FORMAT statement, it is printed "as is" for every case. The date symbols (Y, M, D, h, m, and s) are used to format dates in your output and are discussed in Chapter 6.

7.5 Picture format example

The following example uses picture format:

```
LIST name$ age total drugdose /,
      FORMAT = '<<<<<<<<<  ## | ###### ##.##'
```

– The nine characters of *NAME$* are left-justified, followed by two spaces
– The *AGE* values are right-justified, followed by a space, a vertical bar and another space

- *TOTAL* values are right-justified in a field of six digits followed by a space
- *DRUGDOSE* values are displayed with two digits after the decimal point

---

Note: *If you want to display case numbers, include the built-in variable CASE in the variable list of your LIST statement.*

7.6 Displaying many variables in one panel

This example uses data from a survey to illustrate picture format. In Los Angeles (circa 1980), interviewers from the Institute for Social Science Research at UCLA surveyed a multi-ethnic sample of community members for an epidemiological study of depression and help-seeking behavior among adults (Afifi and Clark). The CESD depression index was used to measure depression. The index is constructed by asking people to respond to twenty items: "I felt I could not shake off the *blues...*", "My sleep was *restless,*" etc. For each item, respondents answered "less than 1 time per day" (score 0); "1 to 2 days per week" (score 1); "3 to 4 days per week" (score 2), or "5 to 7 days" (score 3). Responses to the 20 items were summed to form a *TOTAL* score. Persons with a CESD *TOTAL* greater than or equal to 16 are classified as depressed. The information available for each subject includes the following:

Variable	Definition
ID	Subject identification number
SEX	1 = male; 2 = female
AGE	Age in years at last birthday
MARITAL	1 = never married; 2 = married; 3 = divorced; 4 = separated; 5 = widowed
EDUCATN	1 = less than high school; 2 = some high school; 3 = finished high school; 4 = some college; 5 = finished bachelor's degree; 6 = finished master's degree; 7 = finished doctorate
EMPLOY	1 = full time; 2 = part time; 3 = unemployed; 4 = retired; 5 = houseperson; 6 = in school; 7 = other
INCOME	Thousands of dollars per year
RELIGION	1 = Protestant; 2 = Catholic; 3 = Jewish; 4 = none; 5 = other
BLUE to DISLIKE	The 20 depression items
TOTAL	Total CESD score
CASECONT	0 = normal; 1 = depressed (CESD ≥ 16)
DRINK	1 = yes, regularly; 2 = no

Variable	Definition
HEALTHY	General health? 1 = excellent; 2 = good; 3 = fair; 4 = poor
CHRONIC	Any chronic illnesses in last year? 0 = no; 1 = yes

Often it is beneficial to see many variables in a single panel so that cases can be compared. To do this, use the FORMAT option to specify a picture format:

```
USE survey
LIST id .. total casecont drink / FORMAT=,
```

`'#### # ### # # # ### # | # # # # # # # # # # # # # # # # # # # # || ## || ### #'`

The first 30 and last 30 cases are shown below. It is easy to see who is depressed by scanning the column labeled *TOTAL* (bordered by a double vertical rule):

```
                        R
            M       E
            A D E   I   L
            R E N   N   I            D             F F A H               B         B G   T U
            I E M   C   I            E L           E A S O     P H E H O           A E   A N D
            C P N   O   G            P O           A I _ P H E O F P J R E _       T N E D T   L F I
          S A T L   O   I          B R N       C S F U O F P J R E O E A R E N     T O   L F I   K R S
        S A T A O   M   N        D L E E C S   F U O F P E J R E N N S L K         T A   N L L   N L L
      I E G A T M   O   N        B E S R A U   R O U P O E A R E N N S L K         T L   N N S   K N N
      D X E L N Y   E   N        U E S Y Y D   L E D L Y Y D T T P G D S Y E       A L               N
      --- - -- - - - - - -- -    - - - - - - - - - - - - - - - - - - - - - -     --  -  -- -- --- -
       1  2 68 5 2 4    4 1      0 0 0 0 0 0 0 0 0 0 0 0 0 0 0 0 0 0 0 0      0    0 2
       2  1 58 3 4 1   15 1      0 0 1 0 0 0 0 0 0 0 1 0 0 1 0 1 0 0 0 0      4    0 1
       3  2 45 2 3 1   28 1      0 0 0 1 0 0 0 0 0 0 0 1 1 1 0 0 0 0 0 0      4    0 1
       4  2 50 3 3 3    9 1      0 0 0 0 1 1 0 3 0 0 0 0 0 0 0 0 0 0 0 0      5    0 2
       5  2 33 4 3 1   35 1      0 0 0 0 0 0 3 3 0 0 0 0 0 0 0 0 0 0 0 0      6    0 1
       6  1 24 2 3 1   11 1      0 0 0 0 0 0 0 1 0 0 1 2 0 0 2 1 0 0 0 0      7    0 1
       7  2 58 2 2 5   11 1      2 1 1 2 1 0 0 2 2 0 0 0 0 3 0 0 0 0 0 1     15    0 2
       8  1 22 1 3 1    9 1      0 1 2 0 2 1 0 0 0 0 0 0 0 1 1 1 1 0         10    0 2
       9  2 47 2 3 4   23 2      0 1 1 0 0 3 0 0 0 0 0 3 0 3 2 3 0 0 0 0     16    1 1
      10  1 30 2 2 1   35 4      0 0 0 0 0 0 0 0 0 0 0 0 0 0 0 0 0 0 0 0      0    0 1
      11  2 20 1 2 3   25 4      0 0 1 0 1 2 1 0 0 1 0 1 2 2 1 1 2 3 0 0     18    1 1
      12  2 57 2 3 2   24 1      0 0 0 0 0 0 0 0 0 0 0 0 2 2 0 0 0 0 0 0      4    0 2
      13  1 39 2 2 1   28 1      1 1 0 0 0 0 0 0 0 0 1 0 2 0 1 0 0 1 1        8    0 1
      14  2 61 5 3 4   13 1      0 0 0 1 0 0 1 0 0 0 1 0 0 0 0 0 0 0 1        4    0 1
      15  2 23 2 3 1   15 2      0 0 0 0 0 0 0 0 0 0 0 1 3 1 0 2 1            8    0 1
      16  2 21 1 2 1    6 1      1 1 2 0 1 1 1 1 2 2 0 1 1 2 1 1 1 2 0 0     21    1 1
      17  2 23 1 4 1    8 1      3 3 2 3 3 3 2 2 3 2 2 2 1 2 3 2 0 1 0 3     42    1 1
      18  2 55 4 2 3   19 1      1 0 1 1 1 0 0 0 0 2 0 0 0 0 0 0 0 0          6    0 2
      19  2 26 1 6 1   15 1      0 0 0 0 0 0 0 0 0 0 0 0 0 0 0 0 0 0 0 0      0    0 2
      20  1 64 5 2 4    9 4      0 0 0 0 0 0 0 3 0 0 0 0 0 0 0 0 0 0 0 0      3    0 1
      21  2 44 1 3 1    6 2      0 0 0 0 0 0 0 3 0 0 0 0 0 0 0 0 0 0 0 0      3    0 1
      22  2 25 2 3 1   35 1      0 0 0 1 0 0 0 0 0 0 0 1 0 1 0 1 0 0 0 0      4    0 1
      23  2 72 5 3 4    7 2      0 0 0 0 0 0 0 0 0 0 0 0 2 0 0 0 0 0 0 0      2    0 1
      24  2 61 2 3 1   19 2      0 0 0 0 0 0 0 0 0 0 0 2 0 2 0 0 0 0 0 0      4    0 2
      25  2 43 3 3 1    6 1      0 0 0 0 1 0 1 2 1 0 0 1 0 1 1 2 0 0 0 0     10    0 2
      26  2 52 2 2 5   19 2      1 2 1 0 1 0 0 0 0 0 1 1 0 3 2 0 0 0 0 0     12    0 1
      27  2 23 2 3 5   13 1      0 0 0 0 0 0 3 0 0 0 0 1 1 0 0 0 1 0 0        6    0 2
      28  1 73 4 2 4    5 2      0 1 2 0 2 2 0 0 0 0 0 2 0 0 0 0 0 0 0 0      9    0 1
      29  2 34 2 3 2   19 2      0 2 2 0 1 0 2 1 1 1 1 2 3 2 3 3 2 0 0 2     28    1 1
      30  2 34 2 3 1   20 1      U U 0 0 0 0 0 0 0 0 0 1 0 0 0 0 0 0 0 0      1    0 1
                           ***  We skip cases 31–264  ***
     265  1 48 3 3 1   23 4      0 1 0 0 0 1 0 0 0 0 0 0 1 2 1 0 0 0          7    0 1
     266  1 22 1 3 1    9 4      0 1 1 0 0 0 0 1 0 0 0 1 0 0 1 1 0 0 0 1      7    0 1
     267  1 62 2 3 1   15 3      0 1 1 1 1 0 1 0 1 1 1 1 1 0 1 1 0 1 0 2     15    0 1
     268  2 43 3 4 1   15 3      1 1 0 0 1 0 0 0 0 1 0 2 1 0 0 0 0 0 0 0      8    0 1
     269  2 23 2 5 3   23 4      2 2 0 0 2 0 0 0 0 1 0 0 3 1 3 1 0 0 0 0     15    0 2
     270  1 36 3 7 1   65 4      0 0 0 0 0 0 0 0 0 0 1 0 0 1 1 0 0 0 0        3    0 1
     271  2 32 2 5 1   35 1      0 0 1 0 0 0 0 0 0 0 0 0 0 1 1 0 0 0          3    0 1
     272  1 26 1 5 1   13 2      1 1 0 1 0 0 0 0 0 0 0 1 0 1 1 1 1 0          8    0 1
     273  1 20 1 3 1   15 3      0 1 1 0 1 1 0 0 1 1 0 0 0 1 1 1 1 1 1 0     12    0 1
     274  2 42 5 3 1   11 1      0 0 0 0 0 0 0 2 0 0 0 0 3 0 2 3 0 0 0 0     10    0 1
     275  1 35 1 4 1   11 1      0 1 2 0 1 0 0 0 0 0 0 1 0 0 0 1 0 0 1 1      8    0 1
```

```
276 2 52 4 2 1  8 1   0 0 1 0 0 0 0 0 1 0 0 0 0 0 1 0 0 0 0 0 ‖  3 ‖ 0 1
277 2 77 5 3 4  6 1   0 0 0 0 0 0 0 0 0 0 0 0 0 0 0 0 0 0 0 0 ‖  0 ‖ 0 1
278 1 32 1 5 1 23 2   0 1 0 0 1 1 1 0 2 1 1 1 0 2 1 1 1 0 0 0 ‖ 14 ‖ 0 1
279 2 26 1 5 1  6 4   0 1 0 0 0 1 0 0 0 0 1 3 0 1 1 1 3 0 0 0 ‖ 12 ‖ 0 1
280 1 62 2 3 1 35 1   0 0 0 0 0 0 0 0 0 0 0 0 0 0 0 0 0 0 0 0 ‖  0 ‖ 0 1
281 1 23 1 4 1 45 2   0 0 0 0 0 0 0 0 0 0 0 0 0 0 0 0 0 0 0 0 ‖  0 ‖ 0 1
282 1 32 2 5 1 35 3   1 1 0 0 1 0 0 0 2 1 1 0 0 1 0 2 1 1 0 0 ‖ 12 ‖ 0 1
283 2 30 2 3 1 28 3   1 1 0 0 0 0 0 1 2 1 1 2 0 1 0 3 0 0 0 0 ‖ 13 ‖ 0 1
284 2 83 5 2 5  4 1   0 0 0 0 0 0 0 0 0 0 0 0 0 0 0 0 0 0 0 0 ‖  0 ‖ 0 2
285 1 37 1 4 1 13 4   0 0 0 0 0 0 0 0 2 1 0 0 2 2 1 0 1 1 0 0 ‖ 10 ‖ 0 1
286 2 42 2 3 1 35 2   0 0 0 0 0 0 3 0 0 0 0 0 0 0 0 0 0 0 0 0 ‖  3 ‖ 0 1
287 1 56 2 4 1 35 2   0 1 0 0 0 0 0 0 0 0 0 0 3 2 1 1 0 1 0 0 ‖  9 ‖ 0 1
288 1 61 2 3 1 28 4   2 3 0 0 3 0 0 0 1 3 0 3 1 3 3 3 0 0 0 0 ‖ 28 ‖ 1 1
289 2 19 4 2 5 28 1   3 3 3 3 3 3 3 3 0 3 1 1 3 3 3 0 3 3 0 3 ‖ 47 ‖ 1 2
290 1 49 4 7 1 23 3   0 0 0 0 0 0 0 0 0 0 0 0 0 0 0 0 0 0 0 0 ‖  0 ‖ 0 1
291 1 45 2 5 1 35 3   0 0 0 0 0 0 0 0 0 1 0 1 1 0 0 0 0 0 0 0 ‖  3 ‖ 0 1
292 1 64 2 4 1 55 3   0 0 0 0 1 1 3 0 1 1 1 0 0 1 0 0 0 0 0 0 ‖  9 ‖ 0 1
293 1 43 3 6 1 28 1   0 0 0 0 0 0 0 0 0 0 0 0 0 0 0 2 0 0 0 0 ‖  2 ‖ 0 2
294 2 58 1 3 4  9 1   1 0 0 0 0 0 0 1 1 1 2 0 2 1 0 0 0 0 0 1 ‖ 10 ‖ 0 2
```

From this listing, we can describe individual subjects:

❶ Subject 284 is a woman. She is an 83-year-old widow with an income of $4,000 per year—*and her total depression score is zero.*

❷ Look at person 289. She is a 19-year-old separated woman who is extremely depressed (*TOTAL*=47). She has had some high school (*EDUCATN*=2), is a "houseperson" (*EMPLOY*=5), and says her income is $28,000 per year.

Displaying dates and times

With the FORMAT option of LIST, you can list values in a specified date or time format. For this example, we use the *SICKDATE* data file, which lists the date each patient's illness was diagnosed (*DIAGDATE*) and the date each died (*MORTDATE*). These dates are listed in day-of-the-century format.

NAME$	DIAGDATE	MORTDATE
Jones	32153	33151
Smith	31255	32351
Williams	30251	32512
Jackson	29351	30251
Moore	28351	29351
Iverson	29351	30251
Brown	27351	32512
Long	26351	28351
Nelson	28351	30251
Dennison	24351	25351

To convert dates to day-of-the century format, see the DOC function in Chapter 6.

To demonstrate how the FORMAT option displays these dates, we use three different formats:

mm/dd/yy   mmm.dd,yyyy   dd.mmm,yy

```
USE sickdate
LIST diagdate diagdate diagdate mortdate mortdate,
     mortdate / FORMAT =,
```

'mm/dd/yyyy mmm.dd,yyyy dd.mmm,yy | mm/dd/yyyy mmm.dd,yyyy dd.mmm,yy'

```
DIAGDATE    DIAGDATE      DIAGDATE     MORTDATE    MORTDATE      MORTDATE
----------  -----------   ---------    ----------  -----------   ---------
01/22/1900  Jan.11,1988   11.Jan,88  | 01/23/1900  Oct. 5,1990    5.Oct,90
01/21/1900  Jul.27,1986   27.Jul,85  | 01/22/1900  Jul.27,1988   27.Jul,88
01/21/1900  Oct.27,1982   27.Oct,82  | 01/22/1900  Jan. 4,1909    4.Jan,89
01/20/1900  May.10,1980   10.May,80  | 01/21/1900  Oct.27,1982   27.Oct,82
01/19/1900  Aug.14,1977   14.Aug,77  | 01/20/1900  May.10,1980   10.May,80
01/20/1900  May.10,1980   10.May,80  | 01/21/1900  Oct.27,1982   27.Oct,82
01/18/1900  Nov.18,1974   18.Nov,74  | 01/22/1900  Jan. 4,1989    4.Jan,89
01/18/1900  Feb.22,1972   22.Feb,72  | 01/19/1900  Aug.14,1977   14.Aug,77
01/19/1900  Aug.14,1977   14.Aug,77  | 01/21/1900  Oct.27,1982   27.Oct,82
01/16/1900  Sep. 1,1966    1.Sep,66  | 01/17/1900  May.28,1969   28.May,69
```

Additional features for LIST

When listing data, there are other options you may want to use.

– To display eight variables per panel instead of five (the default), use Edit➧Options or the PAGE WIDE command to specify a wide output format.

– To specify how many lines are printed on each page for printer or file output, use Edit➧Options or PAGE PRINTER = *n*.

– To add up to 10 lines of title material and annotation to the top of each page, use Edit➧Titles or PAGE TITLE = '*text*'. Each line can be 132 characters long and is automatically centered.

You can also use the PRINT command in BASIC to list data values without case numbers and variable names (see Chapter 11).

Sorting Cases

To order all the cases in the current data file in ascending or descending order, select **Data➠Sort** or use the SORT command.

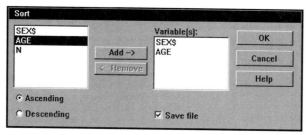

You can specify up to ten numeric or string variables for nested sorting, and you can specify whether values are sorted in ascending or descending order. If you do not specify any variables, SYSTAT sorts by the first variable in the file. If you select **Save file**, SYSTAT prompts you to specify the name for the output file. Otherwise the results are stored in a temporary file.

With commands:

```
SORT
SORT age
SORT name$
SORT sex$ age
SORT sex$ age / D A
```

In the last example, the / D A option specifies that the first variable listed (*SEX$*) is sorted in descending order, the second in ascending order.

Order
By default, SYSTAT orders cases in an ascending order, (1, 2, ..., *n*) for numeric variables and, as follows, for string variables:

```
! " # $ % &þ'( ) * + , - . /
0 1 2 3 4 5 6 7 8 9
: ; < = > ? @
A B C D E F G H I J K L M N O P Q R S T U V W X Y Z
[      \ ] ^ _
a b c d e f g h i j k l m n o p q r s t u v w x y z
{ | } ~
```

This means that words are sorted alphabetically with words in upper case preceding those in lower case. (Notice that if you sort a string variable containing numeric values, those values are sorted from left to right, rather than small to big: 1, 12, 150, 2, 31, 4000, 5.4, etc.)

Cases with missing data for the sort variable are placed at the beginning of the file.

For our examples, we use data from the *CHILDREN* file:

N	SEX$	AGE
1	Female	5
2	Male	6
3	Male	4
4	Female	6
5	Female	5
6	Male	6
7	Male	8
8	Female	3
9	Male	6
10	Female	5
11	Male	4
12	Male	5
13	Female	5
14	Female	6

The variable *N* stores the case number, so each case includes a value for *SEX$*, *AGE*, and its index.

7.7 Simple SORT

The following commands sort the file *CHILDREN* on the variable *SEX$*.

```
USE children
SORT sex$
```

Now list the sorted data:

```
Case number SEX$    AGE      N
          1 Female  5.0    1.0
          2 Female  5.0   13.0
          3 Female  6.0   14.0
          4 Female  5.0   10.0
          5 Female  3.0    8.0
          6 Female  5.0    5.0
          7 Female  6.0    4.0
          8 Male    6.0    2.0
          9 Male    4.0    3.0
         10 Male    6.0    6.0
         11 Male    8.0    7.0
         12 Male    6.0    9.0
         13 Male    4.0   11.0
         14 Male    5.0   12.0
```

Cases where *SEX$* equals Female come before those where *SEX$* equals Male. (*N* represents the original position of each case.)

7.8
Nested
SORT

If you select more than one sort variable, SYSTAT does a nested **SORT**. For example, if you select *SEX$* and *AGE*, in that order, SYSTAT first sorts the males and females into two groups and then sorts each group from youngest to oldest:

```
USE children
SORT sex$ age
```

Within each gender group, SYSTAT now arranges the cases so that the values for *AGE* go from smallest to largest.

```
Case number SEX$     AGE      N
     1       Female   3.0     8.0
     2       Female   5.0     1.0
     3       Female   5.0    10.0
     4       Female   5.0     5.0
     5       Female   5.0    13.0
     6       Female   6.0    14.0
     7       Female   6.0     4.0
     8       Male     4.0     3.0
     9       Male     4.0    11.0
    10       Male     5.0    12.0
    11       Male     6.0     2.0
    12       Male     6.0     6.0
    13       Male     6.0     9.0
    14       Male     8.0     7.0
```

7.9
Sorting in
ascending or
descending order

Using commands, you you can sort in ascending or descending order. Specify **D** or **A** for each variable. For example:

```
SORT sex$ age / D A
```

sorts the file in descending order for *SEX$* (males preceed females) and then, within each sex, in ascending order for *AGE* (from youngest to oldest).

Selecting a Subset of Cases

If you want subsequent graphical displays and analyses to use only those cases that meet the conditions you set, use **Data➧Select cases** or the SELECT command. Cases that do not meet the specified condition are excluded from the analysis. For example, for data with variables *AGE* and *SEX*, you could restrict analyses and graphs to:

- Adults only: *AGE* > 21   *or*
- Adult males: *AGE* > 21 *AND* *SEX$* = 'Male'

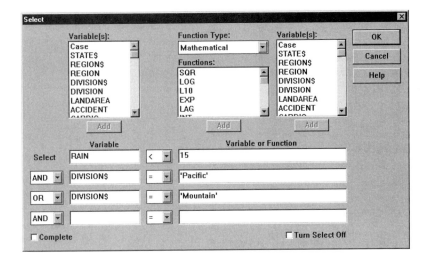

Use whatever combination of selecting, pasting, and typing is necessary to build the test condition. You can specify any number of conditions, connecting them with logical **AND** or **OR**. Use parentheses if needed for logic or clarity.

7.10 Selecting cases

For example, using the *USSTATES* data file, select states in the Pacific and Mountain divisions that have low rainfall.

```
SELECT rain < 15 AND (division$ = 'Pacific' OR,
                      division$ = 'Mountain')
LIST rain state$
```

```
Case number RAIN    STATE$
         38    11.0 MT
         39    11.0 ID
         42    10.0 NM
         43     7.0 AZ
         44    14.0 UT
         45     8.0 NV
```

Turning off SELECT

Your selection stays in effect until you quit SYSTAT, open a new data file, or turn selection off using **Data➧Unselect** or the **Turn Select Off** option in the dialog box.

With commands, you can turn off selection by typing:

    SELECT

with *no expression* following SELECT.

Grouping Variables and By Groups

For each case, a grouping variable contains a value that identifies group membership. For example, for the string variable *SEX$*, the values might be *Male* and *Female*, or for the numeric variable *SEX*, the codes 1 and 2. Values of grouping variables are used to define categories, cells, subpopulations, or groups of cases for:

- Each factor in a frequency table
- Analyses where group means are compared such as *t* tests, analysis of variance, discriminant analysis
- Stratifying an analysis—for example, computing descriptive statistics separately for males and females using SYSTAT's **By Groups** feature
- Univariate graphical displays, such as bar charts, pie charts, dot plots, and profile displays
- Symbols or names that label plot points in bivariate and 3-D scatterplots

The values of grouping variables can be entered and stored as a column in your data file or generated while executing any SYSTAT procedure via the **Label** and **Order** features or the COD, INC, and CUT functions.

This chapter describes how to:

- Recode values of numeric or string grouping variables
- Assign labels to categories or intervals
- Order categories for displays and analyses
- Specify cutpoints to define intervals along a continuous variable
- Identify when the value of a numeric or string variable *matches* (1=yes, 0=no) one of a set of codes that you list
- Define **By Groups** variables for stratified analyses

Grouping Variables and By Groups

Overview

This chapter describes and illustrates the use of the **Data➡Label** and **Data➡Order** features and the COD, INC, and CUT transformation functions for defining, ordering, and labeling groups and categories.

One important difference between **Label** and the transformation functions is that values generated using COD, INC, or CUT are stored in the data file, while those created by **Label** are not (however, it is possible to save labels by using the LAB$ function).

New group codes and labels produced remain available during your current SYSTAT session. For example, if you specify labels for the numeric variable *SEX* as you request a two-sample t test:

```
LABEL sex / 1='Male', 2='Female'
```

and next use *SEX* as a two-way table factor, the labels *Male* and *Female* will label the categories.

Note: *To use categories specified with **Label**, you must use **Data➡Category** to define the variable as categorical before requesting statistical analyses or charts.*

Using Label and Order

We discuss the **Label** and **Order** features here and the COD, INC, and CUT functions in the next section.

Label

You can use **Data⇒Label** or the LABEL command to:

- Group cases into categories or subpopulations
- Assign a character name to each code or group of codes for use as a label in the output
- Order categories for graphical displays and statistical analyses
- Define intervals along a continuous variable
- Include a category or group for missing code values
- Assign new labels for string variables

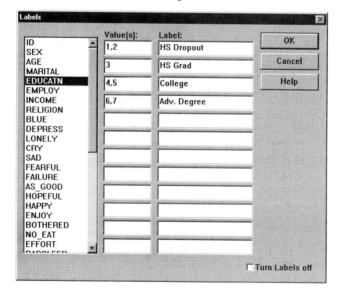

Once labels are defined for a variable, cases with unspecified codes are omitted from subsequent analyses that use the variable. This means that you must include all values of the variable in the label specification unless you want to exclude some cases from subsequent analyses.

Note: *To use categories specified with **Label**, you must use **Data⟹Category** to define the variable as categorical before requesting statistical analyses or charts.*

In the **Label** dialog box, select a variable and then specify the codes and labels for that variable (See "Label statements" below for details). Use this syntax for labeling or recoding numeric codes:

```
LABEL varlist  /  n1=text1, n2=text2, . . .
            or
                 n1,n2,...=text1,
                 n3,n4,...=text2, . . .,
            or
                 n1 .. n2=text1,
                 n3 .. n4=text2, . . .
```

For string codes, specify:

```
LABEL varlist$ / 'oldtext1'=newtext1,
                 'oldtext2'=newtext2,  . . .
```

Saving labels with the data. When **Label** is used with the LAB$ function, the names you specify can be saved along with the data. If the data for *SEX* are 1 and 2, *Male* and *Female* are displayed in the listing. Then, if you specify

```
LET age$ = LAB$(age)
```

and save the data, the values specified with **Label** are saved as data.

Use of quotes. With the **Label** dialog box, you do not need to type quotes. With commands, if the name of a category or interval contains no imbedded blanks or symbols, you may omit the quotes—however, when quotes are omitted, SYSTAT prints the name in capital letters.

Canceling Label. To turn off the previous **Label** specification and return to the default of using all values in numeric (or alphanumeric) order, specify:

```
LABEL var   (or 'var$')
```

Label statements

Options for **Label** statements include:

n1=text1, n2=text2, ...	The labels for codes *n1, n2,...* in the data file become *text1, text2, ...*, respectively, and the resulting categories are ordered as you list them. See ❶ below.
n1,n2, ...=text1, *n3,n4, ...=text2, ...*	The cases with codes *n1, n2, ...* become the first group with label *text1*, the cases with codes *n3,n4, ...* become the second group with label *text2*, etc. See ❹ below. (The codes *ni* do not have to be consecutive values or specified in order).
n1 .. n2=text1 *n3 .. n4=text2, ...*	Include the codes *n1* and *n2* and all the codes between them as the first group with label *text1*; for the second group, include codes *n3* and *n4* (and all codes in between) and assign label *text2*; and so on. In other words, assign intervals along a continuous variable. See ❺ below.
'oldtext1'=newtext1 *'oldtext2'=newtext2, ...*	Assign new names to string codes (and possibly reorder them). See ❻ below.

> **Note:** To recode character values as numbers, see the **COD** function below. Also consider the **VAL** function.

8.1 Recoding and labeling categories and intervals

Let's say your SYSTAT file contains these variables with the following data values:

MARITAL	1, 2, 3, 4
MARITAL$	Never, Married, Divorced, Separated
EMPLOY	1, 2, 3, 4, 5, 6
EDUCATN	1, 2, 3, 4, 5, 6, 7
AGE	18, 19, ... , 83
SEX$	M, F, and a blank for missing
DOSE$	None, Low, Medium, and High

You can use the LABEL command to group the cases, order the resulting groups, and create labels for the output:

```
LABEL marital / 1=Never, 2=Married, 3=Divorced,
                4=Separated                              ❶
LABEL marital / 2='Married', 3='Divorced',
                1='Never'                                ❷
LABEL employ  / 1='Full time', 2='Part time',
                3='Unemployed'                           ❸
LABEL educatn / 1,2='HS Dropout',
                3='HS grad', 4,5='College',
                6,7='Degree +'                           ❹

LABEL age     /    .. 29 ='18 to 29',
                30 .. 45 ='30 to 45',
                46 .. 60 ='46 to 60',
                60 ..    ='Over 60'
or  LABEL age     /    .. 29 ='18 to 29',
                   .. 45 ='30 to 45',
                   .. 60 ='46 to 60',
                   ..    ='Over 60'                      ❺


LABEL sex$    / 'M'=Male, 'F'=Female                     ❻
LABEL sex$    / 'M'=Male, 'F'=Female, ' '= Missing       ❼

SELECT dose$ <> 'none'
ORDER  dose$ / SORT='high', 'medium', 'low'             ❽
```

Note that the slashes (/) need not be aligned as we show here. The highlighted numbers below correspond to those in the commands above:

❶ The numeric codes 1 through 4 stored in the variable *MARITAL* assign each subject to one of four marital status categories. The labels *Never* through *Separated* will identify these groups in graphical displays and statistical analyses.

❷ Subjects with code 4 will not be used in subsequent displays or analyses that use the variable *MARITAL*, and the order of the categories in, for example, a bar chart will be *Married, Divorced,* and *Never*.

❸ SYSTAT will use only those subjects with codes 1, 2, and 3 when *EMPLOY* is specified.

❹ The seven codes for educational level are collapsed into four categories and assigned names.

❺ The age of each subject is used to assign the person to one of four age groups. That is, ages 29, 45, and 60 are used as cutpoints along the continuous variable *AGE* to form four intervals. The second specification is a shortcut and works when the intervals are identified in the same order as they fall across the range of the distribution. SYSTAT forms the category as it encounters each specification. Thus, if we specify

```
LABEL age /  .. 30 = 'label1'
           30 .. 45 = 'label2'
```

SYSTAT assigns 30-year-olds to the first group and anyone 30.00001 or older to the next group.

❻ The character codes *M* and *F* define two subpopulations—they are labeled *Male* and *Female*, respectively.

❼ When this LABEL statement is specified, *SEX$* will have three categories—the third is for those subjects who did not report their sex.

❽ For character codes, you may need to eliminate a category and/or specify a specific order. Here, **Select** is used to delete the subjects who had no drug (none) and order the doses from high to low for use in graphs and analyses.

Note: *Label* and *Select* both select a subset of cases (see ❷, ❸, and ❽ above); however, the subset identified via *Select* applies to all subsequent displays and analyses and that for *Label* to only those subsequent procedures where the same *Label* variables are specified.

Including a category for missing codes

If you want to include a category (group) for cases with missing codes, your option list should include a period (.) for missing numbers or a space surrounded by quotation marks (" " or ' ') for missing character data. For example,

```
LABEL gnp$ / ' '=Missing, 'D'=Developed,'U'=Emerging
```

forms three economic categories for the countries in the *OURWORLD* file. See also the **Missing values** option for **Order** later in this chapter.

Grouping information for multiple variables

Using commands, if you have several variables with the same codes, you can specify grouping information for them in one statement. For example, if your data file has the same doses (6.25, 12.5, and 25) for three drugs (each drug is a variable), specify labels as follows:

```
LABEL drug_A drug B drug_C / 6.25='low dose',
                            12.5='medium dose',
                              25='high dose'
```

Alternatively, if the three drug variables are stored consecutively in the data file, use shortcut notation, represented by double periods (..):

```
LABEL drug_A .. drug_C / 6.25='low dose',
                         12.5='medium dose',
                           25='high dose'
```

Or, as an example using character data, consider a study about smoking cessation in which researchers questioned subjects about their desire to have a cigarette in different situations (after eating, at a party, and after a stressful event). To each question, the subjects responded "always," "sometimes," or "never." For quick data entry, you could name the questions 1 through 10 and enter the responses as *a*, *s*, and *n*. Then specify

```
LABEL q1$ .. q10$ / 'a'=always 's'=sometimes 'n'=never
```

to tell SYSTAT to use the full response to label the output.

Collapsing categories

If you assign the same label to two codes (or groups of codes), the codes form a single category. In *SYSTAT: Statistics*, data is used from a breast cancer study in which 764 women have tumors classified in one of four categories. Two of the categories describe malignant tumors, and the other two, benign tumors. To find out how the overall malignant or benign status relates to survival, the LABEL command is used to collapse the four categories into two:

```
XTAB
   USE cancer
   FREQ = number
   LABEL tumor$ / 'MinMalig'=Malignant,
                  'MaxMalig'=Malignant,
                  'MinBengn'=Benign,
                  'MaxBengn'=Benign
   TABULATE survive$ * tumor$
```

```
Frequencies
  SURVIVE$ (rows) by TUMOR$ (columns)

                 MALIGNANT    BENIGN      Total
               +---------------------+
     Alive     |    256         298  |     554
               |                     |
     Dead      |    120          90  |     210
               +---------------------+
     Total          376         388        764

  Test statistic                       Value        DF         Prob
     Pearson Chi-square                 7.283     1.000        0.007
```

The proportion of women with benign tumors who remained alive at the end of the study is significantly greater than that for those with malignant tumors (*p* value=0.007). Note that because we did not insert quotes around *Malignant* and *Benign*, they are printed in all capital letters in the output.

Order

You can use **Data**➠**Order** or the ORDER command to specify how SYSTAT sorts categories for output including table factors, statistical analyses, and graphical displays.

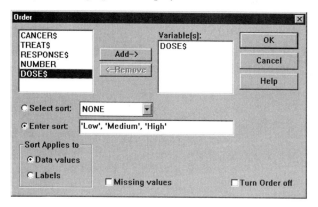

Select Sort. Specify one of the following options for ordering categories:

- **None.** Categories are ordered as SYSTAT first encounters them in the data file.

- **ASC.** Ascending sort. Numeric category codes are ordered from smallest to largest, and string codes, alphabetically. This is the default.

- **DESC**. Descending sort. Numeric category codes are ordered from largest to smallest, and string codes, backwards alphabetically.

- **FASC or FDESC**. Categories are ordered by the frequency of cases within each, placing the category with the largest (or smallest) frequency first. Use **FASC** for an ascending sort, and **FDESC** for a descending sort.

Enter sort. Specify a custom order for numeric codes or string codes. Values must be separated by commas, with string values enclosed in quotes (for example, 1, 3, 2, or 'low,' 'medium,' 'high').

Missing values. Include an additional category for missing values if the value of *var* or *var$* is missing.

Sort Applies to. Indicate whether the sort applies to data values or labels specified with **Data⟶Labels**.

Turn Order off. Return to the default order.

With commands:

```
ORDER varlist or varlist$ / MISS  DATA or LABEL,
                          SORT=option
```

where the option is NONE, ASC, DESC, FASC, FDES, numlist, or charvallist.

Specify:

```
ORDER var or var$
```

to return to the default order.

Note: ***Order*** *is not a filter like* ***Label***. *For example, if the data for a variable contain four unique values and you identify three of them using the* ***Sort*** *option, then the fourth (unspecified) value becomes a fourth category automatically. With* ***Label***, *cases with the fourth (unspecified) category are not used.*

Using COD, INC, and CUT

Use the functions described in this section to:

– Recode values of numeric or string grouping variables: COD
– Identify when the value of a numeric or string variable *matches* (1=yes, 0=no) one of the specific codes you list: INC
– Define intervals along a continuous variable: CUT
– Separate the values of a string variable alphabetically: CUT

These functions are specified using LET... and IF...THEN... LET statements, available with **Data ➡ Transform** (see Chapter 6).

> **Note:** Unlike **Label** and **Order**, these functions modify the actual data values. If you save the data after specifying **COD**, **INC**, or **CUT**, the results are stored in the data file.

8.2 Recoding numeric and string variables: COD

Use the COD function to recode values of a grouping variable.

Function	Result
COD(*var*,*num1*,*num2*,...)	Values of *var* are replaced: *num1* becomes 1, *num2* becomes 2, etc.
COD(*var$*,'*text1*','*text2*',...)	Values of *var$* are replaced: *text1* becomes 1, *text2* becomes 2, etc.

Suppose the variable *OCCUPATN* contains 30 or 40 numeric occupation codes including: 21 (brick layer), 32 (carpenter), 53 (day laborer), and 65 (plumber). For a particular analysis, you need to study these four jobs and want to recode the values as 1 (day laborer), 2 (carpenter), 3 (plumber), and 4 (brick layer). Use the COD function to do this:

```
LET new_job = COD (occupatn, 53,32,65,21)
```

The values of *OCCUPATN* and the corresponding values of *NEW_JOB* are shown below:

OCCUPATN	NEW_JOB
53	1
32	2
65	3
21	4
all else	.

The **COD** function always produces consecutive integers (starting with 1) that correspond, respectively, to the original codes specified in the statement. Periods (SYSTAT's marker for missing data) are stored in *NEW_JOB* for every subject whose original occupation code is not among the four values specified.

Skipping integers. If you specify

```
let new_job = cod (occupatn, 53, ,32, ,65,21)
```

the new codes would become:

OCCUPATN	NEW_JOB
53	1
32	3
65	5
21	6
all else	.

Characters to numbers. The **COD** function also works for string variables. Let's say the string variable *OCCUPATN$* has 30 or 40 string codes. The values of *NEW_JOB* will be the same codes as in the last example (1, 2, 3, and 4) if we specify:

```
LET new_job = COD (occupatn$  'day laborer',
                   'carpenter'  'plumber',
                   'brick layer')
```

Use quotes to surround all string codes.

8.3
Is it or
isn't it a
match?
INC

The INC (for included) function compares each value of a numeric or string variable with a list of values that you specify. If a match is found, SYSTAT returns a 1; if not, a 0.

Function	Result
INC(*var,num1,num2,…*)	A 1 (true) if the value in *var* matches one of the numbers *num1, num2,…*; 0 (false) otherwise
INC(*var$,'text1','text2',…*)	A 1 (true) if the value in *var$* matches *text1, text2, …,* ; 0 (false) otherwise

Valid INC statements are:

```
LET driver = INC(job,63,47,85)
LET driver = INC(job$, 'truck driver','bus driver',
                      'cab driver')
```

In the first example, if *JOB* contains a 63, 47, or 85, *DRIVER* will contain a 1. All other values of *JOB* receive a 0.

In the second example, if *JOB$* contains 'truck driver,' 'bus driver,' or 'cab driver,' the new variable *DRIVER* will contain a 1. All other values for *JOB$* receive a 0 for *DRIVER*.

8.4
Defining
intervals:
CUT

Use CUT to define intervals on a quantitative (continuous) variable or to divide the values of a string variable alphabetically.

Function	Result
CUT(*var,num1,num2,…*)	Use to define intervals along a continuous variable. Values in *var* less than or equal to *num1* get value 1. Values greater than *num1* and less than or equal to *num2* get value 2, etc.
CUT(*var$,'text1','text2',…*)	Use to group variables alphabetically. Values in *var$* less than *text1* (alphabetically), including *text1*, get value 1. Values between *text1* and *text2*, including *text2*, get value 2, etc.

Defining
age groups

Sometimes you need to categorize a quantitative variable, such as age. For example, this statement uses each subject's age to assign him or her to one of four age groups:

```
LET age_grp = CUT (age, 12, 19, 64)
```

The values of *AGE* and the corresponding values of the new variable *AGE_GRP* are shown below:

AGE		AGE_GRP
$-\infty <$	ages <= 12	1
$12 <$	ages <= 19	2
$19 <$	ages <= 64	3
$64 <$	ages	4

The numbers you list in the CUT function (12,19, and 64) are the upper limits of the intervals. For example, a 64-year-old subject falls into the adult category, and someone who reports their age as 64.01 is in the senior category. Note that *n* cutpoints define *n + 1* intervals, so you always have one more interval (and label) than the number of cutpoints.

Alternatively, you could use **Data➡Label** to do the same task as the above CUT function, and define labels at the same time:

```
LABEL age /    .. 12 = child, .. 19 = teen,
               .. 64 = adult, .. = senior
```

Defining intervals alphabetically

The CUT function also divides string variables alphabetically into intervals. Suppose the variable *NAME$* contains the following values:

Richards, Carson, Young, Stern, Parker, Buck, Smith, Martin, Howe

The CUT function:

```
LET group = CUT(name$, 'Howe', 'Richards')
```

assigns codes alphabetically to the variable *GROUP*:

NAME$	GROUP
Richards	2
Carson	1
Young	3
Stern	3
Parker	2
Buck	1
Smith	3
Martin	2
Howe	1

The new variable *GROUP* contains a 1 for Howe and the names preceding Howe alphabetically, a 2 if the name falls between Howe and Richards (including Richards), and a 3 if it follows Richards.

Stratifying the Analysis: By Groups

You can use **Data➠By Groups** or the BY command to request separate results for each level of one or more grouping variables. For example, you could obtain separate graphs and statistical analyses for male children, female children, male teens, female teens, and so on. Here, *SEX* and *AGE$* (categorized as child, teen, etc.) would be the grouping variables.

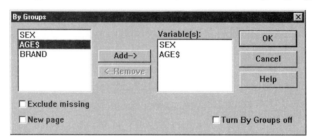

You can select up to 10 grouping variables. After specifying grouping variables, run your analyses as normal; all subsequent SYSTAT procedures and graphs perform analyses separately for each unique combination of the group codes.

Exclude missing. Exclude categories defined by missing values from the analysis. If this option is not selected, a separate category is created for cases with missing values for the grouping variable, and a separate analysis is carried out for them.

New page. Begin output for each unique combination of the grouping variables on a new page.

With commands, specify the BY command before you request a graph or analysis:

```
BY grpvar1, grpvar2, ...
```

For example, if the variable *SEX* has code 1 for males and code 2 for females, and *CITY$* has the codes Chicago, New York, and Los Angeles, specify

```
BY sex, city$
```

to form six groups (Chicago males, Chicago females, New York males, New York females, and so on).

By Groups and the plot Group option

When **By Groups** is used with a graphical display, each group (or each unique combination of the grouping variables) is displayed in a separate chart, and the scale is set using only the values within the group. For example, if *SEX$* is the grouping variable, separate charts are produced for males and females. The scale for each chart is defined by the maximum and minimum values within each gender.

However, for many graphical displays, a **Group** option is available. With this option, displays for all subgroups appear on a single chart and share a common scale.

Note: *To obtain separate charts that share a common scale, use the minimum and maximum values for the complete sample to define the scale, rather than the minimum and maximum within each group.*

Turning off By Groups

Grouping variables stay in effect until you exit SYSTAT, open a new data file, or select **Turn By Groups off** in the By Groups dialog box.

Options

Michael Pechnyo

Use the **Options** dialog box to:

– Specify the destination of your statistical and graphical output (screen only, screen and printer, screen and file)
– Request extended statistical results
– Turn *Quick Graphs* on or off
– Specify the format of numeric output in data listings and numeric results
– Select the page width for your output (wide or narrow output)
– Select either file order or alphabetical order for variable lists in dialog boxes
– Specify Enter key navigation behavior in the Data window
– Specify data precision (single or double) for saving data and casewise results
– Turn the command prompt on or off

Options settings are automatically saved at the end of a session and remain in effect for subsequent sessions.

In addition to the options available on the **Options** dialog box, you can also insert titles into your SYSTAT output (**Edit**➠**Titles**). This setting is *not* saved at the end of a session.

Options Dialog Box

Titles

Options

Options Dialog Box

To change **Options** settings, from the menus in any SYSTAT window select **Edit ⟹ Options**.

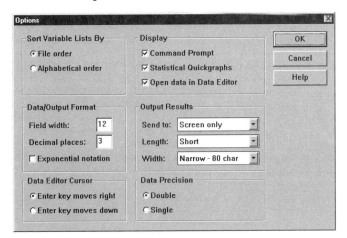

Sort variable lists

You can display source variable lists in dialog boxes sorted in **File order** or in **Alphabetical order**. For data files with a large number of variables, it is often easier to find variables in source lists if the variables are sorted alphabetically. If variables are grouped together in the file for a specific reason, it may be easier to select related groups of variables if the variables are sorted in file order.

Display

The settings in the Display group control the display of the command prompt, *Quick Graphs*, and data in the Data window.

Command prompt. Turns the command prompt in the Main window on and off. When the command prompt is on, you can enter and run commands in the Main window, and commands generated by dialog box choices are automatically displayed in the Main window.

Statistical Quick Graphs. Turns the display of *Quick Graphs* on and off. Many statistical procedures automatically display useful diagnostic graphs. Turn off *Quick Graphs* if you only want to view statistical output.

Open data in Data Editor. Turns the automatic display of the Data window on and off. By default, SYSTAT automatically opens the Data Editor (if it isn't already open) whenever you open a data file and displays the data in the window.

Data/output format

These settings control the display of numeric data in the Data window and in output. Field width is the total number of digits in the data value, including decimal places. Exponential notation is used to display very small values. This is particularly useful for data values that might otherwise appear as 0 in the chosen data format. For example, a value of 0.00001 is displayed as 0.000 in the default 12.3 format but is displayed as 1.00000E-5 in exponential notation.

Output results

These settings control the display of the results of your analyses.

Send to. You can display output results on the screen, automatically print them as you run your analyses, or automatically save them to a file.

Length. Specifies the amount of statistical output that is generated. **Short** provides standard output (the default). Some statistical analyses provide additional results when you select **Medium** or **Long**. Note that some procedures have no additional output.

To identify the results printed with each setting for a particular procedure, see the "Extended Results" section of the documentation for that procedure.

In command mode, DISCRIM, LOGLIN, and XTAB allow you to selectively add or delete items in command mode. Specify Print=None and then individually specify the items you want to print.

Width. Select **Narrow** (80 characters wide) or **Wide** (132 characters wide). This applies to screen output—how output is saved and printed. If you have a large screen, a wide printer, or a printer with a condensed font, select **Wide** so that more columns of text can be shown per line. The Wide setting is useful for data listings and correlation matrices when there are more than five variables.

Data Editor cursor

This setting controls the navigation behavior of the Enter key in the Data window. The Enter key can either move to the next cell on the right or down to the next row.

Data precision

This setting controls the precision for data saved in SYSTAT data files. **Double** tells SYSTAT to save numeric values using 8 bytes per value and retains up to 15 significant decimal digits. **Single** stores values in 4 bytes, which ensures approximately 7 significant digits. All character values are stored in 12-byte strings.

Titles

To insert titles at the top of each output page, use **Edit**➡ **Titles**.

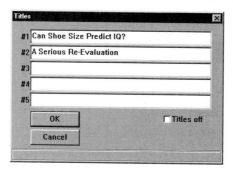

Use **Titles off** to toggle titles on and off as you generate output.

Title specifications affect only new text output displayed in the Main window. Graphs and existing text output are not affected by changes in titles.

Using Commands

Most SYSTAT commands are accessible from the menus and dialog boxes. When you make selections, SYSTAT generates the corresponding commands. However, some users may prefer to bypass the menus and just type the commands directly at the command prompt. This is particularly useful because some options are available only by using commands, not by selecting from menus or dialog boxes.

A command file is simply a text file that contains SYSTAT commands. Saving your analysis in a command file allows you to repeat it at a later date. In addition, many government agencies require that command files be submitted with reports that contain computer generated results. You can create a command file by typing commands in the Command Editor, or by making selections in the menus and dialog boxes and then editing the resulting command log or output file.

Whenever you run an analysis—whether you use the menus or type the commands—SYSTAT stores the commands in the command log.

For help on a command or procedure, type HELP followed by the name of the command. In any SYSTAT dialog box, click the **Help** button for help on the corresponding command.

The Command Interface

Using Commands

The Command Interface

When you make selections from the menus and dialog boxes, SYSTAT generates the corresponding commands. The commands are displayed at the command prompt in the main window and are stored in the command log. Alternatively, you can bypass the menus entirely and simply type commands at the command prompt.

What do commands look like?

Here are some examples of SYSTAT commands:

```
XTAB                                                        1
    USE food                                                2
    PRINT / LIST                                            3
    TAB food$ brand$ diet$                                  4
STATS                                                       5
    STATISTICS                                              6
    BY diet$                                                7
    STAT / MEDIAN  MIN  MAX  MEAN  CI                       8
    BY                                                      9
CORR                                                       10
    PEARSON calories fat protein cost / BONF               11
    SPLOM   calories fat protein cost                      12
    PLOT calories * protein / LABEL=brand$                 13
```

The **STATISTICS** command on line 6 produces a set of descriptive statistics for all seven numeric variables in the *FOOD* data file. Line 8 asks for the median, minimum, maximum, means, and the confidence intervals for all the variables.

The command prompt

You enter SYSTAT commands at the command prompt (indicated by the ">" sign, as shown below). To display the command prompt in the main window, select **Edit➠Options** and select **Command Prompt**.

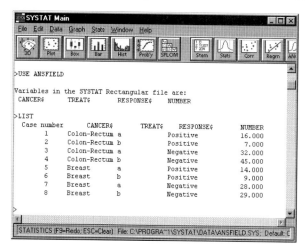

If you prefer to make selections from the menus and dialog boxes, the command prompt displays the corresponding commands.

Entering commands

To issue a command, simply type the command and press Enter. SYSTAT's commands are grouped into 21 procedures:

ANOVA	BASIC	CLUSTER	CORR	DESIGN	DISCRIM	EDIT
FACTOR	GLM	LOGLIN	MATRIX	MDS	NONLIN	NPAR
QC	RAMONA	REGRESS	SERIES	STATS	TTEST	XTAB

To enter a procedure, type the name of the procedure after the prompt and press Enter. For example, type:

    STATS

Next, identify which data to use. For example, type

    USE ourworld

and press Enter.

Now type a command line:

    STATISTICS urban babymort pop_1990 / MEAN SEM MEDIAN

Press Enter to obtain the following output:

```
                      URBAN    BABYMORT   POP_1990
    N of cases          56        57         57
    Median            53.000    22.000     10.354
    Mean              52.821    48.140     22.800
    Std. Error         3.049     6.256      4.022
```

Command syntax

Most SYSTAT commands have three parts: a command, an argument(s), and options:

    command argument / options

For example, in the command:

    STATISTICS urban babymort / MEAN SEM MEDIAN

- The *command* specifies the task—in this case, to display statistics.

- The *arguments* are the names of the variables, *URBAN* and *BABYMORT*.

- The *options* (following the slash) specify which statistics you want to see. If you don't specify any options, SYSTAT displays a default set of statistics.

Hot versus cold commands

Some commands execute a task immediately, while others do not. We denote these *hot* and *cold* commands, respectively.

Hot commands. These commands initiate immediate action. For example, if you type LIST and press Enter, SYSTAT lists cases for all variables in the current data file.

Cold commands. These commands set formats or specify conditions. For example, PAGE WIDE specifies the format for subsequent output, but output is not actually produced until you issue further commands.

Rules for entering commands

Upper or lower case. Commands are not case sensitive. You can type commands in upper or lower case or both:

    STATISTICS *or* statistics *or* StatISTics

The only time SYSTAT distinguishes between upper and lower case is in the values of character variables. In other words, for a variable named *SEX$*, SYSTAT considers the text values "male" and "MALE" to be different.

Abbreviating commands. You can shorten commands to the first three letters (in some cases, the first two). For example, for STATISTICS, you can type either:

STATI   *or*   STAT

Note: *Variable names must be typed in full; they cannot be abbreviated.*

Retrieving and editing commands. SYSTAT holds the last six command lines you enter in memory. Use the F9 key to scroll through the commands. Press F9 once to bring back the previous command, press it again to see the command before that, and so on.

Continuing long commands onto a second line. To continue a command onto another line, type a comma at the end of the line. For example, typing

        STATISTICS urban babymort pop_1990 / MEAN SEM MEDIAN

is the same as:

        STATISTICS urban babymort,
                  pop_1990 / MEAN SEM,
                  MEDIAN

Do not use a comma at the end of the last line of a command; this would cause SYSTAT to wait for the rest of the command.

Commas and spaces. Except when used to continue a command from one line to the next, commas and spaces are interchangeable as delimiters. For example, the following are equivalent:

    STATISTICS urban babymort pop_1990
    STATISTICS urban, babymort, pop_1990
    STATISTICS urban,babymort, pop_1990

Quotation marks. You must put quotation marks around any character (string) data. For example, type:

        FIND country$ = 'Peru'

You can use either double (" ") or single (' ') quotation marks.

Shortcuts

There are several shortcuts you can use to minimize typing for transformation statements.

Listing consecutive variables. When you want to specify more than two variables that are consecutive in the data file, you can type the first and last variable and separate them with two periods (..) instead of typing the entire list. For example, instead of typing

```
STATISTICS babymort life_exp gnp_82 gnp_86 gdp_cap
```

you can type:

```
STATISTICS babymort .. gdp_cap
```

Multiple transformations: the @ sign. When you want to perform the same transformation on several variables, you can use the @ sign instead of typing a separate line for each transformation. For example,

```
LET gdp_cap = L10(gdp_cap)
LET     mil = L10(mil)
LET  gnp_86 = L10(gnp_86)
```

is the same as:

```
LET (gdp_cap, mil, gnp_86) = L10(@)
```

The @ sign acts as a placeholder for the variable names. The variable names *must* be separated by commas and enclosed within parentheses ( ).

Command files

A command file is simply a text file that contains SYSTAT commands. Saving your analyses in a command file allows you to repeat them at a later date.

You can create a command file by typing commands in the Command Editor, or by making selections in the menus and dialog boxes and then editing the resulting command log or output file.

To open the Command Editor window, select **Window➧Command Editor**.

The command log

SYSTAT records the commands you specify during your *current* session in a temporary file called the command log. To edit the command log, select **File➧Open Command Log** in the Command Editor window. This is an easy way to build a command file—as you make selections from the menus and dialog boxes, SYSTAT builds a file containing the corresponding commands.

Note: *The command log records only the commands from your current session. You cannot use the command log to recover commands from a previous session, unless you saved those commands in a command file before exiting SYSTAT.*

Submitting command files

When you submit a command file, SYSTAT executes the commands as if they were typed line-by-line at the command prompt. For example, suppose you have a text file of SYSTAT commands named *TUTORIAL.CMD*. You can execute the commands in the file in three ways:

1. Issue a **SUBMIT** command from any SYSTAT procedure:

   ```
   SUBMIT tutorial
   ```

2. In the main window, select **File➡Submit**.

3. Open the file in the Command Editor. Options on the **File** menu then allow you to submit either the entire file or from the currently selected line (wherever the cursor is) to the end.

Comments in command files

The **REM** command can be used for inserting comments in command files and for making a command inactive during the current run. All text following **REM** on the same line is ignored.

```
REM Now we merge files side-by-side
REM MERGE a b
USE baseline labtest
```

The text following the first **REM** command remains in the command file. The **MERGE** statement in the second line is not invoked.

Note: *To add comments that appear in your output, use the **NOTES** command, described below.*

Saving commands along with output

Whenever the command prompt is displayed, the commands are printed, and the results are interspersed at the appropriate place in the output stream. This allows you to use the OUTPUT command to save your commands along with the results from subsequent statistical analyses.

Be sure the command prompt is displayed before running your analysis. To save the results from the current session, including commands and any error and/or warning messages produced, type:

    OUTPUT *filename* / COMMANDS ERRORS WARNINGS

Use OUTPUT without an argument to close the file.

Commands to control output

SYSTAT provides a number of commands to save and print output, as well as to control its appearance. These commands may be particularly useful when creating command files.

OUTPUT command. Allows you to route subsequent text output to a file or a printer. See Chapter 9.

PAGE command. Allows you to specify a narrow (80 columns, the default) or wide format (132 columns) for output. You can also specify a title that appears at the top of each printed output page. See Chapter 9.

FORMAT command. Allows you to specify the number of character spaces per field displayed in data listings and matrix layouts, and the number of digits printed to the right of the decimal point. You can also display very small numbers in exponential notation (instead of being rounded to zero). See Chapter 9.

NOTES command. Allows you to add comments to your output. For example:

    NOTE "THIS IS A COMMENT.",
         "This is second line of comment",
         "It's the 'third' line here!"

Each character string enclosed in either single or double quotation marks is printed on a separate line. A note can span any number of lines, but a single string cannot exceed 132 characters.

Help on commands

HELP provides information about SYSTAT commands. At the command prompt, type HELP followed by the name of a procedure or command for which you want help.

For example, from any procedure, you can access help on the CORR procedure by typing:

HELP CORR

If you are already in the CORR procedure, you can just type HELP, or HELP followed by the name of a command (for example, HELP CLUSTER).

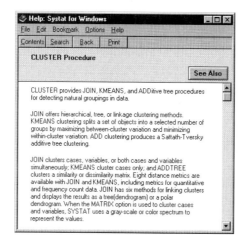

Once you are in Help, use the **Contents**, **Search**, and **See Also** buttons to locate additional topics.

Note: *You can start help by selecting from the **Help** menu or by clicking the **Help** button in a SYSTAT dialog box. From a dialog box, you access help on the corresponding command.*

Programming in BASIC

SYSTAT's BASIC procedure allows you to do transformation and complex data manipulation tasks that require a programming language. The BASIC procedure allows you to:

- Read ASCII text files with multiple lines per case, multiple cases per record, unequal length records, or a fixed format.
- Enter data case by case at the command prompt.
- Enter or read matrices with or without a diagonal and specify their type as correlation, covariance, similarity, dissimilarity, and so on.
- Delete cases that meet (or fail to meet) a specified condition.
- List data without variable names or case numbers.

For more complicated programming tasks, you can:

- Use array (subscripted) variables.
- Do FOR...NEXT loops.
- Include ELSE, GOTO, PRINT, and DELETE in IF...THEN statements.
- Specify commands that operate on subgroups of cases (beginning and end of group and file).

This chapter presents applications of SYSTAT transformation commands. There are simpler ways to accomplish many of these tasks, but the programs in this chapter are selected to illustrate the full range of SYSTAT's capabilities.

Note: In former versions of SYSTAT, the BASIC procedure was named DATA, and it included LET, IF...THEN...LET, SORT, LIST, STANDARDIZE, and RANK. These commands can now be executed within any procedure.

Reading and Entering Data

Exporting Data to an ASCII Text File

Selecting, Listing, and Saving Cases

Programming Examples

Reading and Entering Data

Chapter 3 describes how to read ASCII files into SYSTAT using **File**➠
Open or the IMPORT command. This chapter describes how BASIC
provides more flexibility for reading ASCII data files. You can read files
with:

- More than one line of data per case
- Fixed format
- Special data structures like multiple cases per line
- Varying numbers of variables per case

Here is an outline of the commands for reading a text file:

```
BASIC
    NEW
    GET input filename
    INPUT varlist
    SAVE output filename
    RUN
```

Input filename is the name of the ASCII file with a *.DAT* extension to be
imported; *varlist* is a list of variable names; and *output filename* is the
name of the SYSTAT file that is created. SYSTAT uses the number of
variable names you list to determine how many values to read for each
case.

Entering data after the RUN command. Rather than use a GET statement to
read an existing file, you can type small data sets after the RUN command:

```
BASIC
    NEW
    INPUT varlist
    SAVE output filename
    RUN
      [type data here]
```

Free- or fixed-format input. You can use *free format* or *fixed format* to input
data with BASIC commands or to format data in an ASCII text file.

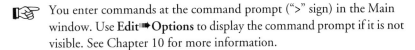 You enter commands at the command prompt (">" sign) in the Main
window. Use **Edit**➠**Options** to display the command prompt if it is not
visible. See Chapter 10 for more information.

Free-format input

Free-format input is easier to use than fixed format because it reads delimited data.

- Each data value is separated by a tab, a comma, and/or one or more spaces.
- Each new case begins on a new line. A single case can extend over several lines, but the next case must start on a new line. (If you have several cases per record, see the backslash option in Example 11.7.)
- Character values that contain blanks, commas, or special characters are surrounded by single (' ') or double (" ") quotation marks.
- Missing numeric data are recorded as a period (.), and missing character data are recorded as a blank surrounded by single (' ') or double (" ") quotation marks. They can also be indicated by typing two commas (, ,) with no characters between them.

The file should be ASCII text without nonprinting characters such as page breaks, margin indicators, or control characters. The data can be aligned or unaligned:

```
Sloan          male    31   158.5              Sloan male 31 158.5
'Mike Johnson' male    45   165       or       'Mike Johnson'  male
Smythe         female  37   126.5              45 165
                                               Smythe      female      37
                                               126.5
```

SYSTAT counts the number of variable names listed in the INPUT command to determine how many data values to read for each case. After reading the specified number of values, SYSTAT moves to the next line to begin reading the next case.

The following examples use INPUT to name the variables in the order they are read into SYSTAT:

    INPUT *varlist*

where *varlist* is a list of variable names. You can identify a range of variables in *varlist* using subscript notation, such as:

    INPUT *var*(1)...*var*(10)   or   INPUT *var*(1...10)

Variable names can be up to 12 characters long. Names of string variables must end with a dollar sign ($). Subscripts can be used for numeric or character variables (for example, *QUESTION(1)*,...,*QUESTION(35)*) as long as the total length does not exceed 12 characters.

11.1
Input data
at the command
prompt

You can create a data file by typing data directly in the SYSTAT Main window. For example, to create a SYSTAT data file called *MYFILE*, type:

```
BASIC
    NEW
    SAVE MYFILE
    INPUT A B C
    RUN
```

Now enter data one case to a line, pressing Enter at the end of each line:

```
1 2 3
4 5 6
7 8 9
~
```

The last character (a tilde) tells SYSTAT to end data input. SYSTAT responds:

```
3 cases and 3 variables processed and saved.
```

Typing data at the command prompt is particularly useful if you are creating a command file and want to include the data in that file rather than in a separate data file.

11.2
Reading
an ASCII
text file:
GET

Suppose you want to read an ASCII text file named *INFILE.DAT* that has the following data:

```
1 2 3
4 5 6
7 8 9
```

Then you want to write it as a SYSTAT file named *MYFILE1.SYS* that has three variables named *A*, *B*, and *C*. Type:

```
BASIC
    NEW
    GET infile
    SAVE myfile1
    INPUT a b c
    RUN
```

```
3 cases and 3 variables processed.
SYSTAT file created.
```

11.3
Reading
multiple lines
per case

To demonstrate how to read ASCII files with multiple lines per case, we use the *MINIWRLD.DAT* file. This file contains 15 variables for each country and has two lines of data per case. The variables are:

1. Name of the country
2. Population in 1990
3. Percentage of the population living in cities
4. Number of births per 1000 people per year
5. Number of infants (per 1000 live births) who die during their first year
6. Gross domestic product per capita
7. Average expenditure for education (per person)
8. Average expenditure for health (per person)
9. Average expenditure for military (per person)
10. Type of government
11. Years of life expectancy for males
12. Years of life expectancy for females
13. Percentage of population who can read
14. Type of country
15. Ratio of birth to death rates

The following illustration shows the file in a text editor. (*Note*: The first two rows of column numbers are not part of the file.)

```
1              2        3    4    5  6           7        8        9        10
11   12   13      14         15
France       56.358  73   14    6  14542.657  648.069  728.249  432.780  Democracy
73   82   99.00   Europe       1.556
Greece       10.028  65   11   10   5614.184  115.000  158.700  260.400  Democracy
75   80   95.00   Europe       1.222
Switzerland   6.742  58   12    5  17723.499  853.538 1209.077  330.769  Democracy
75   83   99.00   Europe       1.333
Spain        39.269  91   11    6  10153.121  166.675  224.923  117.964  Democracy
75   82   97.00   Europe       1.375
UK           57.366  76   14    7  14259.401  474.488  479.064  447.473  Democracy
73   79   99.00   Europe       1.273
Hungary      10.569  54   12   15   6112.397  234.340  196.792  146.321  OneParty
67   75   99.00   Europe       0.923
Iraq         18.782  68   46   67   1863.509   87.875   19.000  760.000  OneParty
66   68   55.00   Islamic      6.571
Pakistan    114.649  28   43  110    376.801    7.655    0.697   23.268  Military
56   57   26.00   Islamic      3.071
Ethiopia     51.667  14   45  116    127.742    4.943    1.185   10.137  Military
49   52   55.20   Islamic      3.000
Afghanistan 15.862  16   44  154    189.128    1.000       .        .    OneParty
47   46   12.00   Islamic      2.444
Brazil      152.505  68   26   69   2472.049   59.449   22.729   16.260  Democracy
62   68   76.00   'New World'  3.714
Canada       26.538  76   14    7  19353.214 1052.813  936.211  316.797  Democracy
74   81   99.00   'New World'  2.000
Venezuela    19.698  76   28   27   2944.446  193.989   78.652   45.562  Democracy
71   77   85.60   'New World'  7.000
ElSalvador    5.310  39   34   49   1035.808   17.647    7.647   29.020  Military
62   68   65.00   'New World'  4.857
```

To store these data in the SYSTAT file called *MINIWRLD.SYS*, type:

```
BASIC
    GET miniwrld
    SAVE miniwrld
    INPUT country$ pop_1990 urban birth_rt babymort,
          gdp_cap educ health mil gov$ lifeexpm,
          lifeexpf literacy group$ b_to_d
    RUN
```

After the commands are executed, SYSTAT responds:

```
14 cases and 15 variables processed.
SYSTAT file created.
```

11.4
Unequal length records

For each new case, SYSTAT reads as many data values as are named in the INPUT statement, one value per variable, even if it has to read several lines of data to do so. The following example illustrates what happens when the rows have records that vary in length. The data in the text file *MYDATA1.DAT* are:

```
10    20    30    40
50    60
70    80
90    100   110   120
```

To create a SYSTAT file named *MYFILE2.SYS*, type:

```
BASIC
    NEW
    SAVE myfile2
    GET mydata1
    INPUT a b c d
    RUN
```

After the commands are executed, SYSTAT responds:

```
3 cases and 4 variables processed.
SYSTAT file created.
```

To view the contents of the SYSTAT file, type:

```
    LIST
```

```
                       A          B          C          D
Case     1         10.000     20.000     30.000     40.000
Case     2         50.000     60.000     70.000     80.000
Case     3         90.000    100.000    110.000    120.000

3 cases and 4 variables processed.
No SYSTAT file created.
```

Line by line, this is how SYSTAT processes the file:

Case 1   SYSTAT reads 10, 20, 30, and 40 as the first case of the new data file.

Case 2   It next reads two data values from the second line (50 and 60) as variables *A* and *B* for case 2. It still must fill variables *C* and *D*, so it continues to the next line and reads 70 and 80.

Case 3   SYSTAT finally reads 90, 100, 110, and 120 as case 3 of the new file.

11.5 Coding missing values

SYSTAT uses a period to represent missing numeric data and a space to represent missing character data.

– Code missing *numeric* data as periods in your data. Do not code missing numeric data as characters such as NA, M, *, or ? because SYSTAT does not read character data into a numeric field. If missing numeric data are left as blank spaces, SYSTAT moves the next value in the file where the missing value should be. All subsequent data are also moved (see example below).

– Code missing *character* data as a blank space enclosed in single (' ') or double quotation marks (" ").

This example demonstrates what happens when you do not code missing values as periods. The values in the *MYDATA2.DAT* text file are:

```
100 200 300
400     600
700 800 900
```

To create a SYSTAT file named *NEWFILE.SYS*, type:

```
BASIC
   SAVE newfile
   GET mydata2
   INPUT a b c
   RUN
```

The SYSTAT file *NEWFILE.SYS* does not contain the correct number of cases or values:

	A	B	C
Case 1	100.000	200.000	300.000
Case 2	400.000	600.000	700.000

Instead of three cases, SYSTAT produces two, omitting 800 and 900. SYSTAT reads the first line of data correctly, but treats the missing value in the second line as a space delimiter separating the values 400 and 600. Therefore, SYSTAT reads 600 as variable *B*. It completes case 2 by reading 700, the first value of the next line. SYSTAT is ready to start a new case, so it moves to the next line of original data. There are no more lines of data to read, so SYSTAT closes the file.

To read these data correctly, use a period or consecutive commas to mark where data are missing. Data in the *MYDATA2.DAT* file can be either:

```
100 200 300                100,200,300
400  .  600       or       400,  ,600
700 800 900                700,800,900
```

11.6
Multiple cases per record: backslash

If you want SYSTAT to read more than one case per line, append a backslash (\) to your **INPUT** statement. The backslash forces SYSTAT to use all the data in the row, even if it has to start a new case. It also forces SYSTAT to start a new case whenever it starts reading a new row of values. Without a backslash, SYSTAT ignores extra values in a row and moves to the next line to find data for the next case.

This example shows how to use the backslash to read data where you have more than one case per line of original data. Data in the text file *MYDATA3.DAT* are:

```
Tom 23 Jerry 51 Marilyn 50 Lynne 18
Mark 22 Andrew 8 Henry 70 Chris 23
```

To create the SYSTAT file *MULTIPLE.SYS*, type:

```
BASIC
    NEW
    SAVE multiple
    GET mydata3
    INPUT name$ age \
    RUN
```

```
8 cases and 2 variables processed.
SYSTAT file created.
```

To view the contents of the SYSTAT file, type:

```
LIST
```

```
                    NAME$        AGE
Case    1            Tom      23.000
Case    2          Jerry      51.000
Case    3        Marilyn      50.000
Case    4          Lynne      18.000
Case    5           Mark      22.000
Case    6         Andrew       8.000
Case    7          Henry      70.000
Case    8          Chris      23.000

8 cases and 2 variables processed.
No SYSTAT file created.
```

With the backslash, SYSTAT reads the entire line of original data even though each line fills up four cases in the SYSTAT file. Without the backslash, SYSTAT would read only the first two values from each line and generate only two cases.

11.7 Incomplete records: backslash

This example shows how to use the backslash to read records that do not have an equal number of values per case. The data in the text file *MYDATA4.DAT* are:

```
1 2 3
4 5 6 7
8 9
```

To create the SYSTAT file *UNEQUAL.SYS*, type:

```
BASIC
    NEW
    SAVE unequal
    GET mydata4
    INPUT a b c d \
    RUN
```

```
3 cases and 4 variables processed.
SYSTAT file created.
```

The SYSTAT data file looks like this:

```
                    A        B        C        D
Case    1       1.000    2.000    3.000        .
Case    2       4.000    5.000    6.000    7.000
Case    3       8.000    9.000        .        .
```

Fixed-format input

With *fixed-format* input, you tell SYSTAT exactly where the values for each variable are located in the data records. Values for a variable must be in the same place for every record.

A fixed-format input statement consists of two parts. The first part provides the variable names that will appear in the SYSTAT file. The second part contains the format that tells SYSTAT where to read values for each variable. The number of items specified in the format must match the number of input variables. Enclose the variable names and the input format in separate sets of parentheses:

```
INPUT (age,sex$,income) (#3,$6,#8)
```

SYSTAT checks the number of items you specify in the format against the number of variables. If they do not match, an error message is displayed.

Formats

Formats control a pointer that tells SYSTAT where to read the next variable value. These formats specify the location and width of fields that contain values. Leading and trailing blanks are ignored for numeric data. All characters within the formatted field, except leading blanks, are read into a character value. Character strings are left-justified.

Format items for fixed-format input include the following:

#*n*	Read a numeric value in the next *n* columns
$*n*	Read a character value in the next *n* columns
>	Move the pointer one column to the right
<	Move the pointer one column to the left
^*n*	Move the pointer to column *n*
/	Move the pointer to the first column on the next record
%*n*	Move the pointer to the first column on the *n*th record
\	Leave the pointer on the current record for next case
n*r	Repeat *r* *n* times, where *r* is any of the above

Some examples:

>>>	Move the pointer three columns to the right
3*>	Move the pointer three columns to the right
^10	Move to column 10 of the current record
#4	Read the numeric value in the next four columns beginning at the current column
$5	Read the character value in the next five columns beginning at the current column

^3	Move the pointer to column 3
>>>>>	Move the pointer five columns to the right
5*>	Move the pointer five columns to the right
%2	Move the pointer to column 1 of the second record (You cannot move back to an earlier record.)
/	Move the pointer to column 1 of the next record
//	Move the pointer to column 1 two records ahead (For example, if you are starting on the first record, %3 and // mean the same thing.)
#3	Read the numeric value in the next three columns beginning at the current column
2*$3	Read a character value in three columns and then another in the next three columns

You can use a backslash (\) to keep the pointer at the current position—rather than move to the next row—to begin the next case. This feature allows you to read files with multiple cases per record.

Note: Use % and ^ rather than / and >. In this way, you know precisely which record and column you are on. Furthermore, if you have seven records per observation, you need a %7 at the end of your format, even if you read nothing from the seventh field, to ensure that the pointer is positioned correctly for the next observation.

11.8 Simple fixed-format example

Suppose you have an ASCII file *TESTDATA.DAT* like this (the two lines at the top help you count columns):

```
0         1         2
1234567890123456789012345 6
_____
1232 BILLY 0 1 1 1 0 BACDD
BCEAD
7384 SUSAN 1 1 0 1 1 BDAEA
DDEAE
2837   TIM 1 1 1 0 1 CBADE
DDBCA
7484   TOM 0 0 1 0 1 BCDEC
AAEDC
5678 WAYNE 1 1 0 1 0 ADEAA
DACBB
```

The first variable in the file is a four-column ID number. The second is the first name of a student. The next five variables are answers to true-false questions and are separated by spaces. The last five variables on the first line are answers to multiple-choice questions and are not delimited.

The variables on the second line are answers to five more multiple-choice questions.

SYSTAT reads the data into a SYSTAT file called *TEST.SYS*. Because the INPUT statement takes up more than one line, commas are used to continue it onto subsequent lines.

```
BASIC
    GET testdata
    SAVE test
    INPUT (id,name$, q(1) .. q(5), q$(6) .. q$(15)),
          (#4,$6,5*#2,>,5*$1,%2,5*$1)
    RUN
```

Here is how each variable is read by its format description:

#4	Read numeric value from first four columns into variable ID
$6	Read character value from next six columns into NAME$
5*#2	Read five consecutive two-column numeric values into Q(1), Q(2), Q(3), Q(4), and Q(5)
>	Move pointer one space to the right
5*$1	Read five consecutive one-column character values into Q$(6), Q$(7), Q$(8), Q$(9), and Q$(10)
%2	Move pointer to second line of input record
5*$1	Read five consecutive one-column character values into Q$(11), Q$(12), Q$(13), Q$(14), and Q$(15)

Entering triangular matrices

By default, data in ASCII files take cases-by-variables (rectangular) form. Both BASIC and the regular worksheet allow you to enter triangular matrices, such as those produced by CORR. See *SYSTAT: Statistics* for definitions of **SSCP**, **Dissimilarity**, and **Similarity** matrices.

Specifying file type: TYPE

Use the TYPE command to indicate what type of matrix you are entering. Valid types are RECTANGULAR, SSCP, COVARIANCE, CORR, DISSIMILARITY, and SIMILARITY. The default is RECTANGULAR.

COVARIANCE designates a covariance matrix and CORR, a correlation matrix. When CORR outputs a triangular matrix to a SYSTAT file, it automatically sets the type. If you LIST a triangular matrix in BASIC, the upper triangular portion contains missing values, since the matrices are symmetric and only half the values are needed by the statistical routines.

11.9
A covariance matrix

This example reads a covariance matrix from an ASCII file named *MYDATA5.DAT* and saves it in a SYSTAT file named *TURTLE.SYS*. *MYDATA5* contains the following data records:

```
451.39
271.17 171.73
168.70 103.29 66.65
```

To create the SYSTAT file, type:

```
BASIC
    SAVE turtle
    GET mydata5
    INPUT length, width, height
    TYPE COVARIANCE
    RUN
```

11.10
A matrix with a missing diagonal: DIAGONAL

For some types of data, the values on the diagonal are undefined or constant. In these cases, you can input only the values below the diagonal and leave the diagonal missing.

Use **DIAGONAL ABSENT** to signal to BASIC that the diagonal values are missing. If you do not use the command, **DIAGONAL PRESENT** is assumed. If you input a correlation matrix with **DIAGONAL ABSENT**, SYSTAT sets the diagonal elements to 1.0; otherwise, the diagonal elements are set to missing values.

The following example reads a correlation matrix with no diagonal elements. The matrix is a text file named *MYCORR.DAT* that looks like this:

```
.96
.90  .91
.72  .11  .99
.09  .42  .89  .98
.59  .51  .73  .90  .92
.88  .79  .52  .82  .89  .97
```

To store this matrix as the SYSTAT file *COLORS.SYS*, type:

```
BASIC
    SAVE colors
    GET mycorr
    INPUT red,orange,yellow,green,blue,indigo,violet
    TYPE CORR
    DIAGONAL ABSENT
    RUN
```

Notice that there are only six rows and columns to fill seven variables. The diagonal elements are set to missing.

Trouble-shooting ASCII files

You must be sure that your ASCII file does not contain any nonprinting ASCII characters such as page breaks, control characters, and column markers. SYSTAT can read numbers, alphabetical and keyboard characters, delimiters (spaces, commas, or tabs that separate consecutive values from each other), and carriage returns.

Numeric fields must contain only numeric data; therefore, exclude variable labels or column headings when using GET to read from an ASCII file. Note that SYSTAT can import ASCII data files containing variable names with **Import** on the **File** menu (see Chapter 3).

Most text editors, such as Microsoft Word and WordPerfect, can save files in an ASCII text format without nonprinting characters. If you do not know if your file is in an ASCII format, use the TYPE command in DOS to view it. If you see any strange characters, your file was not saved in ASCII format, and SYSTAT will not be able to read it.

Errors and error messages

Following are some of the error messages encountered when reading ASCII files.

Empty file error. Make sure you spelled the filename correctly and that it is in the current directory. If it is not, either copy it to the current directory or specify the complete filename (path plus full filename).

Long INPUT statement. If your INPUT statement is too long for one line, type a comma at the end of the first line and press Enter. Continue typing the statement on the next line. Do this for as many lines as you need.

Data lost or in the wrong columns. If SYSTAT places data incorrectly or data are lost when you read them, make sure you correctly specify missing values in your data file. If you are using free-format input, enter missing numeric values as periods (.) and missing character values as blanks surrounded by quotation marks (" "). If you are using fixed-format input, you can leave missing values as blank spaces. If you are using free-format input to read a file that does not have the same number of values in every record, add the backslash (\) to the end of your INPUT statement (see above).

Unexpected data error. Make sure the ASCII file includes no field headings or variable labels and make sure variable types match data types. Do not put character data under a numeric variable or vice versa. Make sure you correctly specify missing values. If you are using free-format input, enter missing numeric values as periods (.) and missing character values as blanks surrounded by quotation marks (" "). If you are using free-format input to read a file that does not have the same number of values in every record, add the backslash (\) to the end of your INPUT statement. If you are using fixed-format input, make sure you specify the variable types in the format section correctly.

Non-ASCII character warning. Check for nonprinting characters in your file. Such characters include control characters, tab markers, margin and page-break indicators, and so on.

Nonmatching number of variables error. The number of variables defined in the format of your INPUT statement does not match the number of variables named in the variable list.

Input past end of record error. The format of your INPUT statement tells SYSTAT to read your ASCII file records further than allowed. This message should rarely occur.

Unpacking records

This example shows how to reorganize several repeated measures on a single record as one measure per record and how to generate a sequence number for each value.

Begin with the *TRIAL.SYS* data file that has two records:

```
10 20 30 40 50 Male
11 21 31 41 51 Female
```

The following examples generate a file with 10 cases. First, you create a temporary ASCII text file with 10 cases, each containing one data value plus its sequence number and label:

```
BASIC
    USE trial
    OUTPUT temp
    FOR I=1 to 5
        PRINT X(I),I,sex$
    NEXT
    RUN
    OUTPUT *
```

SYSTAT's **FOR...NEXT** statement lists the five data values (and the values of *SEX$* and *I*, the index, as a sequence number). The **OUTPUT** * command closes the text file.

Then, you read the data from the text file *TEMP* into the SYSTAT file *NEWTRIAL*:

```
NEW
  INPUT x,i,sex$
  GET temp
  SAVE newtrial
  RUN
```

Here are the values in the SYSTAT file *NEWTRIAL*:

	X	I	SEX$
1	10.000	1.000	Male
2	20.000	2.000	Male
3	30.000	3.000	Male
4	40.000	4.000	Male
5	50.000	5.000	Male
6	11.000	1.000	FeMale
7	21.000	2.000	Female
8	31.000	3.000	Female
9	41.000	4.000	Female
10	51.000	5.000	Female

Exporting Data to an ASCII Text File

For use in a word processor or in another program, you may need to write data in SYSTAT files as text. You can use the PUT command, the PRINT command, or the LIST command to store data in a text file.

If you want a command conversion procedure, use PUT:

```
BASIC
    USE filename
    PUT output filename
    RUN
```

where USE identifies the SYSTAT input file and PUT assigns a filename for the output ASCII file. PUT saves your data in a text file that has up to 11 columns, with each column separated by commas. Character values (strings) are surrounded by double quotation marks (" "). Variable names are not included in the ASCII file. SYSTAT automatically adds a *.DAT*.

11.11 Converting a data file to a text file

The following commands convert the SYSTAT file *MINIWRLD* to a text file:

```
BASIC
    USE miniwrld
    PUT textfile
    RUN
```

You can use a word processor to view *TEXTFILE.DAT*. The first case in the file appears as follows:

```
"France       ",      56.358,      73.000,      14.000,       6.000,
14542.657,      648.069,      728.249,     432.780,"Democracy   ",      73.000,
      82.000,      99.000,"Europe       ",       1.556
```

A hard carriage return appears only at the end of the text. The text "wraps around" here for display purposes. Notice that PUT adds commas as data separators and surrounds character values in quotes. This is not true if you use PRINT, as shown in the following example.

11.12
Saving data as text without quotes: PRINT

If you do not want commas as delimiters and quotation marks around character data, use the PRINT command to send the output to a file.

```
BASIC
    USE miniwrld
    ID=country$
    OUTPUT subset2
    PRINT country$ literacy urban birth_rt gov$
    RUN
    OUTPUT *
```

The OUTPUT * command closes the text file. The resulting file, *SUBSET2.DAT*, looks like this:

```
France        99.0    73.0    14.0    Democracy
Greece        95.0    65.0    11.0    Democracy
Switzerland   99.0    58.0    12.0    Democracy
Spain         97.0    91.0    11.0    Democracy
UK            99.0    76.0    14.0    Democracy
Hungary       99.0    54.0    12.0    OneParty
Iraq          55.0    68.0    46.0    OneParty
Pakistan      26.0    28.0    43.0    Military
Ethiopia      55.2    14.0    45.0    Military
Afghanistan   12.0    16.0    44.0    OneParty
Brazil        76.0    68.0    26.0    Democracy
Canada        99.0    76.0    14.0    Democracy
Venezuela     85.6    76.0    28.0    Democracy
ElSalvador    65.0    39.0    34.0    Military
```

Selecting, Listing, and Saving Cases

Use IF...THEN DELETE statements to select a subset of cases and store them in a SYSTAT data file, or use PUT or PRINT to save them in a text file. (You can also save selected cases using the SELECT command with EXTRACT, as described in Chapter 7.)

```
BASIC                                    BASIC
    USE myfile                               USE myfile
    IF condition THEN DELETE    or           IF condition THEN
    SAVE subfile                             PUT subtext
    RUN                                      RUN
```

**11.13
Deleting
selected
cases**

The following commands drop certain cases and list the variable *COUNTRY$* to show the cases SYSTAT retained:

```
BASIC
    USE miniwrld
    IF CASE<=9 THEN DELETE
    RUN

    LIST country$
```

SYSTAT responds:

```
Case number     COUNTRY$
        1       Afghanistan
        2       Brazil
        3       Canada
        4       Venezuela
        5       ElSalvador
```

**11.14
Saving
selected cases
to a new file**

The following commands save only those cases in *MINIWRLD* where *GDP_CAP* is greater than 10,000. The results are stored in *NEWFILE*.

```
BASIC
    USE miniwrld
    SAVE newfile
    IDVAR=country$
    IF gdp_cap < 10000 THEN DELETE
    RUN

    LIST
```

```
* Case ID * COUNTRY$    POP_1990     URBAN        BIRTH_RT     BABYMORT
* Case ID * GDP_CAP     EDUC         HEALTH       MIL          GOV$
* Case ID * LIFEEXPM    LIFEEXPF     LITERACY     GROUP$       B_TO_D
France       France           56.358       73.000       14.000          6.000
France                14542.657      648.069      728.249      432.780 Democracy
France                   73.000       82.000       99.000 Europe          1.556
Switzerland  Switzerland       6.742       58.000       12.000          5.000
Switzerland           17723.499      853.538     1209.077      330.769 Democracy
Switzerland              75.000       83.000       99.000 Europe          1.333
Spain        Spain            39.269       91.000       11.000          6.000
Spain                 10153.121      166.675      224.923      117.964 Democracy
Spain                    75.000       82.000       97.000 Europe          1.375
UK           UK               57.366       76.000       14.000          7.000
UK                    14259.401      474.488      479.064      447.473 Democracy
UK                       73.000       79.000       99.000 Europe          1.273
Canada       Canada           26.538       76.000       14.000          7.000
Canada                19353.214     1052.813      936.211      316.797 Democracy
Canada                   74.000       81.000       99.000 NewWorld        2.000
```

Instead of using an IF...THEN DELETE statement to delete cases that are less than 10,000, you could have used SELECT:

```
SELECT gdp_cap >= 10000
EXTRACT newfile
```

11.15
Omitting variable names and case numbers

The PRINT command is similar to LIST, except that case numbers and variable names are not printed. Also, PRINT can be used with REPEAT, allowing you to print the first *k* cases. Type:

```
BASIC
    USE miniwrld
    REPEAT 3
    PRINT country$ literacy urban birth_rt
    RUN
```

SYSTAT responds:

```
France          99.000      73.000      14.000
Greece          95.000      65.000      11.000
Switzerland     99.000      58.000      12.000
```

Case numbers and variables are not printed. SYSTAT prints numeric and character values in 12-column, right-justified fields. Blanks pad the left side of numeric fields. With PAGE set to WIDE, you can display up to 10 variables per line. If you use FORMAT to set the field width to fewer than 12 characters per field, you can display more than 10 variables per line.

11.16
Using PRINT
to save
selected cases

You can select specific cases by using the IF...THEN PRINT... command. The example uses the OUTPUT command to store the values of *GROUP$*, *COUNTRY$*, *LITERACY*, *BIRTH_RT*, and *LIFEEXPF* (for Islamic countries only) in the text file *TEXTFILE.DAT*:

```
BASIC
    USE ourworld
    OUTPUT textfile
    IF group$='Islamic' THEN PRINT country$ literacy,
                                birth_rt lifeexpf
    RUN
    OUTPUT *
```

After RUN, the OUTPUT * command closes the text file. The ASCII file *TEXTFILE.DAT* looks like this:

```
Gambia      25.100    48.000    50.000
Iraq        55.000    46.000    68.000
Pakistan    26.000    43.000    57.000
Banglades   29.000    42.000    53.000
Ethiopia    55.200    45.000    52.000
Guinea      20.000    47.000    44.000
Malaysia    65.000    29.000    71.000
Senegal     28.100    44.000    56.000
Mali        18.000    51.000    47.000
Libya       50.000    37.000    70.000
Somalia     11.600    47.000    54.000
Afghanist   12.000    44.000    46.000
Sudan       31.000    44.000    55.000
Turkey      70.000    29.000    67.000
Algeria     52.000    37.000    64.000
Yemen       15.000    52.000    49.000
```

11.17
Printing
the first three
cases

In BASIC, if you want to see only some of the cases, you can specify a number of cases with REPEAT. The following example sends the first three cases of *MINIWRLD* to the *NEWFILE.DAT* file:

```
BASIC
    USE miniwrld
    OUTPUT newfile
    REPEAT 3
    PRINT
    RUN
    OUTPUT *
```

Programming Examples

The examples in this section show more applications of SYSTAT transformation commands, including statistical calculations and data management procedures. There are simpler ways to accomplish many of these tasks, but the programs in this chapter are selected to illustrate the full range of SYSTAT BASIC capabilities.

**11.18
Example:
A calendar for
the year 2000**

The commands to generate a calendar for the year 2000 are shown below, and defined throughout the sections that follow.

```
BASIC
    LET year=2000
    DIM DAY$(7)
    DIM DATE(7)
    FORMAT 9 0
    FOR MONTH=1 TO 12
        LET   BASE=DOC(YEAR,MONTH,1)-1
        LET   LAST=BASE+31
        LET   FIRST=INT((BASE+1)/7)*7
        LET   MONTH$=STR$(BASE+1,'MMMMMMMMM/YY')
        PRINT '   +-----------------------',MONTH$,YEAR,
                  '-------------------------+'
        FOR I=1 TO 7
            LET DAY$(I)=DOW$(i-1)
        NEXT
        PRINT '  | ',DAY$(1),DAY$(2),DAY$(3),DAY$(4),
                DAY$(5),DAY$(6),DAY$(7),'|'
        FOR I=FIRST TO LAST STEP 7
            FOR L=I TO I+6
                LET DATE(L+1-I)=L-BASE
                IF (DAT(L,'M')<>MONTH) THEN,
                        LET DATE(L+1-I)=.
            NEXT
            PRINT DATE(1),DATE(2),DATE(3),DATE(4),
                    DATE(5),DATE(6),DATE(7)
        NEXT
    NEXT
NEXT
RUN
```

```
+-------------------- January      2000 --------------------+
| Sunday    Monday    Tuesday   Wednesday Thursday  Friday    Saturday  |
                                                              1
   2         3         4         5         6         7         8
   9         10        11        12        13        14        15
   16        17        18        19        20        21        22
```

```
     23        24        25        26        27        28        29
     30        31                   .         .         .
+----------------------- February     2000 ------------------------+
| Sunday    Monday    Tuesday   Wednesday Thursday  Friday    Saturday |
                         1         2         3         4         5
      6         7         8         9        10        11        12
     13        14        15        16        17        18        19
     20        21        22        23        24        25        26
     27        28        29         .         .         .         .
+----------------------- March        2000 ------------------------+
| Sunday    Monday    Tuesday   Wednesday Thursday  Friday    Saturday |
                                   1         2         3         4
      5         6         7         8         9        10        11
     12        13        14        15        16        17        18
     19        20        21        22        23        24        25
     26        27        28        29        30        31         .
+----------------------- April        2000 ------------------------+
| Sunday    Monday    Tuesday   Wednesday Thursday  Friday    Saturday |
                                                                 1
      2         3         4         5         6         7         8
      9        10        11        12        13        14        15
     16        17        18        19        20        21        22
     23        24        25        26        27        28        29
     30         .         .         .         .         .         .
+----------------------- May          2000 ------------------------+
| Sunday    Monday    Tuesday   Wednesday Thursday  Friday    Saturday |
                1         2         3         4         5         6
      7         8         9        10        11        12        13
     14        15        16        17        18        19        20
     21        22        23        24        25        26        27
     28        29        30        31         .         .         .
+----------------------- June         2000 ------------------------+
| Sunday    Monday    Tuesday   Wednesday Thursday  Friday    Saturday |
                                             1         2         3
      4         5         6         7         8         9        10
     11        12        13        14        15        16        17
     18        19        20        21        22        23        24
     25        26        27        28        29        30         .
+----------------------- July         2000 ------------------------+
| Sunday    Monday    Tuesday   Wednesday Thursday  Friday    Saturday |
                                                                 1
      2         3         4         5         6         7         8
      9        10        11        12        13        14        15
     16        17        18        19        20        21        22
     23        24        25        26        27        28        29
     30        31         .         .         .         .         .
+----------------------- August       2000 ------------------------+
| Sunday    Monday    Tuesday   Wednesday Thursday  Friday    Saturday |
                1         2         3         4         5
      6         7         8         9        10        11        12
     13        14        15        16        17        18        19
     20        21        22        23        24        25        26
     27        28        29        30        31         .         .
+----------------------- September    2000 ------------------------+
| Sunday    Monday    Tuesday   Wednesday Thursday  Friday    Saturday |
                                                       1         2
      3         4         5         6         7         8         9
     10        11        12        13        14        15        16
     17        18        19        20        21        22        23
     24        25        26        27        28        29        30
      .         .         .         .         .         .
+----------------------- October      2000 ------------------------+
| Sunday    Monday    Tuesday   Wednesday Thursday  Friday    Saturday |
      1         2         3         4         5         6         7
      8         9        10        11        12        13        14
     15        16        17        18        19        20        21
     22        23        24        25        26        27        28
     29        30        31         .         .         .         .
+----------------------- November     2000 ------------------------+
| Sunday    Monday    Tuesday   Wednesday Thursday  Friday    Saturday |
                                   1         2         3         4
      5         6         7         8         9        10        11
     12        13        14        15        16        17        18
     19        20        21        22        23        24        25
     26        27        28        29        30         .         .
+----------------------- December     2000 ------------------------+
| Sunday    Monday    Tuesday   Wednesday Thursday  Friday    Saturday |
                                                       1         2
      3         4         5         6         7         8         9
     10        11        12        13        14        15        16
     17        18        19        20        21        22        23
     24        25        26        27        28        29        30
```

Setup

You will typically use the following setup:

```
BASIC
    USE filename
    program statements
    .
    .
    .
    SAVE newfile
    RUN
```

When you enter the RUN command, SYSTAT executes the commands you have entered. SYSTAT executes the commands for each case in your data file before moving to the next case.

To preserve your work, you must save the transformed values to a new file. SYSTAT does not add these values to the original file. If you do not save your file, SYSTAT stores the results in a temporary data file.

Errors

When you enter a SYSTAT transformation command statement, SYSTAT reads it, checks for syntax errors, and then stores it in memory for later execution. If SYSTAT finds an error, it tells you and lets you enter a new statement and continue programming. The statement with an error is forgotten.

Statements and expressions

SYSTAT transformation commands make use of operators and functions in expressions and statements.

Note: *For a list of these operators and functions and an introduction to* LET *and* IF...THEN *statements, see Chapter 11.*

When the data are incomplete (values are missing), it is important to think about the consequences for results of transformation command statements. Arithmetic involving missing values propagates missing values. SYSTAT lists missing values first in numeric and alphabetical sorts and evaluates them as missing in relational comparisons.

You can number the lines in your transformation commands. When you begin a command with a line number in BASIC, SYSTAT assumes you are entering a program statement. A line number can be any integer between 0 and 32,000. You can increment line numbers by any amount. You can enter lines out of order, but SYSTAT executes them in increasing numerical order.

You do not need to give line numbers to program statements. You can even mix numbered and unnumbered program statements in one RUN. If you do, SYSTAT executes the unnumbered statements first, in the order you enter them. It then executes numbered statements in the order of their statement numbers.

You can use the ERASE command to delete numbered program statements. For example:

```
ERASE 10
```

eliminates statement 10, and

```
ERASE 10-50
```

removes all statements with numbers from 10 to 50.

IF...THEN

With the IF...THEN statement, you can execute actions conditionally, as described in Chapter 11. The syntax for an IF...THEN statement is:

```
IF condition THEN action
```

In BASIC, the action that follows THEN can be any legal BASIC language statement including LET, FOR...NEXT, DELETE, GOTO, and another IF...THEN. For example, legal IF...THEN statements are:

```
IF condition THEN LET variable = expression
IF condition THEN GOTO n
IF condition THEN PRINT variable and/or string
IF condition THEN DELETE
IF condition THEN IF condition THEN...
IF condition THEN FOR...
```

The action that follows THEN *cannot* be RUN, DIM, NEXT, GET, INPUT, TYPE, DIAGONAL, LRECL, NEW, REPEAT, ERASE, ARRAY, or SAVE. These are not BASIC language statements.

Note that IF...THEN can take another IF...THEN statement as its THEN statement.

You can execute more than one conditional transformation per RUN. If you are testing consecutive IF...THEN conditions on the same variable or variables, you should use IF...THEN...ELSE, discussed below.

ELSE

The examples above tested cases for one condition (for example *CARDIO > 325*, or *CARDIO > 325* and *CANCER > 100*). If the case met the condition, SYSTAT executed the transformation. If the case did not meet the condition, SYSTAT did not execute the transformation.

You may want, however, to execute many conditional transformations at once. If you are testing consecutive related conditions on the same variable, SYSTAT provides an ELSE statement to accompany IF...THEN. In its simplest form, IF...THEN and ELSE take the format:

```
IF condition THEN action1
ELSE action2
```

SYSTAT executes *ACTION2* only when the preceding IF condition evaluates to false. Another IF...THEN statement can follow ELSE, enabling you to string together a number of related conditional transformations:

```
IF condition THEN LET variable = expression
ELSE IF condition THEN LET variable = expression
ELSE IF condition THEN LET variable = expression
ELSE LET variable = expression
```

In this case, SYSTAT executes the statement following ELSE only when all preceding IF conditions are false. When a preceding condition is true, SYSTAT ignores subsequent ELSE statements.

11.19
Using
IF...THEN...ELSE

The following examples compare two sets of transformation commands. The first uses only IF...THEN statements to assign values to a new variable called *RATE$* based on values for *CARDIO*:

```
BASIC
   USE usstates
   SAVE newdata
      IF cardio < 275 THEN LET rate$ = 'LOW'
      IF cardio >= 275 AND cardio < 325,
         THEN LET rate$ = 'AVERAGE'
      IF cardio >= 325 THEN LET rate$ = 'HIGH'
   RUN
```

Using IF...THEN and ELSE makes the commands simpler:

```
BASIC
   USE usstates
   SAVE newdata
      IF cardio < 275 THEN LET rate$ = 'LOW'
      ELSE IF cardio <  325 THEN LET rate$ = 'AVERAGE'
      ELSE IF cardio >= 325 THEN LET rate$ = 'HIGH'
   RUN
```

SYSTAT executes these commands once for each case. The order of the IF and ELSE statements is important. The ELSE depends on the truth of the IF conditions before it. SYSTAT executes an ELSE statement only if all preceding conditions are false.

After running these commands, check the values for the first 10 cases for *CARDIO* and *RATE$*:

```
BASIC
   USE newdata
   LIST state$, cardio, rate$ / NUMBER=10
```

```
Case number STATE$    CARDIO    RATE$
       1      ME       330.400   HIGH
       2      NH       278.300   AVERAGE
       3      VT       289.400   AVERAGE
       4      MA       343.900   HIGH
       5      RI       353.600   HIGH
       6      CT       318.800   AVERAGE
       7      NY       376.200   HIGH
       8      NJ       356.100   HIGH
       9      PA       400.600   HIGH
      10      OH       344.600   HIGH
```

FOR...NEXT

The syntax for a FOR...NEXT statement is:

```
FOR index = n1 TO n2 STEP=n3
    statement
    statement
    .
    .
    .
NEXT
```

Note that **STEP** is optional. *INDEX* can be omitted too (but seldom is). Here are some examples:

```
FOR i = 1 TO 10
    PRINT i
NEXT

FOR j = 1 TO 10
    LET x(j) = LOG(x(j))
NEXT

FOR w = 0 TO cardio < 400 STEP URN
    PRINT w
NEXT
```

Instead of the second **FOR...NEXT** statement, you could have stated:

```
LET (X(1)...X(10))=LOG(@)
```

FOR...NEXT loops are executed for each case (or number of times specified in a **REPEAT** statement). In the first example, the **PRINT** statement is executed 10 times for each case. The second example computes the natural log for each of 10 subscripted variables.

The third example illustrates some important points. First, notice that the indices (*n1, n2,* and *n3*) can be expressions. If *CARDIO* is greater than or equal to 400 for a case, then *W* is printed only once (as 0) because the index *W* runs from 0 to 0. Otherwise, *W* runs from 0 to 1 in increments determined by a uniform random number chosen once before the loop is executed. This means that the **PRINT** statement will be executed a random number of times for each case where *CARDIO* is less than 400. This construct can be useful in Monte Carlo simulation.

FOR...NEXT loops without an index are executed once. Otherwise, **FOR...NEXT** loops are tested at the beginning to determine whether they should be executed for the current value of index. See Example 11.28 for an explicit parsing of a FOR...NEXT loop using GOTO statements. Some other languages can execute FOR...NEXT loops once even when a condition is false. The following example will not print anything:

```
FOR i = 6 TO 3 STEP 1
    PRINT i
NEXT
```

Nesting. You can nest up to 10 FOR...NEXT loops:

```
FOR
    FOR
        FOR
            .
            .
            .
            NEXT
        NEXT
    NEXT
```

Always match every FOR with a NEXT.

11.20 Conditional FOR...NEXT

The mean value for the variable *PULMONAR* from the data set *USSTATES* is approximately 34.8 with a standard deviation of 7.7. Suppose you want to set *RATE$* to HIGH and *RATE* to 1 everywhere that *PULMONAR* is more than one standard deviation above average.

```
BASIC
    USE usstates
    IF pulmonar > 34.8 THEN FOR
        LET rate$ = 'HIGH'
        LET rate = 1
        NEXT
    RUN

    LIST pulmonar, rate$, rate
```

Here are the first 10 cases:

```
Case number PULMONAR  RATE$     RATE
     1        46.100  HIGH       1.000
     2        33.500             0.0
     3        45.200  HIGH       1.000
     4        34.400             0.0
     5        34.300             0.0
     6        29.300             0.0
     7        31.000             0.0
     8        29.300             0.0
     9        36.000  HIGH       1.000
    10        37.500  HIGH       1.000
```

For the cases that meet the condition *PULMONAR > 34.8*, SYSTAT executes the two transformations between **FOR** and **NEXT**. For those cases that do not meet the condition, SYSTAT assigns missing values to *RATE$* and *RATE*.

11.21 FOR...NEXT with ELSE

This example shows the IF...THEN...ELSE format with the FOR...NEXT statement and the following assignments:

Where PULMONAR is	Let RATE$ =	Let RATE =
< 20.8	LOW	1
>= 20.8 and < 34.8	MID	2
>= 34.8	HIGH	3

```
BASIC
    USE usstates
    IF pulmonar < 20.8 THEN FOR
        LET rate$ = 'LOW'
        LET rate = 1
    NEXT
    ELSE IF pulmonar < 34.8 THEN FOR
        LET rate$ = 'MID'
        LET rate = 2
    NEXT
    ELSE IF pulmonar >= 34.8 THEN FOR
        LET rate$ = 'HIGH'
        LET rate = 3
    NEXT
    RUN

    LIST pulmonar, rate$, rate
```

Here are the first 10 cases:

```
Case number PULMONAR  RATE$     RATE
         1    46.100  HIGH      3.000
         2    33.500  MID       2.000
         3    45.200  HIGH      3.000
         4    34.400  MID       2.000
         5    34.300  MID       2.000
         6    29.300  MID       2.000
         7    31.000  MID       2.000
         8    29.300  MID       2.000
         9    36.000  HIGH      3.000
        10    37.500  HIGH      3.000
```

If, for a case, *PULMONAR* is less than 20.8, SYSTAT executes the associated FOR...NEXT statements, setting the values of *RATE$* to LOW and *RATE* to 1. It does not execute the subsequent ELSE statements but moves on to the next case.

If *PULMONAR* is greater than or equal to 20.8 but less than 34.8, SYSTAT executes the first **ELSE** statement. SYSTAT sets *RATE$* to **MID** and *RATE* to 2 and does not execute the second **ELSE** statement.

If *PULMONAR* is greater than 34.8, SYSTAT executes the last **ELSE** statement and sets *RATE$* to **HIGH** and *RATE* to 3.

FOR...NEXT loops with subscripted variables

You can use **FOR...NEXT** to define program loops that assign incremental values to an index variable. You can use such a loop to transform a set of subscripted variables. SYSTAT executes the statements between the **FOR** and the **NEXT** statements for each successive value of the index variable you specify. The index variable begins with the initial value you assign, does the transformations, and then increases by one. The cycle repeats until the index variable reaches the limit specified with **TO**.

Some examples are:

```
FOR i = 1 TO 5
FOR trial = 1 TO LAST
FOR j = 2 TO 20 STEP 2
```

The **STEP** option adjusts the size of the increment. If you enter the following, SYSTAT increments *N* by two each time. Its values are 1, 3, 5, 7, and 9 consecutively.

```
FOR n = 1 TO 10 STEP 2
```

With this command, SYSTAT runs through the loop only six times.

If you want to execute a set of commands on a certain number of cases, use the **REPEAT** command (see "REPEAT, for using the first n cases" on p. 240) rather than the **FOR...NEXT** construct. Remember, every set of commands is executed once for each case; therefore, if you use **FOR...NEXT**, BASIC runs through the loop for every case.

Temporary subscripts using the ARRAY statement

If your variable names are not already subscripted, you can use the **ARRAY** statement to assign subscripts temporarily for the purpose of doing transformations inside a **FOR...NEXT** loop. See Example 11.24 for more information.

11.22
Logging 10
variables

Suppose you have a file containing the variables *X(1...10)* and you want to calculate the natural log of each. You could either enter 10 separate LET commands or use the FOR...NEXT looping construct to do this. Type:

```
FOR n = 1 TO 10
  LET x(n) = LOG(x(n))
NEXT
```

SYSTAT runs through the loop 10 times, increasing the value of *N* by one each time. Thus, *N* successively has the values 1, 2, 3, 4, 5, 6, 7, 8, 9, and 10. This FOR...NEXT statement is the same as:

```
LET x(1)  = LOG(x(1))
LET x(2)  = LOG(x(2))
LET x(3)  = LOG(x(3))
LET x(4)  = LOG(x(4))
LET x(5)  = LOG(x(5))
LET x(6)  = LOG(x(6))
LET x(7)  = LOG(x(7))
LET x(8)  = LOG(x(8))
LET x(9)  = LOG(x(9))
LET x(10) = LOG(x(10))
```

Alternatively, you could use the @ shortcut and specify:

```
LET (x(1) .. x(10)) = LOG(@)
```

If you don't want to change the values in *X* by replacing them with their logs, you can assign the transformed values to a new variable *Y*. See the DIM statement below for how to create a new subscripted variable.

The STEP option adjusts the size of the increment. The following increases *N* by two each time to values 1, 3, 5, 7, and 9 successively. SYSTAT runs through the loop only five times.

```
FOR n = 1 TO 10 STEP 2
```

This is the same as:

```
LET x(1) = LOG(x(1))
LET x(3) = LOG(x(3))
LET x(5) = LOG(x(5))
LET x(7) = LOG(x(7))
LET x(9) = LOG(x(9))
```

Dimensioning space for new variables

To add new subscripted variables to a file, use the DIM statement. A DIM statement reserves space for new subscripted variables. String variables can be used.

For example, the following DIM statement creates new variables $X(1)$, $X(2)$, $X(3)$, $X(4)$, and $X(5)$.

```
DIM x(5)
```

You can use subscripted variables defined with DIM in transformations. Suppose you have variables $X(1...10)$. The following program creates new variables $Y(1...10)$ whose values are the natural logarithms of corresponding values in $X(1...10)$.

```
DIM y(10)
FOR n = 1 TO 10
   LET y(n) = LOG(x(n))
NEXT
```

Without the DIM statement, SYSTAT would not understand the Y variable subscript in the LET statement and would respond with an error message. You cannot redimension existing or previously defined arrays of subscripted variables.

Operations within rows

The following examples show you how to use the array capabilities in SYSTAT to perform operations within rows (cases).

11.23 Computing means of subscripted variables

The following commands compute the average of the variables $X(1)$ through $X(10)$ for each case. The statement:

```
IF x(i) <> .
```

checks for missing data. (Of course, you can calculate the mean more easily with the multivariable function AVG.)

```
BASIC
   USE myfile
   SAVE newdata
   LET sumx = 0
   LET n = 0
   FOR i = 1 TO 10
      IF x(i) <> . THEN FOR
```

```
            LET sumx = sumx + x(i)
            LET n = n + 1
        NEXT
    NEXT
    IF n <> 0 THEN LET mean = sumx/n
    ELSE LET mean = .
    RUN
```

The commands beginning with **LET** and ending with **ELSE** are executed once for each case. At the start of each case, **LET SUMX=0** and **LET N=0** set the variables *SUMX* and *N* to 0. *SUMX* sums the nonmissing values across each case, and *N* counts the nonmissing values for each case.

The **FOR...NEXT** loop runs the variables *X(1...10)* through two conditional transformations. In the first, if *X(I)* is not missing, its value is added to *SUMX*. In the second, again if *X(I)* is not missing, the count variable *N* is increased by one.

Upon completion of the **FOR...NEXT** loop, another conditional transformation tests whether *N* is not equal to 0. If *N* is not equal to 0, then the calculation *MEAN=SUMX/N* is executed. If *N* equals 0 (because the values of *X(1...10)* for the current case are all missing), dividing by *N* would cause an error. Therefore, SYSTAT executes the ensuing **ELSE** statement and sets *MEAN* to missing (.).

11.24 Computing means of unsubscripted variables: ARRAY

To average variables that are not subscripted, use the **ARRAY** command to alias the variables with a subscripted variable and then use the same logic as above.

You can have only one **ARRAY** command per set of commands that end with **RUN**. The **ARRAY** command can be used only in conjunction with a **FOR...NEXT** loop.

The example below averages the values of the average expenditures for health, education, and the military (*HEALTH*, *EDUC*, and *MIL*) using the *OURWORLD* data file and tests for missing values.

```
BASIC
    USE ourworld
    SAVE newdata
    ARRAY dollars / health  educ  mil
    LET summoney = 0
    LET n = 0
```

```
FOR i = 1 TO 3
   IF dollars(i) <> . THEN FOR
      LET summoney = summoney + dollars(i)
      LET n = n + 1
   NEXT
NEXT
IF N <> 0 THEN LET mean = summoney/n
ELSE LET mean = .
RUN
```

SYSTAT treats each variable specified in the **ARRAY** statement as an element in a subscripted variable named *DOLLARS*.

HEALTH = DOLLARS(1)
EDUC = DOLLARS(2)
MIL = DOLLARS(3)

Subgroup processing: BOG, EOG, BOF, EOF

You can specify BASIC commands that operate on subgroups of cases in a file. To do this, you must first identify variables in your file that define subgroups. BASIC has four special variables available for processing subgroups:

– **BOF** has value 1 if beginning-of-file, else it is 0

– **EOF** has value 1 if end-of-file, else it is 0

– **BOG** has value 1 if beginning-of-**BY** group, else it is 0

– **EOG** has value 1 if end-of-**BY** group, else it is 0

Before using **BOG** or **EOG**, you must use a **BY** statement to identify the variables that define subgroups in your data. You can name up to 10 variables. To clear a previous **BY** command, type **BY** with no arguments.

Note: *In BASIC, the BY command behaves slightly differently than in other procedures. Rather than causing subsequent commands to be executed on subgroups, it specifies which variable or variables are used for BOG and EOG.*

You can use **BOG**, **EOG**, **BOF**, and **EOF** within conditional expressions in IF...THEN statements. For example, the statement:

```
IF BOG THEN statement
```

causes SYSTAT to execute *STATEMENT* every time it encounters a new value in a **BY** variable. This is because the value of **BOG** is 1 ("true") for every case that begins a new group (and 0 otherwise).

11.25
Printing the last
case in a file

The following procedure prints the value of *CARDIO* for the last case in the *USDATA* file. **EOF** is 0 for every case but the last, where its value is 1.

```
BASIC
    NEW
    USE USDATA
    IF EOF THEN PRINT,
        "The CARDIO value for the last case is",CARDIO
    RUN
```

To print all but the last case, set the condition to one of the following:

```
IF EOF=0 THEN...
IF NOT EOF THEN...
```

11.26
Computing
totals within
groups

Suppose you want to sum values of the variable *X* within *GROUP1* and within *GROUP2*. You start with a file called *OURFILE* and want to write a file called *OURFILE2*.

OURFILE			OURFILE2		
GROUP	X		GROUP	X	TOTAL
1	3		1	3	1
1	4		1	4	7
1	6		1	6	13
2	9		2	9	9
2	-1		2	-1	8
2	2		2	2	10

The commands to do this are:

```
BASIC
    USE ourfile
    SAVE ourfile2
    BY group
    IF BOG THEN LET total=x
    ELSE LET total=LAG(total) + X
    IF EOG THEN PRINT group total
    RUN
```

BOG is true when a case is first in its group; otherwise, it is false.

Saving only the totals with group identifiers

If you want *OURFILE2* to include only the summary record for each group:

```
GROUP     TOTAL
1         13
2         10
```

insert these commands before RUN in the last setup:

```
IF NOT EOG THEN DELETE
DROP X
```

EOG means "end of group."

11.27 Computing subgroup means

The last example added the variable *N* that counts the number of cases within each group. You can use *N* to compute the mean within each group:

MEAN = TOTAL / N

The data in the output file *OURFILE3* are:

```
GROUP     MEAN
1         4.333
2         3.333
```

The commands to do this are:

```
BASIC
    USE ourfile
    SAVE ourfile3
    BY group
    IF BOG THEN LET total=x
    ELSE LET total=total + x
    IF BOG THEN LET n=1
    ELSE LET n=LAG(n) + 1
    IF EOG THEN LET mean=total/n
    IF NOT EOG THEN DELETE
    DROP x, total
    RUN
```

GOTO

A GOTO statement jumps from the current statement to the numbered statement specified. It works only with numbered statements.

For example, GOTO 10 tells BASIC to jump to the statement numbered 10. You can combine GOTO with IF...THEN for programming flexibility:

```
IF CASE = 10 THEN GOTO 50
IF GROUPS > 3 THEN GOTO 100
```

11.28
Simple GOTO

Here is a simple SYSTAT program using GOTO. Assume that *I, J, K,* and *L* are variables in the current file:

```
10 LET i = j - 1
20 LET i = i + 1
30  IF i > k THEN GOTO 60
40  PRINT i
50 GOTO 20
60 STOP
```

It is equivalent to the following program that uses the FOR...NEXT construct:

```
10 FOR i = j TO k STEP 1
40  PRINT i
50 NEXT
60 STOP
```

You can use IF...THEN with GOTO to mimic loops like those provided by other languages such as Pascal or FORTRAN. For example, you could program REPEAT...UNTIL, WHILE, or other flow-of-control constructions that SYSTAT does not directly provide.

PRINT

The PRINT command prints the values of variables you specify. You can also use PRINT to print character strings, which can be used in transformation commands.

Suppose you have a program that sums the values of a variable. Also suppose that instead of recording the answer (sum) somewhere in the worksheet, you just want the program to display its results. You can do this by issuing a PRINT statement:

```
PRINT "The sum of values in A is ", sum
```

BASIC prints numeric values in 12-column, right-justified fields. Blanks pad the left of each field. Character values are left-justified. Character strings that you specify literally (that is, not those that are values of character variables you listed in the PRINT command) are not justified; they are printed exactly the way you specified them, but without the surrounding quotation marks.

STOP

The STOP command halts work on the current observation and clears memory for work on the next observation. You will rarely need to use STOP. A possible case where you might want STOP is to terminate a loop when a certain value is reached.

REPEAT, for using the first n cases

For any set of BASIC commands, you can use the REPEAT command to limit the computations to a certain number of cases—just as you can use REPEAT 10 to limit the action of commands like LIST to the first 10 cases.

11.29 REPEAT example

You can use REPEAT to test complex transformations. If you use REPEAT before RUN, you can see whether the commands are correct or if you need to change them before running it on an entire file. For example,

```
BASIC
    REPEAT 3
    USE myfile
    LET x = LOG(x)
    LET y = LOG(y)
    PRINT x y
    RUN
```

If you made a mistake writing the program, you would find the error before running the program on the entire file. For files with several hundred cases, a brief trial run can save time. After you correct any errors, type REPEAT with no arguments to restore the counter.

Selecting random subsamples

The examples below illustrate two methods of taking random samples without replacement from data files. The first extracts a percentage of cases from a file; the second, a specific number of cases.

11.30 Selecting a percentage of cases

To pick a random sample of approximately three-fourths of a file, type:

```
BASIC
    USE usstates
        IF URN > .75 THEN DELETE
    RUN
```

To vary the sample size, change the 0.75 proportion to another number between 0 and 1.

Here is another method which keeps both selected and deselected cases in the same file. The *WEIGHT* variable can be used with statistical procedures to select the random subsample for cross-validation.

```
BASIC
    USE usstates
    IF URN > .75 THEN LET weight = 0
    ELSE LET weight = 1
    RUN
```

Matrix

12

Laszlo Engelman

Most of the classical analyses provided by statistical software packages can be expressed using matrix algebra; thus, they can be computed in the **Matrix** procedure. Students will find **Matrix** useful for gaining an understanding of matrix algebra and how statistical computations work. Researchers can prototype state-of-the-art procedures before they become available in statistical packages and can execute complex data management tasks.

For references about matrix algebra, see *Applied Linear Statistical Models* by Neter, Wasserman, and Kutner (1985), *Linear Statistical Inference and Its Applications* by C. R. Rao (1973), and *Linear Regression Analysis* by G. A. F. Seber (1977). Each of these books devotes a chapter or an appendix to the algebra of vectors and matrices.

Overview

Entering Data and Defining Matrices

Transformations and Statistical Functions

Matrix Algebra

Matrix

Overview

Matrix provides commands and functions that allow you to use matrix algebra to specify statistical analyses and perform data management tasks. For most tasks, you use the MAT and CALL commands. Some of the functions available with MAT are:

TRP	Transpose	DIAG	Extract the diagonal
INV	Inverse	DIAG3	Extract diagonal and surrounding elements
TRACE	Trace	SWEEP	Pivot on diagonal elements
DET	Determinant	SOLVE	Solve a system of linear equation
LOGDET	Log of the determinant	KRON	Kronecker product of two matrices
EIGVAL	Eigenvalues	CHOL	L of the Cholesky L*L' decomposition

For example, to compute the eigenvalues of the correlation matrix *MYCORR* and store them as the column vector *MYEIGEN*, specify:

```
MAT myeigen = EIGVAL(mycorr)
```

The result of a MAT command function is a single matrix, scalar, row vector, or column vector. These functions are described in the sections that follow.

Some of the functions in **Matrix** yield more than one result. For these functions, use the CALL command. For example, to compute both the eigenvectors and eigenvalues for *MYCORR*, specify:

```
CALL EIGEN(myvector, myeigen, mycorr)
```

Other functions for the CALL command decompose the input matrix into two or more matrices. Use QRD for the QR decomposition, CHOL for the Cholesky decomposition, and SVD for the singular value decomposition.

The MAT command also has functions for transforming each element of a matrix, extracting summary statistics across rows or columns, and performing matrix manipulations such as reconfiguring the number of rows and columns, removing rows with missing data, generating an identity matrix, generating design variables for categorical variables, and so on.

12.1
A multiple
regression
example

This example uses the **Matrix** procedure to estimate the coefficients of a multiple linear regression model for the *LONGLEY* data. Since the late 1960's, statisticians have referred to these data when discussing the accuracy of estimates in multiple regression. The data are considered statistically ill-conditioned because of the near multicollinearity among the independent variables. Five of the 15 correlations are over 0.99; a sixth correlation is 0.978. Researchers argue about the number of digits that are computed accurately, even though there is little meaning to the computation regardless of the numerical accuracy.

The multiple linear regression model is:

$$y = \beta_0 + \beta_1 x_1 + \beta_2 x_2 + \ldots + \beta_6 x_6 + \varepsilon$$

The matrix form of this model is

$$Y = X\beta + \varepsilon$$

where Y is the dependent variable vector, X is a matrix containing a column of 1's for β_0 and a column for each independent variable, β is the vector of regression coefficients, and ε is the vector of random errors. The estimates of the coefficients are:

$$\hat{\beta} = (X'X)^{-1}X'Y$$

However, it is computationally more sound to subtract off the mean vector first:

$$\hat{\beta} = \left((X - \bar{X})'(X - \bar{X}) \right)^{-1} (X - \bar{X})'(Y - \bar{Y})$$

Entering data and defining matrices

You can type data directly into the **Matrix** procedure or read them from a SYSTAT file.

Reading data from a SYSTAT file. The *LONGLEY* data are distributed with your software, so you do not need to type them. They are listed in *SYSTAT: Statistics*. The following commands read the *LONGLEY* file, define *TOTAL* as the vector for the dependent variable, and define *DEFLATOR*, *GNP*, *UNEMPLOY*, *ARMFORCE*, *POPULATN*, and *TIME* as the matrix of independent variables:

```
MATRIX
    USE longley
    MAT x = longley( ;deflator..time)
    MAT y = longley( ;total)
```

The syntax of the **MAT** command allows us to select rows and columns. In parentheses, we list the row selection, followed by a semicolon, followed by the column selection. The first **MAT** command extracts the columns *DEFLATOR* through *TIME* (the two periods are a shortcut to denote all of the variables between two variables). We want to use all of the rows, so we leave the row selection blank. The second **MAT** command extracts the *TOTAL* column.

Typing data into Matrix. If your data are not in a file, you can type them in. To enter the *LONGLEY* data, type:

```
MATRIX
    MAT longley = [83     234289 2356 1590 107608 1947 60323;
                   88.5 259426 2325 1456 108632 1948 61122;
```

*** *we omit cases 3-13* ***

```
                   115.7 518173 4806 2572 127852 1961 69331;
                   116.9 554894 4007 2827 130081 1962 70551]

    COLNAME longley = deflator gnp unemploy armforce,
                      populatn time total

    MAT x = longley( ;deflator..time)
    MAT y = longley( ;total)
```

Estimating the coefficients

Using the **X** matrix and **Y** vector from above, we obtain estimates of the regression coefficients. Note that we didn't add a column of 1's to the **X** matrix, so we have to compute b_0, the intercept (constant). Again, the equation is:

$$\hat{\beta} = \left((X - \bar{X})'(X - \bar{X}) \right)^{-1} (X - \bar{X})'(Y - \bar{Y})$$

```
MAT beta = INV(SSCP(x))*TRP(x-COLMEAN(x))*(y-COLMEAN(y))
MAT constant = COLMEAN(y) - COLMEAN(x)*beta
FORMAT 13 7
SHOW constant beta
```

```
Matrix: CONSTANT

 -3.482259E+06

Matrix: BETA
  DEFLATOR        15.0618723
       GNP        -0.0358192
  UNEMPLOY        -2.0202298
  ARMFORCE        -1.0332269
  POPULATN        -0.0511041
      TIME      1829.1514646
```

We used four **MAT** command functions to request these results:

SSCP	The cross-products of deviations of the X matrix
INV	The inverse of the **SSCP** matrix
TRP	The transpose of the $X - \bar{X}$ matrix
COLMEAN	The column means for **Y** and **X**

The **FORMAT** command writes the results in a field 13 characters wide with seven digits following the decimal point.

Computing multiple R²

To compute multiple R^2, we first compute multiple R (the correlation between the observed value of *TOTAL* and the predicted value from the model), and then square the result.

```
MAT mult_r = CORR(y||constant + x*beta)
MAT mult_rsq = mult_r(2;1)^2
SHOW mult_r mult_rsq
```

```
Matrix: MULT_R
                        TOTAL
        TOTAL     1.0000000    0.9977369
                  0.9977369    1.0000000

Matrix: MULT_RSQ
                        TOTAL
                  0.9954790
```

We use the **CORR** function to compute the correlation between Y and the predicted value of Y (constant + x * beta). That is, the argument of the **CORR** function is a matrix with two columns. The first column is Y and the second is the predicted values. In **Matrix**, double vertical bars concatenate matrices side by side. The estimate of multiple R is printed in the second row and first column of the output matrix. It is 0.9977369. This agrees with the result from **Linear Regression** (0.998). To square multiple R, we first extract it from the matrix using the notation (2;1). The result is 0.9954790.

Eigenvalues and the condition number

Continuing from above, we use the **EIGEN** function of the **CALL** command to compute the eigenvalues of the correlation matrix of the independent variables and then compute the condition number (the ratio of the largest eigenvalue to the smallest).

```
CALL EIGEN (e_value, e_vector, CORR(x))
MAT cond_num = e_value(1;1) / e_value(6;6)
```

```
FORMAT 10 8 / UNDERFLOW
SHOW e_value cond_num
```

```
Matrix: E_VALUE
                     DEFLATOR        GNP  UNEMPLOY  ARMFORCE  POPULATN      TIME
    DEFLATOR        4.603E+00          0         0         0         0         0
         GNP                0  1.175E+00         0         0         0         0
    UNEMPLOY                0          0 2.034E-01         0         0         0
    ARMFORCE                0          0         0 1.493E-02         0         0
    POPULATN                0          0         0         0 2.552E-03         0
        TIME                0          0         0         0         0 3.767E-04

Matrix: COND_NUM
    1.222E+04
```

The EIGEN function computes both the eigenvalues and eigenvectors, but we print only the former. Note that they are printed as the diagonal of a matrix. We use the notations (1;1) and (6;6) to reference the first (largest) and last (smallest) eigenvalues when computing the condition number. Several of the eigenvalues are close to 0, indicating that the predictor variables have redundancies among them. Example 12.6 will illustrate how ridge regression can adjust for this problem.

Transformations and statistical functions

For transforming each element of a matrix, **Matrix** provides many of the functions available for single variables.

SQR	Square root	ABS	Absolute value	TNH	Hyperbolic tangent
LOG	Log base e	INT	Integer part	ASN	Arc sine
L10	Log base 10	SIN	Sine	ACS	Arc cosine
EXP	Exponentiation	COS	Cosine	ATN	Arc tangent
LGM	Log gamma	TAN	Tangent	ATH	Arc tangent hyperbolic
				AT2	Arc tangent

For example, to transform each element of the matrix *MYDATA* to base 10 logarithms, type:

```
MAT log_data = L10(mydata)
```

If you want to transform only one column, use a LET statement as usual. For the *LONGLEY* data, for example, you could transform *POPULATN* to log units:

```
LET populatn = L10(populatn)
```

Note: The argument of a MAT command function is the name of a matrix. The argument of a LET statement is a column (variable) name.

The MAT command also has functions that yield vectors of statistics to summarize the rows or columns of a matrix:

ROWMEAN	COLMEAN	Mean of each row or column
ROWSTD	COLSTD	Standard deviation of each row or column
ROWSUM	COLSUM	Sum of the elements in each row or column
ROWMIN	COLMIN	Minimum of each row or column
ROWMAX	COLMAX	Maximum of each row or column
ROWMIS	COLMIS	Number of missing values in each row or column
ROWNUM	COLNUM	Number of values present in each row or column

Statistical functions that yield results as matrices include:

ROWZSC	COLZSC	Z scores computed using row or column statistics
ROWRANK	COLRANK	Rank of values within each row or column
SSCP		Cross-products of deviations of columns
COVA		Covariance matrix of columns
CORR		Correlation matrix or columns

Design variables

If you are using **Matrix** to request an analysis of variance or if you need to generate a set of design variables for each categorical variable in a regression model, use one of these MAT command functions:

DESIGN0	"0, 1" design variables
DESIGN1	"1, 0, –1" design variables
DESIGNF	Full rank design variables
ORTHEQ	Equally spaced orthogonal components
ORTHNUM	Unequally spaced orthogonal components

Generating matrices

At the beginning of Example 12.1, we used the MAT command to type data and to extract part of a SYSTAT data file as a matrix. Sometimes, you may find it easier to have **Matrix** generate values for you. You can then alter specific values as needed. **Matrix** can generate an identity matrix of rank n or an $n \times p$ matrix filled with a user-specified element. **Matrix** can also generate five types of design variables for categorical variables (see the previous section).

Identity and rectangular matrices

The I function of the MAT command generates an identity matrix. The M function generates a rectangular matrix filled with a value you specify. For example, to generate a 10×10 identity matrix named *MY_I* and a 3×4 rectangular matrix named *MY_RECT* filled with the square root of 2, specify:

```
MAT my_I = I(10)
MAT my_rect = M(3,4,SQR(2))
```

Matrix manipulations

Matrix has the following commands for manipulating matrices:

DELETE	Delete specified rows
DROP	Drop specified columns
SELECT	Use only those rows meeting a specified condition
CLEAR	Remove listed matrices from memory

The following functions, available with the **MAT** command, also alter matrices:

ROWSORT	Sort rows using the values in a column you specify
COLSORT	Sort columns using the values in a row you specify
STRING	Convert the lower triangular portion of a matrix to a column vector
GNIRTS	Convert a vector to a lower triangular matrix
SHAPE	Reconfigure the number of rows and columns
TRP	Transpose a matrix
FILL	Recode missing values
COMPLETE	Remove rows with missing data
NUMERIC	Retain only columns containing numeric data

Entering Data and Defining Matrices

This section discusses the basics of the **Matrix** procedure. You will learn how to:

- Enter the **Matrix** procedure
- Type in a matrix: MAT
- Name the rows and columns of a matrix: ROWNAME, COLNAME
- Read a SYSTAT file as a matrix: USE
- View a matrix: SHOW
- Clear a matrix from memory: CLEAR
- Save a matrix to a file: SAVE
- Generate an identity matrix or a matrix of any dimensions filled with the value you specify: M

Creating a matrix

To enter the **Matrix** procedure, type MATRIX, and SYSTAT responds:

```
********** Active Matrix: none     **********
```

indicating that there is no active matrix in SYSTAT's memory. You can now enter a matrix or open a SYSTAT file as a matrix.

Use the **MAT** command to create a matrix. The **MAT** command syntax is

    MAT name = expression

where *name* is the name of the matrix and *expression* is either the entries of a matrix or an algebraic expression involving matrices, operators, and functions.

Typing a matrix

To enter a matrix, type the entries separated by commas or spaces, with an open bracket before the first entry and a closed bracket after the last entry. Separate each row with a semicolon, especially if you type several rows on one line. You can type each row on a separate line:

    MAT name = [first row;
                second row;
                .
                .
                .
                last row]

or on one line:

```
MAT name = [first row;second row;...;last row]
```

To enter a missing numeric value, type a period. To enter a missing character value, type a space surrounded by quotation marks. To enter the 2 × 3 matrix,

$$A = \begin{bmatrix} 2 & 4 & 3 \\ 1 & 1 & 5 \end{bmatrix}$$

type:

```
MAT a = [2 4 3;        or        MAT a = [2 4 3;1 1 5]
         1 1 5]
```

SYSTAT responds:

```
********** Active Matrix: A          **********
```

Naming rows and columns

You can use the ROWNAME and COLNAME commands to name the rows and columns of a matrix. The command syntax is:

```
ROWNAME matrix = name1 name2 name3…
COLNAME matrix = name1 name2 name3…
```

Each name should be no more than eight characters and start with a letter. If you open a SYSTAT file in **Matrix**, the variable names are the names of the columns. You can use COLNAME to change these names if you want.

Let's enter a matrix, *GRADES*, with test scores for six students.

```
MAT grades = [85 77 92 89 95 95;
              97 90 95 100 85 97;
              59 .  73 81 64 75;
              80 84 78 90 87 92;
              67 80 77 .  90 95;
              85 89 84 91 82 93]
```

These scores are for four quizzes, a midterm, and a final. We can label the columns as follows:

```
COLNAME grades = quiz1 quiz2 midterm quiz3 quiz4 final
```

This matrix has a row for each student. We can label the rows with the students' names:

```
ROWNAME grades = Mark Cindy Jeff Greg Michele Nicky
```

Now the matrix looks like this:

	QUIZ1	QUIZ2	MIDTERM	QUIZ3	QUIZ4	FINAL
MARK	85	77	92	89	95	95
CINDY	97	90	95	100	85	97
JEFF	59	.	73	81	64	75
GREG	80	84	78	90	87	92
MICHELE	67	80	77	.	90	95
NICKY	85	89	84	91	82	93

If you save a matrix to a file, the column names are considered variable names, and the row names are saved as a variable named *ROWNAME$*, added as the last column. Let's save the *GRADES* matrix to a file:

```
SAVE grades
```

Using a column of a matrix to label rows. You can name the rows of a matrix with the entries in a column of another matrix. This is useful for matrices with a large number of rows. Suppose that the names for the students are stored in the *NAME$* column of a matrix named *IDMTX*. You could name the rows of *GRADES* by typing:

```
ROWNAME grades = idmtx(name$)
```

Reading a matrix

Use the **USE** command to read a SYSTAT file into **Matrix**:

```
USE filename
```

The file is now considered a matrix with the same name as the file. You can perform matrix arithmetic and use matrix functions on the data. If you want to give the matrix a different name, add the **MATRIX** argument. For example,

```
USE longley / MATRIX=m1
```

reads the file *LONGLEY* and is known to **Matrix** as a matrix named **M1**.

Character values. Most of the discussion in this chapter involves matrices with numeric entries only. A matrix can also contain columns of character data. However, you cannot use most of the **Matrix** functions and operators on such a matrix. Thus, if you read a SYSTAT file with character variables into **Matrix**, you may want to delete the character columns. See p. 260 for information about deleting columns.

Note: *To extract a submatrix from a file, see "Extracting a submatrix" on p. 258.*

Viewing a matrix	You can view matrices with the SHOW command:

SHOW *matrix1 matrix2 … matrixn*

SYSTAT prints the specified matrices to the current output device. To view the matrix **A** entered above, type

SHOW a

and SYSTAT displays:

```
Matrix: A
        2.000        4.000
        3.000        1.000
        1.000        5.000
```

If you want to eliminate trailing zeros and move the columns closer together, type:

FORMAT 5 0
SHOW a

```
Matrix: A
    2    4
    3    1
    1    5
```

Saving a matrix

Use the SAVE command to save a matrix to a file. You can save a matrix to a file with the same name as the matrix, or you can specify a different filename. For example, the command

SAVE a

saves the matrix **A** to a file named *A.SYS*. The command

SAVE myfile / MATRIX=a

saves the matrix **A** to a file named *MYFILE.SYS*.

Requesting a directory of matrices

For a description of the matrices known to **Matrix**, use the DIR command. The syntax for the DIR command is

DIR
DIR *matrix1, matrix2, ...*

where *matrixi* is used to request information about specific matrices.

For example, if you have been working with matrices named **A**, **B**, and **C**, type:

DIR *or* DIR A, B, C

```
#1 -- Matrix: A has 3 rows and 2 columns
Col.Names:
           ------------  ------------
#2 -- Matrix: B has 2 rows and 3 columns.
Col.Names:
           ------------  ------------  ------------
#3 -- Matrix: C has 2 rows and 2 columns.
Col.Names:      AGE           INCOME
           ------------  ------------
********** Active Matrix: C **********
```

The output tells us that **A** is a 3×2 matrix, **B** is a 2×3 matrix, and **C** is a 2×2 matrix. The columns of **C** are named *AGE* and *INCOME*.

The active matrix. The DIR report shows that matrices **A**, **B**, and **C** are *known* to the **Matrix** procedure. In addition, the last line of the report identifies matrix **C** as the **active** matrix.

The distinction between *active* and *known* matrices is important for the DELETE, DROP, and SELECT commands and also for LET statements because they operate on the last matrix used—that is, the *active* matrix. Other commands and functions include an argument that identifies the input matrix.

Clearing matrices from memory

The CLEAR command removes the matrices you list from memory. The syntax for the CLEAR command is:

CLEAR *matrix1 matrix2 ... matrixn*

Generating matrices

The MAT command has functions for generating an identity matrix with a rank you specify and for generating a matrix with any dimensions filled with a value you specify.

Function	Result
I(*n*)	An identity matrix of order *n*.
M(*n*,*p*,*num*)	An $n \times p$ matrix filled with *num*s. If you do not specify a value for *num*, the matrix is filled with zeros.

An identity matrix. An identity matrix of order n is an $n \times n$ matrix, **I**, with 1's on the diagonal and zeros elsewhere. For example, to store the identity matrix of order 3 as **I3** and print the result, type:

```
MATRIX i3 = I(3)
SHOW i3
```

```
Matrix:     I3
            1           0           0
            0           1           0
            0           0           1
```

Generating a matrix with a specified value. You can create a matrix of any size filled with a number you choose with the **M** function. To create a 9×6 matrix named *THREE* and filled with 3's, type:

```
MAT three = M(9,6,3)
```

The third parameter of the **M** function can be a mathematical expression. For example, to create a 25×13 matrix filled with the square root of 2, type:

```
MAT sq2 = M(25,13,SQR(2))
```

If you do not specify a third parameter, the matrix is filled with zeros. To create a 3×4 matrix named *ZERO* and filled with zeros, type:

```
MAT zero = M(3,4,0)   or just   MAT zero = M(3,4)
```

Filling in missing values

You can use the **FILL** function to replace the missing values in your matrix with specified values.

Function	Result
FILL(*matrix*,*num*)	Fill the missing values of matrix with nums.

For example, in the *GRADES* matrix above, you could replace missing test scores with zeros:

```
MAT newgrade = FILL(grades,0)
```

Increasing workspace size

When you enter the **Matrix** procedure, it reports the amount of workspace available:

```
Program limits:
   Maximum number of matrices=15.
   Maximum number of row and column names is 230.
   Maximum number of numeric data elements is 4100 (32800 bytes).
   Maximum number of character data elements is 1100 (13200 bytes).
********** Active Matrix:  n o n e **********
```

Use the SET command to increase the size of the workspace:

```
SET MATRIX=#
    MAXNAMES=#
    NUMERIC=#
    CHARACTER=#
```

MATRIX sets the maximum number of matrices: MAXNAMES, the maximum number of row and column names; NUMERIC, the maximum number of numeric data elements; and CHARACTER, the maximum number of characters in the data.

Specifying submatrices

You can select a portion of a matrix for analysis. Use the:

- MAT command to extract a subset of rows and/or columns.
- DELETE command to delete rows that you specify by name or number.
- DROP command to delete columns that you specify by name or number.
- SELECT command to retain only those rows that satisfy a condition you specify; all other rows are deleted.
- NUMERIC function to drop all columns with non-numeric data.
- COMPLETE function to drop all rows containing missing data.

Extracting a submatrix

Within a MAT command, you can extract a submatrix from a matrix. Simply specify the name of the original matrix and the numbers (or names) of the rows and columns of the submatrix. The syntax for the MAT command is:

  mat_name (*reference to rows;reference to columns*)

where:

- *mat_name* is the name of the matrix.

— *reference to rows* is a list of row numbers, a list of row names (see ROWNAMES), or a condition involving column names (for example, *AGE*>21).

— *reference to columns* is a list of column numbers, a list of variable (or column) names (see COLNAMES), or a condition involving row names.

If no row (or column) reference is stated, all rows (or columns) are selected. Separate the list of row or column numbers (or names) by blanks or commas. Use a double period (..) to specify a range of rows or columns. Separate the row reference from the column reference with a semicolon. For example, given the matrix **H**, you could extract the matrix **SUB**

$$H = \begin{bmatrix} 3 & 1 & 4 & 0 & 1 & 7 \\ 0 & 5 & 2 & 9 & 4 & 3 \\ 6 & 3 & 0 & 7 & 1 & 1 \end{bmatrix} \qquad SUB = \begin{bmatrix} 2 & 9 & 4 \\ 0 & 7 & 1 \end{bmatrix}$$

by specifying:

```
MAT sub = h(2..3;3..5)    or    MAT sub = h(2,3;3,4,5)
```

For an example that uses column names, see p. 247.

You don't have to name a submatrix in order to use it. To multiply a 2×2 matrix **B** by the submatrix called **SUB** above, type:

```
MAT product = b*h(2..3;3..5)
```

Extracting the diagonal or tri-diagonal

The DIAG function of the MAT command extracts the diagonal elements of a matrix as a row vector (a $1 \times n$ matrix). The DIAG3 function extracts the main diagonal and the elements above and below the diagonal. The result is a matrix with the elements above the diagonal as the first row, the diagonal as the second row, and the elements below the diagonal as the third row.

Function	Result
DIAG(*matrix*)	The diagonal of matrix as a row vector
DIAG3(*matrix*)	A matrix with the upper subdiagonal as the first row, the main diagonal as the second row, and the lower subdiagonal as the third row

Using the matrix **P** as input to the **DIAG3** function, the result is matrix **Q**:

```
(MAT q = DIAG3(p)):
```

$$
P = \begin{bmatrix} 1 & 2 & 3 & 4 \\ 5 & 6 & 7 & 8 \\ 9 & 10 & 11 & 12 \\ 13 & 14 & 15 & 16 \end{bmatrix} \qquad Q = \begin{bmatrix} \text{sub-diag} & . & 2 & 7 & 12 \\ \text{diagonal} & 1 & 6 & 11 & 16 \\ \text{sub-diag} & 5 & 10 & 15 & . \end{bmatrix}
$$

Deleting rows and columns: DELETE and DROP

Use the **DELETE** command to delete rows of the active matrix (the last matrix referenced). You can specify rows by name or by number. Use a double period (..) to specify a range of rows. For example, to delete the rows named *CAT* and *DOG* and the rows numbered 2, 5, 7, 8, 9, and 10, type:

```
DELETE cat, dog, 2, 5, 7..10
```

Use the **DROP** command to delete columns. You can specify the columns you want to delete by name or by number. Use a double period (..) to specify a range of columns. For example, to delete the columns named *RED*, *YELLOW*, and *BLUE* through *VIOLET* and columns numbered 2, 10, 11, and 12, type:

```
DROP red, yellow, blue..violet, 2, 10..12
```

Conditionally deleting rows: SELECT

Use the **SELECT** command on the active matrix (the last matrix referenced) to retain only those rows satisfying a specified condition; all other rows are dropped. For example, the command

```
SELECT height > SQR(weight)
```

retains only those rows with a value in the *HEIGHT* column greater than the square root of the value in the *WEIGHT* column.

Deleting non-numeric columns: NUMERIC

If you want to delete all of the columns of character data from a matrix, use the **NUMERIC** function of the **MAT** command instead of the **DROP** command. For example, to drop all of the character columns of a matrix *MYDATA* and save the new matrix as *MY_NUM*, type:

```
MAT my_num = NUMERIC(mydata)
```

Deleting rows with missing values: COMPLETE

Use the COMPLETE function (of the MAT command) to delete all rows with missing values. For example,

```
MAT no_miss = COMPLETE(mydata)
```

deletes the rows with missing values from the matrix *MYDATA* and saves the resulting matrix as *NO_MISS*.

Manipulating matrices

This section discusses the following:

- Transposing a matrix: TRP
- Concatenating matrices
- Reordering the rows and columns of a matrix: ROWSORT, COLSORT
- Reshaping a matrix: SHAPE
- Transforming the lower triangular portion of a matrix to a vector and vice versa: STRING and GNIRTS
- Transforming and creating columns using a LET statement

Transposing a matrix

Given a matrix **P**, the transpose of **P** is the matrix obtained by interchanging the rows and columns of **P**.

$$P = \begin{bmatrix} 3 & 1 & 4 & 0 & 1 & 7 \\ 0 & 5 & 2 & 9 & 4 & 3 \\ 6 & 3 & 0 & 7 & 1 & 1 \end{bmatrix}$$

To find the transpose of matrix **P**, type:

```
MAT p_trans=TRP(p)
SHOW p_trans
```

```
Matrix: P_TRANS
                    3          0          6
                    1          5          3
                    4          2          0
                    0          9          7
                    1          4          1
                    7          3          1
```

Concatenating matrices

You can concatenate matrices side by side, end to end, or corner to corner.

Side-by-side concatenation. You can concatenate matrices side by side.

$$A = \begin{bmatrix} 1 \\ 0 \\ 4 \end{bmatrix} \quad B = \begin{bmatrix} 4 & 3 & 7 & 1 \\ 2 & 0 & 2 & 1 \\ 0 & 6 & 0 & 8 \end{bmatrix} \quad C = \begin{bmatrix} 9 & 0 \\ 1 & 5 \\ 3 & 3 \end{bmatrix}$$

To concatenate matrices **A**, **B**, and **C** side by side, use the symbol ‖ (two vertical slashes):

```
MAT wide = a||b||c
SHOW wide
```

```
Matrix: WIDE
      1         4         3         7         1         9         0
      0         2         0         2         1         1         5
      4         0         6         0         8         3         3
```

You can join matrices with different numbers of rows side by side. The number of rows in the resulting matrix is determined by the matrix with the largest number of rows; matrices with fewer rows are filled with missing values.

End-to-end concatenation. You can concatenate matrices end to end.

$$D = \begin{bmatrix} 2 & 7 & 4 & 0 \end{bmatrix} \quad E = \begin{bmatrix} 1 & 1 & 4 & 3 \\ 0 & 3 & 0 & 5 \\ 2 & 5 & 1 & 8 \end{bmatrix} \quad 280F = \begin{bmatrix} 4 & 3 & 3 & 0 \\ 2 & 3 & 1 & 1 \end{bmatrix}$$

To concatenate **D**, **E**, and **F** end to end, use the symbol // (two slashes):

```
MAT long = d//e//f
SHOW long
```

```
Matrix: LONG
      2         7         4         0
      1         1         4         3
      0         3         0         5
      2         5         1         8
      4         3         3         0
      2         3         1         1
```

You can join matrices with different numbers of columns end to end. The number of columns in the resulting matrix is determined by the matrix with the largest number of columns; matrices with fewer columns are filled with missing values.

Corner-to-corner (block-diagonal) concatenation. You can concatenate matrices corner to corner. The lower right corner of the first matrix is joined to the upper left corner of the second matrix, and so on. For example,

$$G = \begin{bmatrix} 1 & 2 & 1 \\ 2 & 1 & 2 \end{bmatrix} \qquad H = \begin{bmatrix} 3 & 4 \\ 4 & 3 \end{bmatrix} \qquad I = \begin{bmatrix} 5 & 6 \\ 6 & 5 \\ 5 & 6 \end{bmatrix}$$

```
MAT corner = g/|h/|i
FORMAT 5 0
SHOW corner
```

```
Matrix: CORNER
        1       2       1       .       .       .       .
        2       1       2       .       .       .       .
        .       .       .       3       4       .       .
        .       .       .       4       3       .       .
        .       .       .       .       .       5       6
        .       .       .       .       .       6       5
        .       .       .       .       .       5       6
```

Note that SYSTAT fills the empty positions with missing values. The symbol for corner-to-corner concatenation is /| (or |/). You can fill the missing value entries of the above matrix via the FILL function.

Reordering rows and columns

The ROWSORT and COLSORT functions of the MAT command reorder the rows and columns of your matrix.

Function	Result
ROWSORT(*matrix,colnum*)	*Matrix* with rows ordered according to the values in column number *colnum*
COLSORT(*matrix,rownum*)	*Matrix* with columns ordered according to the values in row number *rownum*

For example, given the matrix **M**,

$$M = \begin{bmatrix} 2 & 4 & 6 & 2 \\ 1 & 1 & 3 & 7 \\ 5 & 3 & 0 & 6 \\ 3 & 6 & 1 & 3 \end{bmatrix}$$

the command

```
MAT neword = ROWSORT(m,3)
```

sorts the rows of **M** according to the values in column 3. Let's look at the result:

```
SHOW neword
```

```
Matrix:   NEWORD
        5         3         0         6
        3         6         1         3
        1         1         3         7
        2         4         6         2
```

Now we sort the columns of **M** according to the values in the last row:

```
MAT neword2 = COLSORT(m,4)
SHOW neword2
```

```
Matrix:   NEWORD2
        6         2         2         4
        3         7         1         1
        0         6         5         3
        1         3         3         6
```

FOLD

The FOLD function of the MAT command copies the lower triangular portion of a matrix to the portion of the matrix above the diagonal such that the matrix is symmetric about the diagonal.

Function	Result
FOLD(*sqrmat*)	Copy the lower triangular portion of *sqrmat* to the upper triangular portion.

FOLD operates only on square matrices. Think of folding the matrix on the diagonal and replacing each element above the diagonal, with each element of the lower triangular portion "matched up" with it.

Suppose we have a 5 × 5 matrix, *SQRMAT*, containing the integers from 1 through 25, ordered from left to right. Following are the commands to fold *SQRMAT* and display the original matrix and the result:

```
MAT folded = FOLD(sqrmat)
FORMAT=0
SHOW sqrmat folded
```

```
Matrix: SQRMAT
        1         2         3         4         5
        6         7         8         9        10
       11        12        13        14        15
       16        17        18        19        20
       21        22        23        24        25
```

```
Matrix: FOLDED
         1              6             11             16             21
         6              7             12             17             22
        11             12             13             18             23
        16             17             18             19             24
        21             22             23             24             25
```

Reconfiguring a matrix

You can change the dimensions of a matrix with the **SHAPE** function. For example, you can change a 4 × 4 matrix to a 2 × 8 matrix, or you can change a 12 × 36 matrix to a 24 × 18 matrix.

Function	Result
SHAPE(*matrix,m,n*)	An *m* × *n* matrix containing the elements of *matrix*. All columns of the matrix must be the same type (that is, all numeric or all character).

SHAPE fills in the new matrix with the values of the original matrix, starting with the element in the first row and first column and working from left to right across the rows. **SHAPE** uses only as many elements as it needs. For example, if the original matrix is 4 × 5 and you specify dimensions 3 × 3 for the new matrix, **SHAPE** uses only the first nine elements of the original matrix. Conversely, if the original matrix does not contain enough elements to fill the new matrix, **SHAPE** fills the extra positions with missing values. Given the 5 × 3 matrix **D**,

$$
\mathbf{D} = \begin{bmatrix} 1 & 2 & 3 \\ 4 & 5 & 6 \\ 7 & 8 & 9 \\ 10 & 11 & 12 \\ 13 & 14 & 15 \end{bmatrix}
$$

we create a 4 × 4 matrix and a 2 × 4 matrix:

```
MAT iv_by_iv = SHAPE(d,4,4)
MAT ii_by_iv = SHAPE(d,2,4)
SHOW iv_by_iv ii_by_iv
```

```
Matrix: IV_BY_IV
         1              2              3              4
         5              6              7              8
         9             10             11             12
        13             14             15              .

Matrix: II_BY_IV
         1              2              3              4
         5              6              7              8
```

The 4 × 4 matrix has a missing value because **D** had only 15 elements. The 2 × 4 matrix contains only the first 8 elements of **D**.

12.2
Packing two
records
into one

You may have to restructure your data for a statistical analysis. For example, suppose you record the age and blood cholesterol levels for two groups of women. Women in the first group use contraceptive pills; women in the second group do not. The data in the *MYSTUDY* file look like this:

PILL	AGE	CHOL
1	25	200
2	25	211
1	33	230
2	33	243
1	19	180
2	19	215
1	39	215
2	39	175
1	28	189
2	28	163
1	20	179
2	20	175
1	35	300
2	35	224

A *PILL* value of 1 indicates that the woman takes the pill; a value of 2 indicates that she does not. You want to use a matched pairs *t* test to test the hypothesis that the mean difference in blood cholesterol between women who take the pill and women who do not is 0. First, using the **SHAPE** function, match a woman who takes the pill with a woman of the same age who does not:

```
MAT matched = SHAPE(mystudy,7,6)
```

or

```
MAT matched = SHAPE(mystudy, NROW(mystudy)/2,
                     NCOL(mystudy)*2)
```

Now the data look like this:

```
1      25      200      2      25      211
1      33      230      2      33      243
1      19      180      2      19      215
1      39      215      2      39      175
1      28      189      2      28      163
1      20      179      2      20      175
1      35      300      2      35      224
```

Each case has the cholesterol value for a pill user and for her age-matched control. You can drop all of the columns except the two that contain cholesterol and rename them *P_CHOL* and *NOP_CHOL*, respectively:

```
DROP 1,2,4,5
COLNAME matched = p_chol, nop_chol
SAVE matched
```

Now you can request the matched pairs *t* test:

```
TTEST
    USE matched
    TEST p_chol, nop_chol
```

Determining the dimensions of a matrix

The MAT command has DIM, NROW, and NCOL functions for determining the number of rows and columns of a matrix.

Function	Result
DIM(*matrix*)	The number of rows and columns of *matrix*
NROW(*matrix*)	The number of rows in *matrix*
NCOL(*matrix*)	The number of columns in *matrix*

The NROW and NCOL functions return the number of rows and columns of a specified matrix. The DIM function returns both the number of rows and the number of columns as a 2×1 matrix. For example, if you open a SYSTAT data file in **Matrix** and delete the non-numeric columns and the rows with missing data, you can use these functions to determine the dimensions of the resulting matrix.

Changing a matrix to a vector and vice versa

The STRING function (of the MAT command) writes the lower-triangular portion of a matrix as a vector. The GNIRTS (STRING spelled backwards) function writes a row or column vector to the lower-triangular portion of a matrix.

Function	Result
STRING(*matrix*) or STRING(*matrix*,1)	Column vector containing the elements in the lower-triangular portion of *matrix*
STRING(*matrix*,0)	Column vector containing the elements below the diagonal of *matrix*
GNIRTS(*vector*) or GNIRTS(*vector*,1)	Matrix with the elements of *vector* as the lower-triangular portion and missing values above the diagonal
GNIRTS(*vector*,0)	Matrix with the elements of *vector* below the diagonal and missing values on and above the diagonal

12.3 Writing a correlation matrix as a vector

As an example of the STRING function, we examine correlations among 21 variables from the *USSTATES* file. These variables include death rates from nine causes, crime rates, median household income and other economic indicators, weather information, and health care data.

Following are the variable names:

```
ACCIDENT   CARDIO    CANCER     PULMONAR   PNEU_FLU
DIABETES   LIVER     MSTROKE    FSTROKE    VIOLRATE
PROPRATE   AVGPAY    TEACHERS   TCHRSAL    GOVSLRY
POVRTY91   INCOME91  HIGHTEMP   LOWTEMP    HOSPITAL
DOCTOR
```

You can compute the correlation matrix in **Matrix** or **Correlations**. We computed the correlation matrix, named it *USCORR*, and then used the STRING function to write the correlations as a vector:

```
MATRIX
    USE uscorr
    MAT corrstr = STRING(uscorr,0)
    SAVE corrstr
    FORMAT 6 2
    SHOW uscorr corrstr
    FORMAT
```

```
MATRIX: USCORR
 ACCID CARDI CANCE PULMO PNEU_ DIABE LIVER MSTRO FSTRO VIOLR PROPR AVGPA TEACH TCHRS GOVSL POVRT INCOM HIGHT LOWTE HOSPI DOCTO
  1.00    .     .     .     .     .     .     .     .     .     .     .     .     .     .     .     .     .     .     .     .
 -0.27  1.00    .     .     .     .     .     .     .     .     .     .     .     .     .     .     .     .     .     .     .
 -0.32  0.92  1.00    .     .     .     .     .     .     .     .     .     .     .     .     .     .     .     .     .     .
  0.01  0.39  0.48  1.00    .     .     .     .     .     .     .     .     .     .     .     .     .     .     .     .     .
 -0.30  0.63  0.52  0.48  1.00    .     .     .     .     .     .     .     .     .     .     .     .     .     .     .     .
 -0.14  0.61  0.69  0.28  0.13  1.00    .     .     .     .     .     .     .     .     .     .     .     .     .     .     .
 -0.14  0.12  0.29  0.26 -0.15  0.14  1.00    .     .     .     .     .     .     .     .     .     .     .     .     .     .
  0.41  0.23  0.12 -0.17 -0.07  0.12 -0.24  1.00    .     .     .     .     .     .     .     .     .     .     .     .     .
  0.35  0.15  0.03 -0.11 -0.09 -0.06 -0.19  0.94  1.00    .     .     .     .     .     .     .     .     .     .     .     .
  0.04  0.09  0.10 -0.19 -0.18 -0.10  0.50  0.18  0.22  1.00    .     .     .     .     .     .     .     .     .     .     .
 -0.06 -0.34 -0.24 -0.15 -0.39 -0.31  0.36 -0.13 -0.03  0.65  1.00    .     .     .     .     .     .     .     .     .     .
 -0.24 -0.15 -0.08 -0.40 -0.27 -0.20  0.41 -0.26 -0.30  0.49  0.28  1.00    .     .     .     .     .     .     .     .     .
  0.32 -0.07 -0.22  0.04  0.18 -0.01 -0.44 -0.05 -0.11 -0.52 -0.44 -0.35  1.00    .     .     .     .     .     .     .     .
 -0.28 -0.15 -0.02 -0.33 -0.27 -0.11  0.45 -0.30 -0.36  0.40  0.24  0.91 -0.41  1.00    .     .     .     .     .     .     .
 -0.18 -0.01  0.00 -0.25 -0.21 -0.14  0.37  0.11  0.14  0.59  0.34  0.49 -0.54  0.52  1.00    .     .     .     .     .     .
  0.53  0.17  0.02  0.07 -0.04  0.16 -0.01  0.50  0.51  0.22  0.04 -0.38  0.15 -0.50 -0.07  1.00    .     .     .     .     .
 -0.41 -0.32 -0.17 -0.35 -0.25 -0.31  0.32 -0.45 -0.47  0.19  0.24  0.81 -0.31  0.83  0.33 -0.75  1.00    .     .     .     .
  0.09  0.04 -0.07  0.35  0.35 -0.25 -0.03  0.02  0.15  0.08  0.16 -0.35 -0.06 -0.40 -0.14  0.31 -0.37  1.00    .     .     .
 -0.18  0.23  0.31 -0.23 -0.19  0.29  0.04  0.36  0.36  0.36  0.37 -0.01 -0.36 -0.05  0.17  0.08 -0.02 -0.24  1.00    .     .
  0.27 -0.06 -0.17  0.14  0.28 -0.14 -0.41 -0.10 -0.15 -0.56 -0.48 -0.58  0.69 -0.55 -0.58  0.13 -0.42  0.27 -0.46  1.00    .
 -0.62  0.14  0.25 -0.16  0.10  0.07  0.42 -0.34 -0.32  0.41  0.23  0.62 -0.40  0.65  0.47 -0.39  0.61 -0.34  0.18 -0.54  1.00
```

We show the beginning and end of the *CORRSTR* vector:

```
MATRIX: CORRSTR
  LTMat
  -0.27
  -0.32
   0.92
   0.01
   0.39
   0.48
  -0.30
   0.63
   0.52
   0.48
  -0.14
   0.61
   0.69
   0.28
   0.13

    .
    .

   0.07
   0.42
  -0.34
  -0.32
   0.41
   0.23
   0.62
  -0.40
   0.65
   0.47
  -0.39
   0.61
  -0.34
   0.18
  -0.54
```

Following is a stem-and-leaf diagram of the 210 correlations:

```
STATISTICS
    USE corrstr
    STEM ltmatrix
```

```
            STEM AND LEAF PLOT OF VARIABLE: LTMatrix   , N =   210

MINIMUM IS:       -0.748
LOWER HINGE IS:     -0.245
MEDIAN IS:        -0.010
UPPER HINGE IS:      0.273
MAXIMUM IS:        0.944

            -7   4
            -6   2
            -5   8755432
            -4   976653310000
            -3   999877655544332211100
            -2 H 9998666554444332110
            -1   99887776655544444443321000
            -0 M 99877666655433221100
             0   011233344466677889
             1   00111333444455556677789
             2 H 1233344566777888
             3   1112344455556778
             4   00112467788
             5   0011128
             6   00125589
             7
             8   02
             9   114
```

Let's use a SPLOM (scatterplot matrix) with 90% confidence ellipses to examine the bivariate distributions of the variables with sizeable correlations (–0.74, 0.80, 0.82, 0.91, 0.91, and 0.94).

```
USE usstates
SPLOM cancer cardio mstroke fstroke,
      avgpay tchrsal income povrty91 / HALF ELL=.99
```

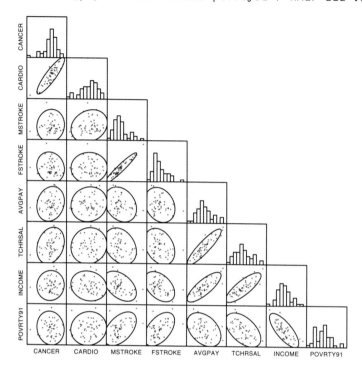

Five of the positive correlations are much larger than the others. Two of these involve death rates due to *CANCER*, *CARDIO*, *MSTROKE* (for males), and *FSTROKE* (for females). The other three involve economic indicators: *AVGPAY* (average pay), *TCHRSAL* (average salary of teachers), and *INCOME* (median family income). One negative correlation, *POVRTY91* (percentage of the population living below the poverty level) and *INCOME*, is fairly large.

Transformations and Statistical Functions

Matrix provides operators and functions for manipulating matrices element by element and matrix by matrix. The latter are the typical matrix algebra operations such as matrix multiplication and matrix inversion and are discussed in the next section. This section focuses on operators that are executed on each element of a matrix and introduces arithmetic, relational, and logical operators and functions.

The overview of this chapter listed 16 functions that produce element-by-element transformations in matrices. For example, the command

```
MAT log_data = L10(mydata)
```

takes the base 10 log of every element of the *MYDATA* matrix and stores the result in the matrix *LOG_DATA*.

This section also introduces statistical functions that output the mean or standard deviations of each row or column. Other statistical functions transform each element to ranks or z scores (these are computed within rows or columns). Finally, functions that generate design variables for categorical variables are introduced.

Element-by-element operators and functions

For element-by-element operations, you can think of each matrix entry as a separate entity. For example, to add two matrices with the same dimensions, just add the corresponding elements. This section discusses

+	Addition	#	Scalar multiplication
−	Subtraction	/	Scalar division
		##	Raising each element to a power

and a variety of other element-by-element matrix functions, such as square root, log, and trigonometric functions. For the examples in this section, we use small matrices with integer entries so that you can easily follow the calculations.

Addition and subtraction

You add or subtract matrices with the same dimensions (number of rows and columns) by adding or subtracting corresponding elements. For example, given

$$A = \begin{bmatrix} 2 & 4 \\ 3 & 1 \\ 1 & 5 \end{bmatrix} \qquad B = \begin{bmatrix} 1 & 3 \\ 6 & 0 \\ 4 & -2 \end{bmatrix}$$

the sum $A + B$ is

$$A + B = \begin{bmatrix} 2 & 4 \\ 3 & 1 \\ 1 & 5 \end{bmatrix} + \begin{bmatrix} 1 & 3 \\ 6 & 0 \\ 4 & -2 \end{bmatrix} = \begin{bmatrix} 3 & 7 \\ 9 & 1 \\ 5 & 3 \end{bmatrix}$$

and the difference $A - B$ is

$$A - B = \begin{bmatrix} 2 & 4 \\ 3 & 1 \\ 1 & 5 \end{bmatrix} - \begin{bmatrix} 1 & 3 \\ 6 & 0 \\ 4 & -2 \end{bmatrix} = \begin{bmatrix} 1 & 1 \\ -3 & 1 \\ -3 & 7 \end{bmatrix}$$

Now, enter matrices **A** and **B**. The commands to add and subtract **A** and **B** and store the results as *SUM* and *DFFRNCE*, respectively, are:

```
MAT sum = a + b
MAT dffrnce = a - b

SHOW sum dffrnce
```

```
Matrix: SUM

          3              7
          9              1
          5              3

Matrix: DFFRNCE

          1              1
         -3              1
         -3              7
```

Matrix performs several variations of matrix addition and subtraction. In addition to adding or subtracting two matrices with the same dimensions element by element, you can:

- Add (subtract) the same number to (from) each element of a matrix
- Add (subtract) a row vector to (from) each row of a matrix
- Add (subtract) a column vector to (from) each column of a matrix

Following is an example of each:

$$\begin{bmatrix} 1 & 2 & 3 \\ 4 & 5 & 6 \end{bmatrix} + \begin{bmatrix} 3 \end{bmatrix} = \begin{bmatrix} 4 & 5 & 6 \\ 7 & 8 & 9 \end{bmatrix} \qquad \begin{bmatrix} 1 & 2 & 3 \\ 4 & 5 & 6 \end{bmatrix} - \begin{bmatrix} 3 \end{bmatrix} = \begin{bmatrix} -2 & -1 & 0 \\ 1 & 2 & 3 \end{bmatrix}$$

$$\begin{bmatrix} 1 & 2 & 3 \\ 4 & 5 & 6 \end{bmatrix} + \begin{bmatrix} 3 & 2 & 1 \end{bmatrix} = \begin{bmatrix} 4 & 4 & 4 \\ 7 & 7 & 7 \end{bmatrix} \qquad \begin{bmatrix} 1 & 2 & 3 \\ 4 & 5 & 6 \end{bmatrix} - \begin{bmatrix} 3 & 2 & 1 \end{bmatrix} = \begin{bmatrix} -2 & 0 & 2 \\ 1 & 3 & 5 \end{bmatrix}$$

$$\begin{bmatrix} 1 & 2 & 3 \\ 4 & 5 & 6 \end{bmatrix} + \begin{bmatrix} 3 \\ 2 \end{bmatrix} = \begin{bmatrix} 4 & 5 & 6 \\ 6 & 7 & 8 \end{bmatrix} \qquad \begin{bmatrix} 1 & 2 & 3 \\ 4 & 5 & 6 \end{bmatrix} - \begin{bmatrix} 3 \\ 2 \end{bmatrix} = \begin{bmatrix} -2 & -1 & 0 \\ 2 & 3 & 4 \end{bmatrix}$$

Element-by-element multiplication and division

The element-by-element multiplication and division operators are # and /, respectively. These operators are most often used to multiply or divide a matrix by a scalar.

Note: *Do not confuse element-by-element multiplication with matrix multiplication. Matrix multiplication is discussed in "Matrix multiplication" on p. 284.*

Multiply the matrix **A** (used in the addition example above) by 3 as follows:

$$3 \, \#\mathbf{A} = 3\# \begin{bmatrix} 2 & 4 \\ 3 & 1 \\ 1 & 5 \end{bmatrix} = \begin{bmatrix} 6 & 12 \\ 9 & 3 \\ 3 & 15 \end{bmatrix}$$

In SYSTAT, type:

```
MAT scalprod = 3#a
SHOW scalprod
```

```
Matrix: SCALPROD
        6          12
        9           3
        3          15
```

Now divide each element of **A** by 2. Some of the elements of the result are not integers, so use the FORMAT command to change the number of decimal places displayed to 2.

```
MAT scalquot = A/2
FORMAT=2
SHOW scalquot
```

```
Matrix: SCALQUOT
            1.00          2.00
            1.50          0.50
            0.50          2.50
```

In addition to scalar multiplication and division, the # and / have other uses. You can:

- Multiply or divide two matrices of the same size element by element.
- Multiply or divide each row of a matrix element by element by a row matrix.
- Multiply or divide each column of a matrix element by element by a column matrix.

Following are examples of each:

$$\begin{bmatrix} 2 & 4 & 6 \\ 8 & 10 & 12 \end{bmatrix} \# \begin{bmatrix} 1 & 2 & 3 \\ 4 & 5 & 6 \end{bmatrix} = \begin{bmatrix} 2 & 8 & 18 \\ 32 & 50 & 72 \end{bmatrix} \qquad \begin{bmatrix} 2 & 4 & 6 \\ 8 & 10 & 12 \end{bmatrix} / \begin{bmatrix} 1 & 2 & 3 \\ 4 & 5 & 6 \end{bmatrix} = \begin{bmatrix} 2 & 2 & 2 \\ 2 & 2 & 2 \end{bmatrix}$$

$$\begin{bmatrix} 2 & 4 & 6 \\ 8 & 10 & 12 \end{bmatrix} \# \begin{bmatrix} 4 \\ 2 \end{bmatrix} = \begin{bmatrix} 8 & 16 & 24 \\ 16 & 20 & 24 \end{bmatrix} \qquad \begin{bmatrix} 2 & 4 & 6 \\ 8 & 10 & 12 \end{bmatrix} / \begin{bmatrix} 4 \\ 2 \end{bmatrix} = \begin{bmatrix} 0.5 & 1 & 1.5 \\ 4 & 5 & 6 \end{bmatrix}$$

$$\begin{bmatrix} 2 & 4 & 6 \\ 8 & 10 & 12 \end{bmatrix} \# \begin{bmatrix} 1 & 2 & 3 \end{bmatrix} = \begin{bmatrix} 2 & 8 & 18 \\ 8 & 20 & 36 \end{bmatrix} \qquad \begin{bmatrix} 2 & 4 & 6 \\ 8 & 10 & 12 \end{bmatrix} / \begin{bmatrix} 1 & 2 & 3 \end{bmatrix} = \begin{bmatrix} 2 & 2 & 2 \\ 8 & 5 & 4 \end{bmatrix}$$

Raising each element to a power

The power operator (##) can be used in several different ways. You can:

- Raise each element of a matrix to the same power.
- Raise each element of a matrix to the power of the corresponding element of a second matrix with the same dimensions.
- Raise the elements of each row of a matrix to the powers of the corresponding elements of a row matrix.
- Raise the elements of each column of a matrix to the powers of the corresponding elements of a column matrix.

For example, to raise each element of **A** to the third power, type:

```
MAT cube = a##3
SHOW cube
```

Following are other uses of ##:

$$
\begin{bmatrix} 2 & 4 \\ 3 & 1 \\ 1 & 5 \end{bmatrix} \#\# \begin{bmatrix} 3 & 2 \\ 3 & 7 \\ 5 & 0 \end{bmatrix} = \begin{bmatrix} 2^3 & 4^2 \\ 3^3 & 1^7 \\ 1^5 & 5^0 \end{bmatrix} = \begin{bmatrix} 8 & 16 \\ 27 & 1 \\ 1 & 1 \end{bmatrix}
$$

$$
\begin{bmatrix} 2 & 4 \\ 3 & 1 \\ 1 & 5 \end{bmatrix} \#\# \begin{bmatrix} 4 \\ 3 \\ 2 \end{bmatrix} = \begin{bmatrix} 2^4 & 4^4 \\ 3^3 & 1^3 \\ 1^2 & 5^2 \end{bmatrix} = \begin{bmatrix} 16 & 256 \\ 27 & 1 \\ 1 & 25 \end{bmatrix}
$$

$$
\begin{bmatrix} 2 & 4 \\ 3 & 1 \\ 1 & 5 \end{bmatrix} \#\# \begin{bmatrix} 3 & 2 \end{bmatrix} = \begin{bmatrix} 2^3 & 4^2 \\ 3^3 & 1^2 \\ 1^3 & 5^2 \end{bmatrix} = \begin{bmatrix} 8 & 16 \\ 27 & 1 \\ 1 & 25 \end{bmatrix}
$$

Functions

The element-by-element functions of the MAT command are listed below. The argument of each function is a matrix, except for AT2 (the arc tangent function), which has two arguments (sine and cosine of each angle):

SQR	Square root	LGM	Log gamma
LOG	Log base e	INT	Integer part (truncation)
L10	Log base 10	TNH	Hyperbolic tangent
EXP	Exponentiation	ASN	Arc sine
ABS	Absolute value	ACS	Arc cosine
SIN	Sine	ATN	Arc tangent
COS	Cosine	AT2	Arc tangent
TAN	Tangent	LGM	Log gamma
TNH	Hyperbolic tangent		

For example, given the matrix

$$
\mathbf{K} = \begin{bmatrix} 49 & 9 & 16 \\ 4 & 0 & 36 \\ 25 & 4 & 1 \end{bmatrix}
$$

you can take the square root of each element by typing:

```
MAT sqrt_k = SQR(k)
SHOW sqrt_k
```

```
Matrix:  SQRT_K
         7          3          4
         2          0          6
         5          2          1
```

Relational operators

You can use the relational operators <, >, <=, >=, <>, and == to compare two matrices with the same dimension element by element. The result is a matrix containing only 0's and 1's— 0's in positions where the relation is false, and 1's where the relation is true. (Determining equality is discussed in "Determining whether two matrices are equal" on p. 278.)

$$A = \begin{bmatrix} 2 & 4 & 6 & 2 \\ 1 & 1 & 3 & 7 \\ 5 & 3 & 0 & 6 \\ 3 & 6 & 1 & 3 \end{bmatrix} \qquad B = \begin{bmatrix} 3 & 5 & 3 & 2 \\ 3 & 0 & 3 & 5 \\ 9 & 1 & 3 & 6 \\ 4 & 1 & 0 & 4 \end{bmatrix}$$

The command

```
MAT c = a<b
SHOW c
```

produces the following output:

```
Matrix: C
         1          1          0          0
         1          0          0          0
         1          0          0          0
         1          0          0          1
```

Because the element in the first row and first column of A is less than the element in the first row and first column of B (that is, 2<3 is true), the element in the first row and first column of C is 1. Because the element in the third row and second column of A is greater than the element in the third row and second column of B (that is, 3<1 is false), the element in the third row and second column of C is 0.

Logical operators

The **Matrix** procedure has logical AND, OR, and NOT operators. The matrices that result from these operators are matrices of 0's (false values) and 1's (true values).

Logical AND. Use AND or the & operator to compare two matrices with the same dimensions element by element. The resulting matrix has 1's in positions where both the original matrices have nonzero values, and 0's elsewhere. In other words, the resulting matrix gets a true value (1) only in positions where the first matrix has a true value *and* the second matrix has a true value.

Logical OR. Use OR or the | operator to compare two matrices with the same dimensions element by element. The resulting matrix has 1's in positions where at least one of the original matrices has a nonzero value, and 0's elsewhere. That is, the resulting matrix gets a true value (1) only in positions where the first matrix has a true value *or* the second matrix has a true value (or both).

Logical negation. Use the exclamation point (!) to negate the elements of a matrix. It operates on a single matrix. The resulting matrix gets a 1 wherever the original matrix is 0, and a 0 wherever the original matrix is nonzero. In other words, the resulting matrix gets a true value wherever the original matrix is false, and a false value wherever the original matrix is true. Following are three matrices:

$$
A = \begin{bmatrix} 1 & 0 & 0 & 1 \\ 2 & 1 & 0 & 1 \\ 0 & 1 & 0 & 0 \end{bmatrix} \quad
B = \begin{bmatrix} 0 & 1 & 0 & 1 \\ 1 & 1 & 0 & 0 \\ 0 & 1 & 0 & 3 \end{bmatrix} \quad
C = \begin{bmatrix} 1 & 1 & 0 & 1 \\ 0 & 0 & 1 & 1 \\ 1 & 1 & 1 & 0 \end{bmatrix}
$$

The table below shows **Matrix** commands involving logical operators, with the matrix *RESULT* that the command generates below it.

MAT result = a&b

$$\begin{bmatrix} 0 & 0 & 0 & 1 \\ 1 & 1 & 0 & 0 \\ 0 & 1 & 0 & 0 \end{bmatrix}$$

MAT result = !a

$$\begin{bmatrix} 0 & 1 & 1 & 0 \\ 0 & 0 & 1 & 0 \\ 1 & 0 & 1 & 1 \end{bmatrix}$$

MAT result = a|b

$$\begin{bmatrix} 1 & 1 & 0 & 1 \\ 1 & 1 & 0 & 1 \\ 0 & 1 & 0 & 1 \end{bmatrix}$$

MAT result = !a|!b

$$\begin{bmatrix} 1 & 1 & 1 & 0 \\ 0 & 0 & 1 & 1 \\ 1 & 0 & 1 & 1 \end{bmatrix}$$

MAT result = (a&b)|c

$$\begin{bmatrix} 1 & 1 & 0 & 1 \\ 1 & 1 & 1 & 1 \\ 1 & 1 & 1 & 0 \end{bmatrix}$$

MAT result = b&!(a|c)

$$\begin{bmatrix} 0 & 0 & 0 & 0 \\ 0 & 0 & 0 & 0 \\ 0 & 0 & 0 & 1 \end{bmatrix}$$

Exclusive OR. You can use a combination of operators to form an exclusive OR. The resulting matrix gets a true value (1) only in positions where one matrix or the other has a true value; if both matrices have a true value, the result is false. To specify A or B, but not both, type:

```
(a & (!b)) | ((!a)&b)
```

Determining whether two matrices are equal

The EQUAL function (of the MAT command) compares two matrices element by element and determines whether they are equal.

Function	Result
EQUAL(*matrix1,matrix2*)	1 if *matrix1=matrix2*, 0 if *matrix ≠ matrix2*

The EQUAL function results in a scalar—a 1 if the matrices are equal or a 0 if they are not equal.

Note: *Do not confuse the EQUAL function with the == operator. The EQUAL function results in a scalar (0 or 1). The == operator results in a matrix of 1's (where corresponding elements are equal) and 0's (where corresponding elements are unequal).*

Statistical functions

A row function operates on each row of a matrix. The result of most row functions is a column vector. A column function operates on each column of a matrix. The result of most column functions is a row vector. The following statistical functions operate on rows or columns of a matrix and result in column or row vectors.

Function		Result
ROWMEAN(*matrix*)	COLMEAN(*matrix*)	The mean of values in each row or column
ROWSTD(*matrix*)	COLSTD(*matrix*)	The standard deviation of the values in each row or column
ROWSUM(*matrix*)	COLSUM(*matrix*)	Sum of values in each row or column
ROWMIN(*matrix*)	COLMIN(*matrix*)	The minimum value in each row or column
ROWMAX(*matrix*)	COLMAX(*matrix*)	The maximum value in each row or column
ROWMIS(*matrix*)	COLMIS(*matrix*)	The number of missing values in each row or column
ROWNUM(*matrix*)	COLNUM(*matrix*)	The number of nonmissing values in each row or column

The following statistical functions result in matrices.

Function	Result
ROWZSC(*matrix*) COLZSC(*matrix*)	The z scores for each element relative to its row or column. For each element, x, the row z score is computed as follows: $$z = \frac{x - rowmean}{rowsd}$$ The column z scores are computed similarly.
ROWRANK(*matrix*) COLRANK(*matrix*)	Ranks of the values in each row or column. The result is a matrix with the same dimensions as *matrix*.
CORR(*matrix*)	Correlation matrix of columns of *matrix*.
COVA(*matrix*)	Covariance matrix of columns of *matrix*.
SSCP(*matrix*)	Cross-products of deviations of columns for *matrix*.

12.4 Results across rows and columns

We use the *GRADES* data file (shown on p. 253) to demonstrate some of these functions. First we use some column functions.

```
MATRIX
    USE grades
    MAT count = COLNUM(grades)
    MAT test_avg = COLMEAN(grades)
    MAT testhigh = COLMAX(grades)
```

```
MAT test_low = COLMIN(grades)
SHOW count test_avg testhigh test_low
```

```
COUNT
Matrix: COUNT
                QUIZ1       QUIZ2     MIDTERM       QUIZ3       QUIZ4       FINAL
Non_missing     6.000       5.000       6.000       5.000       6.000       6.000

Matrix: TEST_AVG
                QUIZ1       QUIZ2     MIDTERM       QUIZ3       QUIZ4       FINAL
Mean           78.833      84.000      83.167      90.200      83.833      91.167

Matrix: TESTHIGH
                QUIZ1       QUIZ2     MIDTERM       QUIZ3       QUIZ4       FINAL
Maximum        97.000      90.000      95.000     100.000      95.000      97.000

Matrix: TEST_LOW
                QUIZ1       QUIZ2     MIDTERM       QUIZ3       QUIZ4       FINAL
Minimum        59.000      77.000      73.000      81.000      64.000      75.000
```

The resulting matrices have an entry for each column of the original matrix. The *COUNT* matrix indicates that there is a missing score for both the second and third quiz. The *TEST_AVG* matrix shows that the lowest average score occurred on the first quiz, and the highest average score was for the final. *TESTHIGH* and *TEST_LOW* show the highest and lowest scores on each test.

Now let's try some row functions and concatenate the resulting columns (matrices):

```
MAT count = ROWNUM(grades)
MAT stu_avg = ROWMEAN(grades)
MAT stu_high = ROWMAX(grades)
MAT stu_low = ROWMIN(grades)

MAT results = count || stu_avg || stu_high || stu_low
SHOW results
```

```
             Non_missing       Mean    Maximum    Minimum
MARK               6.000     88.833     95.000     77.000
CINDY              6.000     94.000    100.000     85.000
JEFF               5.000     70.400     81.000     59.000
GREG               6.000     85.167     92.000     78.000
MICHELE            5.000     81.800     95.000     67.000
NICKY              6.000     87.333     93.000     82.000
```

The output provides information about rows (students). The first result (nonmissing) is the number of tests taken by each student. The second is the average of the nonmissing test scores for each student. The third and fourth panels give each student's high and low grade, respectively. The students' names were specified as **ROWNAMES** on p. 253. **Matrix** knows the contents of each column, and it assigns the respective name.

Correlation, covariance, and SSCP matrices

The MAT command has functions for computing the covariance, correlation, and cross-products of deviations (SSCP) matrices. Given an $n \times p$ matrix

$$
X = \begin{bmatrix}
x_{11} & x_{12} & \cdots & x_{1p} \\
x_{21} & x_{22} & \cdots & x_{2p} \\
\vdots & \vdots & & \vdots \\
x_{n1} & x_{n2} & \cdots & x_{np}
\end{bmatrix},
$$

the cross-product of deviations, covariance, and correlation matrices of X are defined, respectively, as

$$
A = \begin{bmatrix}
a_{11} & a_{12} & \cdots & a_{1p} \\
a_{21} & a_{22} & \cdots & a_{2p} \\
\vdots & \vdots & & \vdots \\
a_{p1} & a_{p2} & \cdots & a_{pp}
\end{bmatrix}
\qquad
S = \begin{bmatrix}
s_{11} & s_{12} & \cdots & s_{1p} \\
s_{21} & s_{22} & \cdots & s_{2p} \\
\vdots & \vdots & & \vdots \\
s_{p1} & s_{p2} & \cdots & s_{pp}
\end{bmatrix}
\qquad
R = \begin{bmatrix}
r_{11} & r_{12} & \cdots & r_{1p} \\
r_{21} & r_{22} & \cdots & r_{2p} \\
\vdots & \vdots & & \vdots \\
r_{p1} & r_{p2} & \cdots & r_{pp}
\end{bmatrix}
$$

where, for all $i, j = 1, \ldots, p$:

$$
a_{ij} = \sum_{k=1}^{n} (x_{ki} - \bar{x}_i)(x_{ki} - \bar{x}_j)
$$

$$
s_{ij} = a_{ij}/(n-1)
$$

$$
r_{ij} = \frac{s_{ij}}{\sqrt{s_{ii} \cdot s_{jj}}}
$$

12.5 Correlations for sets of variables

As an example, let's look at correlations among the independent variables for the regression model in the introduction to this chapter (*TIME* is omitted):

```
MATRIX
    USE longley
    MAT xvars = longley ( ;deflator..populatn)
```

```
MAT corrx = CORR(xvars)
SHOW corrx
```

```
Matrix: CORRX
               DEFLATOR       GNP    UNEMPLOY    ARMFORCE    POPULATN
DEFLATOR          1.000     0.992       0.621       0.465       0.979
     GNP          0.992     1.000       0.604       0.446       0.991
UNEMPLOY          0.621     0.604       1.000      -0.177       0.687
ARMFORCE          0.465     0.446      -0.177       1.000       0.364
POPULATN          0.979     0.991       0.687       0.364       1.000
```

Correlations for two sets of variables. When there are many variables, the correlations matrix can be very large and hard to view—especially if you're only interested in correlations among one group of variables against another. Here we define *DEFLATOR* and *GNP* as one set and *UNEMPLOY*, *ARMFORCE*, and *POPULATN* as a second set.

```
MATRIX
   MAT set_A = longley ( ;deflator,gnp)
   MAT set_B = longley ( ;unemploy..populatn)

   MAT SDa = SQR(DIAG(SSCP(set_A)))
   MAT SDb = SQR(DIAG(SSCP(set_B)))
   MAT corr_ab = TRP((set_A-COLMEAN(set_A))/SDa)*,
                     ((set_B-COLMEAN(set_B))/SDb)
   SHOW corr_ab
```

```
Matrix: CORR_AB
             UNEMPLOY    ARMFORCE    POPULATN
DEFLATOR        0.621       0.465       0.979
     GNP        0.604       0.446       0.991
```

Transforming columns

You can use a LET statement to create a new column or alter an existing column in the active matrix. LET works the same here as it does elsewhere in SYSTAT. The syntax for the LET command is:

```
LET name = expression
```

If the active matrix has a column named *NAME*, it is overwritten; if it does not, a new column is added. The *EXPRESSION* can be any combination of column names, constants, mathematical functions, and operators. For example,

```
LET total_pts = test1 + test2 +2*final
```

creates a column named *TOTAL_PTS*, which is the sum of the values in columns *TEST1* and *TEST2* and twice the value in the *FINAL* column. See Chapter 6 for more information about LET statements.

Generating design variables

If you use **Matrix** to request an analysis of variance or if you need to generate a set of design variables for each categorical variable in a regression model, use one of the following MAT command functions:

Function	Result
DESIGN0(*vector*)	"0, 1" design variables
DESIGN1(vector)	"1, 0, –1" design variables
DESIGNF(*vector*)	Full rank design variables
ORTHEQ(*vector*)	Equally spaced orthogonal components
ORTHNUM(*vector*)	Unequally spaced orthogonal components

To generate design variables, the cases in your data file need no special ordering. For example, if you have a data file named *MYDATA* with the variables *CITY$* (Los Angeles, Chicago, and New York) and *DOSE$* (zero, low, medium, and high) and want to generate the "1, 0, –1" type variables for *CITY$* and the orthogonal coefficients for *DOSE$*, specify:

```
MAT my_design = DESIGN1(mydata( ;city$)) ||,
                ORTHEQ(mydata(;dose$))
```

Recall that the double vertical bar concatenates the set of variables for *CITY$* with those for *DOSE$*. Likewise, you could continue by concatenating the five design variables with the data in *MYDATA*.

The DESIGN1 function generates two design variables (*A* and *B*) for values of *CITY$*; ORTHEQ generates three design variables (*C*, *D*, and *E*) for levels of *DOSE$*. Following are the values generated for specific cities and doses:

CITY	A	B		DOSE	C	D	E
LA	1	0		zero	–3	1	–1
Chicago	0	1		low	–1	–1	3
New York	–1	–1		medium	1	–1	–3
				high	3	1	1

Actually, we have misled you regarding the values of the orthogonal components. SYSTAT normalizes each component by dividing by the square root of the sum of the squares of the coefficients (for example, for the design variable *C*, the value for "zero dose" is

$$-\frac{3}{\sqrt{9 + 1 + 1 + 9}}$$

or –0.671). Following are the actual values:

DOSE	C	D	E
zero	-0.671	0.500	-0.224
low	-0.224	-0.500	0.671
medium	0.224	-0.500	-0.671
high	0.671	0.500	0.224

Matrix Algebra

This section discusses how to use **Matrix** to:

- Multiply two matrices
- Invert a matrix
- Compute the determinant of a matrix
- Find the trace of a matrix
- Find eigenvalues and eigenvectors of a matrix
- Solve systems of linear equations
- Compute the Cholesky L*L decomposition
- Compute the single-value decomposition
- Compute the Kronecker product of two matrices
- Compute the QR decomposition

This section concludes with an example of ridge regression.

Matrix multiplication

You can multiply two matrices provided that the number of columns in the first matrix equals the number of rows in the second matrix (that is, multiply an $m \times n$ matrix by an $n \times p$ matrix). Let's multiply a 2×3 matrix by a 3×3 matrix:

$$
A = \begin{bmatrix} a_{11} & a_{12} & a_{13} \\ a_{21} & a_{22} & a_{23} \end{bmatrix} \qquad
B = \begin{bmatrix} b_{11} & b_{12} & b_{13} \\ b_{21} & b_{22} & b_{23} \\ b_{31} & b_{32} & b_{33} \end{bmatrix}
$$

$$
AB = \begin{bmatrix} a_{11} & a_{12} & a_{13} \\ a_{21} & a_{22} & a_{23} \end{bmatrix} \begin{bmatrix} b_{11} & b_{12} & b_{13} \\ b_{21} & b_{22} & b_{23} \\ b_{31} & b_{32} & b_{33} \end{bmatrix} = \begin{bmatrix} c_{11} & c_{12} & c_{13} \\ c_{21} & c_{22} & c_{23} \end{bmatrix}
$$

where: $\quad c_{11} = a_{11}b_{11} + a_{12}b_{21} + a_{13}b_{31}$

$$
\vdots
$$

$$
c_{23} = a_{21}b_{13} + a_{22}b_{23} + a_{23}b_{33}
$$

In general, the cij entry is the product of the ith row of **A** and the jth column of **B**. Here we multiply two matrices and store the results as a matrix named *A_TIME_B*:

$$A = \begin{bmatrix} 2 & 1 & 3 & 0 & 0 & 1 \\ 0 & 2 & 3 & 1 & 3 & 1 \\ 5 & 3 & 2 & 0 & 2 & 2 \\ 1 & 1 & 3 & 4 & 2 & 1 \\ 0 & 0 & 2 & 1 & 4 & 3 \end{bmatrix} \qquad B = \begin{bmatrix} 3 & 4 \\ 0 & 1 \\ 2 & 2 \\ 4 & 2 \\ 3 & 0 \\ 3 & 1 \end{bmatrix}$$

```
MAT a_time_b = a*b
SHOW a_time_b
```

```
Matrix: A_TIME_B
        15          16
        22          11
        31          29
        34          20
        29           9
```

Raising a matrix to a power

Use the ** or ^ operator to raise a matrix to a power. The command

```
MAT a_cubed = a**3
```

is the same as:

```
MAT a_cubed = a*a*a
```

Note that only square matrices can be raised to a power.

Kronecker product

The result of the Kronecker product of $n \times p$ matrix **A** and $p \times s$ matrix **B** contains a $p \times s$ submatrix for each element of **A** (that is, it has $n \times p$ rows and $s \times p$ columns). Each $p \times s$ submatrix is the product of its element in **A** with every element in **B**. For example, the command

```
MAT c = KRON(a,b)
```

uses input matrices **A** and **B** to produce the matrix **C**:

$$A = \begin{bmatrix} 1 & 2 \\ 3 & 4 \\ 5 & 6 \end{bmatrix} \qquad B = \begin{bmatrix} 7 & 8 \\ 9 & 10 \end{bmatrix} \qquad C = \left[\begin{array}{cc|cc} 7 & 8 & 14 & 16 \\ 9 & 10 & 18 & 20 \\ \hline 21 & 24 & 28 & 32 \\ 27 & 30 & 36 & 40 \\ \hline 35 & 40 & 42 & 48 \\ 45 & 50 & 54 & 69 \end{array}\right]$$

The inverse, determinant, and trace

Often, for classical statistical analyses, you need to compute the inverse, determinant, or trace of a matrix.

The inverse and pivoting

The inverse of a matrix **A** is a matrix **B** such that **AB**=**BA**=**I**, where **I** is the identity matrix. Use the INV or SWEEP function to find the inverse of a matrix.

Function	Result
INV(*matrix*)	The inverse of *matrix*
SWEEP(*matrix, vector*)	Elements of *vector* determine which elements of *matrix* are pivoted (a "1" in *vector* means pivot, a "0" means no pivot)

The inverse. To find the inverse of the matrix **K**,

$$K = \begin{bmatrix} 1 & 2 & 3 \\ 2 & 3 & 4 \\ 3 & 4 & 6 \end{bmatrix}$$

type:

```
MAT 1 = INV(k)
SHOW 1
```

```
Matrix: L

      -2             0             1
      -0             3            -2
       1            -2             1
```

To check that **L** is the inverse of **K**, find **KL** and **LK**:

```
MAT prod_kl = k*1
MAT prod_lk = 1*k

FORMAT 8 4
SHOW prod_kl prod_lk
FORMAT
```

```
Matrix: PROD_KL

       1             0             0
       0             1             0
       0             0             1

Matrix: PROD_LK

       1             0             0
       0             1             0
       0             0             1
```

Using SWEEP to partially invert matrices. The SWEEP function pivots on the diagonal elements of a matrix. If pivoting is done to only some elements, the result is a partially inverted matrix. The vector in the SWEEP argument contains 0 or 1 for each element of the diagonal of the input matrix, where 0 means no pivoting and 1 means pivoting.

The determinant

The determinant of a square matrix is a scalar value that, among other things, indicates whether the matrix is invertible. A matrix has an inverse if and only if its determinant is not 0. In the **Matrix** procedure, you use the DET function to find the determinant of a matrix. The LOGDET function calculates the natural log of the determinant.

Function	*Result*
DET(*matrix*)	The determinant of *matrix*
LOGDET(*matrix*)	The log of the determinant of matrix

Given the matrix **Z**,

$$Z = \begin{bmatrix} 1 & 2 & 0 & 1 \\ 1 & 3 & 4 & 0 \\ 0 & 1 & 5 & 6 \\ 1 & 2 & 3 & 4 \end{bmatrix}$$

type:

```
MAT dtrmnt = DET(z)
SHOW dtrmnt
```

```
Matrix: DTRMNT
        -18
```

Note that, since the determinant of **Z** is not 0, **Z** has an inverse.

Trace

The trace of a square matrix is the sum of the elements in its diagonal. Use the TRACE function to find the trace of a matrix. The matrix **Y**

$$Y = \begin{bmatrix} 2 & 1 & 5 & 3 \\ 1 & 1 & 3 & 6 \\ 5 & 3 & 0 & 1 \\ 3 & 6 & 1 & 3 \end{bmatrix}$$

has a trace of 6 (that is, 2 + 1 + 0 + 3). To find the trace using SYSTAT, type:

```
MAT y_trace = trace(y)
SHOW y_trace
```

Eigenvalues

When you multiply a matrix by a column matrix (or vector), the result is another column matrix of the same dimension. Thus, a matrix is a rotation of vectors. A nonzero vector **v** is called an **eigenvector** of a matrix **A** if there exists a scalar s such that:

$$\mathbf{A}\mathbf{v} = s\mathbf{v}$$

A scalar s is called an **eigenvalue** of **A** if there exists a nonzero vector **v** such that:

$$\mathbf{A}\mathbf{v} = s\mathbf{v}$$

The EIGVAL function of MAT

Use the EIGVAL function of the MAT command to compute the eigenvalues of a matrix.

Function	Result
EIGVAL(*matrix*)	Compute the eigenvalues of *matrix*

For example,

```
MAT eigvals = EIGVAL(a)
```

finds the eigenvalues of matrix **A** and stores them in a column matrix named *EIGVALS*.

The EIGEN function of CALL

To compute eigenvalues and eigenvectors, use the EIGEN function of the CALL command.

Function	Result
EIGEN(*vals,vects,matrix*)	The eigenvalues (*vals*) and eigenvectors (*vects*) of *matrix*

For example,

```
CALL EIGEN(eigvals,eigvect,a)
```

finds the eigenvalues and eigenvectors of matrix **A**. The eigenvalues are stored in a column matrix named *EIGVALS*, and the eigenvectors are stored as columns of the matrix *EIGVECTS*.

Cholesky, QR, and SVD decomposition

Following are ways to decompose a matrix:

Function of the MAT Command	Result
MAT result = function(argument)	
CHOL(matrix)	The matrix **L** found by decomposing symmetric matrix into **L•L'**, where **L** has zeros above the diagonal

Function of the CALL Command	Result
CALL function(arguments)	
CHOL(d_matrix,l_matrix,matrix)	The matrices **D** and **L** found by decomposing *matrix* into **L*•D•L*'**, where **L*** has zeros above the diagonal and **D** is 0 everywhere but the diagonal
QRD(q_matrix,r_matrix,matrix)	The matrices **Q** and **R** found by decomposing *matrix* into **Q•R**, where **Q'•Q=I** and **R** is 0 below the diagonal
SVD(u_matrix,d_matrix,v_matrix, matrix)	The matrices **U**, **D**, and **V** found by decomposing *matrix* into **U•D•V**, where **D** is 0 except for its diagonal and **Q•Q'=I** and **V•V'=I**

Cholesky

The Cholesky decomposition is often used to generate data with a specific correlation structure or to standardize correlated data (for example, to compute Mahalanobis distances). The **Matrix** procedure provides two forms of a Cholesky decomposition. The CHOL function of the MAT command yields one matrix. The CHOL function of the CALL command yields two matrices.

The MAT command's CHOL function. If you begin with a symmetric matrix such as a $p \times p$ correlation matrix **R**, the Cholesky decomposition finds **L** such that

$$\mathbf{R} = \mathbf{L} \cdot \mathbf{L}'$$

where **L** has zeros above the diagonal. Since **L** is triangular, it is much easier to invert than **R**. Note that:

$$R^{-1} = (L \cdot L')^{-1}$$

$$= (L')^{-1} \cdot (L)^{-1}$$

$$= (L^{-1})' \cdot L^{-1}$$

To request a Cholesky decomposition for the correlation matrix *MYCORR*, specify:

```
MAT my_L_mat = CHOL(mycorr)
```

The CALL command's CHOL function. An alternative version of the Cholesky decomposition is

$$R = L* \cdot D \cdot L*'$$

where L^* has zeros above the diagonal and D is 0 everywhere but the diagonal. Some prefer this decomposition to the one shown above because the square roots are not computed. Note that L in the definition above is:

$$L = L* \cdot \sqrt{D}$$

The command for computing the decomposition of the matrix *MYCORR* is:

```
CALL CHOL(my_D_mat,my_Lstar,mycorr)
```

The first two arguments are names for the output D and L^* matrices. The last argument is the name of the input matrix.

QR

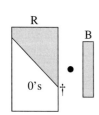

For an $n \times p$ matrix X, the QR decomposition is

$$X = Q \cdot R$$

where Q is an $n \times n$ matrix and R is an $n \times p$ matrix such that:

1. $Q' \cdot Q = I$ and $Q \cdot Q' = I$
2. R is 0 below the diagonal.

This decomposition can make regression computations easier. Note that

$$Y = X \cdot \beta + \varepsilon$$
$$Q' \cdot Y = R \cdot \beta + \varepsilon$$

so by starting at †, computation follows easily via "back solution."

To compute the QR decomposition, use the QRD function of the CALL command:

```
CALL QRD(my_Q_mat, my_R_mat, mydata)
```

The first two arguments are names for the output **Q** and **R** matrices. The last argument is the name of the input matrix.

SVD

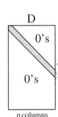

n

p columns

Both the QR and SVD (singular value decomposition) methods can be used to find eigenvalues and eigenvectors. For the $n \times p$ matrix **X**, the SVD decomposition is

$$\mathbf{X} = \mathbf{U} \cdot \mathbf{D} \cdot \mathbf{V}$$

where **U** is an $n \times n$ matrix, **D** is an $n \times p$ matrix that is 0 except for its diagonal, and **V** is a $p \times p$ matrix. In addition:

$$\mathbf{U} \cdot \mathbf{U}' = \mathbf{I_n}$$

$$\mathbf{V} \cdot \mathbf{V}' = \mathbf{I_p}$$

To compute the singular value decomposition, use the SVD function with the CALL command:

```
CALL SVD(my_U_mat, my_D_mat, my_V_mat,mydata)
```

The first three arguments are names for the output **U**, **D**, and **V** matrices. The last argument is the name of the input matrix.

Solving a system of linear equations

You can use **Matrix** to solve a system of linear equations. From the system of n equations in n variables:

$$a_{11}x_1 + a_{12}x_2 + \dots + a_{1n}x_n = b_1$$

$$a_{21}x_1 + a_{22}x_2 + \dots + a_{2n}x_n = b_2$$

$$\vdots$$

$$a_{n1}x_1 + a_{n2}x_2 + \dots + a_{nn}x_n = b_n$$

we form three matrices:

$$A = \begin{bmatrix} a_{11} & a_{12} & \cdots & a_{1n} \\ a_{21} & a_{22} & \cdots & a_{2n} \\ \vdots & \vdots & \vdots & \vdots \\ a_{n1} & a_{n2} & \cdots & a_{nn} \end{bmatrix} \qquad X = \begin{bmatrix} x_1 \\ x_2 \\ \vdots \\ x_n \end{bmatrix} \qquad B = \begin{bmatrix} b_1 \\ b_2 \\ \vdots \\ b_n \end{bmatrix}$$

The system of equations above can be written as:

$$AX = B$$

If **A** is invertible, the equation has a unique solution:

$$AX = B \Rightarrow A^{-1}AX = A^{-1}B \Rightarrow X = A^{-1}B$$

In **Matrix**, you use the SOLVE function to solve a system of equations.

Function	Result
SOLVE(*coefmat,constmat*)	The solution of the system of equations with coefficient matrix *coefmat* and constant matrix *constmat*

If **A** is the matrix of coefficients and **B** is the constant matrix as above, you find the solution matrix **X** as follows:

```
MAT x = SOLVE(a,b)
```

For example, to solve this system of equations,

$$x + y + z = 4$$

$$-x + 2y - z = 2$$

$$2x - y + 3z = 1$$

first type the coefficient and constant matrices, and then use SOLVE to find the solution:

```
MAT a = [1 1 1;-1 2 -1;2 -1 3]
MAT b = [4;2;1]
MAT x = SOLVE(a,b)
SHOW x
```

```
Matrix:   X

       3
       2
      -1
```

The solution is $x = 3$, $y = 2$, and $z = -1$.

12.6 Ridge regression

Ridge regression is a technique that tames the estimates of the regression coefficients when severe multicollinearity exists among the independent variables. The formula for the estimated coefficients is

$$\hat{\beta} = (Z'Z + \lambda I)^{-1} Z' y$$

where Z is the matrix of standardized independent variables, y is the vector of the standardized dependent variable, and I is the identity matrix. The usual least squares estimate is obtained when λ is 0. Before selecting a value for λ, researchers usually try several values and plot the resulting estimates to get an indication of their stability. Then, they choose a value of λ for which the coefficients smooth out and no longer make sudden changes.

```
MATRIX
   USE longley
   FORMAT 11 7
   MAT y = longley(;total)
   MAT x = longley(;deflator..time)
   MAT y = COLZSC(y)
   MAT x = COLZSC(x)
   MAT cpdx = SSCP(x)
   MAT beta = INV(cpdx)*TRP(x)*y
   SHOW  beta
```

```
MATRIX: BETA
  DEFLATOR        0.0462820
       GNP       -1.0137463
  UNEMPLOY       -0.5375426
  ARMFORCE       -0.2047407
  POPULATN       -0.1012211
      TIME        2.4796644
```

```
   MAT ridge = DIAG(cpdx)#I(6)

   MAT betar = INV(cpdx+ridge#0.01)*TRP(x)*y
   MAT beta = beta||betar

   MAT betar = INV(cpdx+ridge#0.02)*TRP(x)*y
   MAT beta = beta||betar

   MAT betar = INV(cpdx+ridge#0.03)*TRP(x)*y
   MAT beta = beta||betar

   MAT betar = INV(cpdx+ridge#0.04)*TRP(x)*y
   MAT beta = beta||betar

   MAT betar = INV(cpdx+ridge#0.05)*TRP(x)*y
   MAT beta = beta||betar
```

```
MAT betar = INV(cpdx+ridge#0.06)*TRP(x)*y
MAT beta = beta||betar

MAT betar = INV(cpdx+ridge#0.07)*TRP(x)*y
MAT beta = beta||betar

MAT betar = INV(cpdx+ridge#0.08)*TRP(x)*y
MAT beta = beta||betar

MAT betar = INV(cpdx+ridge#0.09)*TRP(x)*y
MAT beta = beta||betar

MAT beta = TRP(beta)
MAT ridge = [0.0;0.01;0.02;0.03;0.04;0.05;,
             0.06;0.07;0.08;0.09]
COLNAME ridge = ridge
MAT beta = beta||ridge

SHOW beta
FORMAT
```

```
Matrix: BETA
  DEFLATOR       GNP   UNEMPLOY   ARMFORCE   POPULATN        TIME     RIDGE
 0.0462820 -1.0137463 -0.5375426 -0.2047407 -0.1012211  2.4796644  0.0
 0.2243909  0.3384163 -0.3012889 -0.1203120  0.0900342  0.5684712  0.0100000
 0.2554418  0.3389921 -0.2794636 -0.1027295  0.1713698  0.4314136  0.0200000
 0.2631998  0.3346829 -0.2623944 -0.0895991  0.2023704  0.3776147  0.0300000
 0.2651152  0.3298206 -0.2474496 -0.0784852  0.2177420  0.3480589  0.0400000
 0.2649235  0.3250096 -0.2339612 -0.0686880  0.2262858  0.3289198  0.0500000
 0.2638317  0.3203945 -0.2216270 -0.0598886  0.2312827  0.3152458  0.0600000
 0.2623252  0.3160117 -0.2102638 -0.0519009  0.2342336  0.3048190  0.0700000
 0.2606278  0.3118634 -0.1997416 -0.0445991  0.2359194  0.2964941  0.0800000
 0.2588520  0.3079400 -0.1899598 -0.0378905  0.2367841  0.2896178  0.0900000
```

Plotting ridge estimates

Following is a plot of the results:

```
USE beta
PLOT deflator..time * ridge / OVERLAY  LINE,
                              XMIN=-.01  XMAX=.1,
                              YMIN=-1.1  YMAX=2.5,
                              XLIM=0  YLIM=.02,
                              XLABEL='Ridge Factor',
                              YLABEL='Estimate of Beta'
```

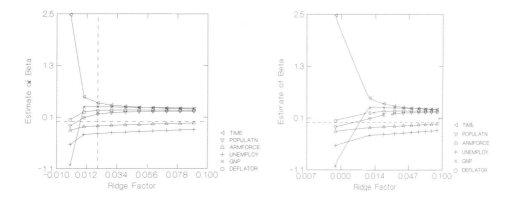

In the plot on the right, we added **Xpow** and **Smooth=Spline** and did not use **Xlimit**=0.02.

References

Neter, J., Wasserman, W., and Kutner, M. (1985). Applied linear statistical models, 2nd ed. Homewood: Richard E. Irwin, Inc.

Rao, C.R. (1973). Linear statistical inference and its applications, 2nd ed. New York: John Wiley & Sons.

Seber, G.A.F. (1977). Linear regression analysis. New York: John Wiley & Sons.

Appendix: Data Files

AFIFI • Afifi and Azen (1974). The dependent variable, *SYSINCR*, is the increase in systolic blood pressure after administering one of four different drugs *(DRUG)* to patients with one of three different diseases *(DISEASE)*. Patients were assigned randomly to one of the four possible drugs.

AGESEX • 1980 U.S. Census. These data show the distribution of *(MALES)* and *(FEMALES)* within age groups. The variable *AGE* labels each age group by the upper age limit of its members.

AIRCRAFT • Bennet and Desmarais (1975). These data show amplitude of vibration *(FLUTTER)* versus time *(TIME)* in an aircraft wing component.

AIRLINE • Box and Jenkins (1976). The variable *PASS* contains monthly totals of international airline passengers for 12 years beginning in January, 1949.

AKIMA • Akima (1978), SAS (1986). These data are topological measurements of a three-dimensional surface using the variables *X, Y,* and *Z.*

AM • Borg and Lingoes (1987), adapted from Green and Carmone (1970). This unfolding data set contains similarities only between the points delineating "A" and "M," and these similarities are treated only as rank orders. Variables include *A1* through *A16.*

ANSFIELD • Ansfield, et al. (1977). This study examines the effects *(RESPONSE$)* of treatments *(TREAT$)* on two patient groups *(CANCER$):* those with cancer of the colon or rectum and those with breast cancer. *NUMBER* gives the number of patients in each cancer/treatment/response group.

BLOCK • Neter, Wasserman, and Kutner (1985). These data comprise a randomized block design. Five blocks of judges *(BLOCK)* analyzed three treatments *(TREAT)*. Subjects (judges) are stratified within blocks, so the interaction of blocks and treatments cannot be analyzed, and the outcome of the analysis is *JUDGMENT*.

BOD • Bates and Watts (1988). Marske created these data from stream samples in 1967 by Marske. Each sample bottle is inoculated with a mixed culture of microorganisms, sealed, incubated, and opened periodically for analysis of dissolved oxygen concentration. The variables are *DAYS* and *BOD*.

BOXES • Messina (1987, p. 126). The ohms of electrical resistance in computer boxes are measured for five randomly selected boxes from each of 20 days of production. Thus, each *SAMPLE* contains five observations of resistance in *OHMS* for each of 20 days *(DAY)*.

BRODLIE • Brodlie (1980). These data are *x* and *y* coordinates taken from a figure in Brodlie's discussion of cubic spline interpolation.

BUSES • Davis (1952). These data count the number of buses failing *(COUNT)* after driving 1 of 10 distances *(DISTANCE)*.

CANCER • Morrison (1973); Bishop, Fienberg, and Holland (1975). These studies examined breast cancer patients in three diagnostic centers *(CENTER$)*, three age groups *(AGE)*, whether they survived after three years post-diagnosis *(SURVIVE$)*, and the inflammation type (minimum/maximum) and appearance of the tumor *(TUMOR$)* (malignant/benign), combined in the variable *INFLAPP$*. The variable *NUMBER* contains the number of women in each cell.

CITIES • Airline distances in hundreds of miles between the following global cities: *BERLIN, BOMBAY, CAPETOWN, CHICAGO, LONDON, MONTREAL, NEW YORK, PARIS, SANFRAN*, and *SEATTLE*.

CITYTEMP • These data consist of low and high July temperatures for eight U.S. cities in 1992.

CLOTH • Montgomery (1991, p. 183). Here, the occurrences of nonconformities *(DEFECTS)* in each of 10 rolls of dyed cloth were counted *(ROLL)*. The rolls were not all the same size in square meters. Thus, the sample unit was defined as 50 square meters of cloth, and roll sizes were expressed in these units *(UNITS)*.

CODDER • These data contain the percentage of reader attention *(PERCENT)* in a certain geographical area *(LOCUS$)* for the local newspaper.

COLAS • Schiffman, Reynolds, and Young (1981). These data consist of judgments by 10 subjects of the dissimilarity (0–100) between pairs of colas, including *DIETPEPS, RC, YUKON, PEPPER, SHASTA, COKE, DIETPEPR, TAB, PEPSI*, and *DIETRITE*.

COLOR • These data provide the proportions of *RED, GREEN*, and *BLUE* that will produce the color specified in *COLOR$*.

COLRPREF • The *COLRPREF* data set contains color preferences *(RED, ORANGE, YELLOW, GREEN, BLUE)* among 15 people *(NAME$)* for five primary colors.

CONDENSE • Messina (1987, p. 22). The *CONDENSE* data file contains nonconformance data (defects) for 15 lots of condensers. *LOT$* is lot number, *TYPE$* is type of defect, and *TALLY* is the frequency of a particular defect in a particular lot. One thousand condensers were inspected in each lot.

COVAR • Winer (1971). Winer uses this artificial data set in an analysis of covariance in which *Y* is the dependent variable, *X* is the covariate, and *TREAT* is the treatment.

COX • Cox (1970). These data record tests for failures among objects after certain times *(TIME)*. *FAILURE* is the number of failures, and *COUNT* is the total number of tests.

DOSE • These data are from a toxicity study for a drug designed to combat tumors. The data show the proportion of laboratory rats dying *(RESPONSE)* at each dose level *(DOSE)* of the drug.

EKMAN • Ekman (1954). These data are judged similarities among 14 different spectral colors (the variable names are the colors' wavelengths named *W584, W600, W610, W628, W651,* and *W674*). The judgments are averaged across 31 subjects.

ENERGY • SYSTAT created this file to demonstrate error bars. The variable *SE* determines the length of the error bar. *ENERGY$* is determined as low, medium, and high.

ENZYME • Greco, et al. (1982). These data measure competitive inhibition for an enzyme inhibitor. *V* is the initial enzyme velocity, *S* is the concentration of the substrate, and *I* is the concentration of the inhibitor.

EURONEW • A subset of the *WORLD* data. These data include 27 European countries. The variable *LABLAT* is the latitude measurement of the capital, and *LABLON* is the longitude.

EX1 • Wheaton, Muthén, Alwin, and Summers (1977). These data are attitude scales administered to 932 individuals in 1967. The attitude scales measure anomia *(ANOMIA)*, powerlessness *(POWRLS)*, and alienation *(ALNTN)*. They also include a variable for socioeconomic index *(SEI)*, socioeconomic status *(SES)*, and years of schooling completed *(EDUCTN)*.

EX2 • Duncan, Haller, and Portes (1971). These data measure peer influences on ambition. These data include the respondent's parental aspiration *(RPARASP)*, socioeconomic status *(RESOCIEC)*, intelligence *(REINTGCE)*, occupational aspiration *(REOCCASP)*, and educational aspiration *(REEDASP)*. These data also include the respondent's best friend's intelligence *(BFINTGCE)*, socioeconomic status *(BFSOCIEC)*, parental aspiration *(BFPARASP)*, occupational aspiration *(BFOCCASP)*, and ambition *(BFAMBITN)*.

EX3 • Mels and Koorts (1989). These data are taken from a job satisfaction survey of 213 nurses. These data include variables for job security *(JOBSEC)*, attitude toward training *(TRAING)*, opportunities for promotion *(PROMOT)*, and relations with superiors *(RELSUP)*.

EX4A and **EX4B** • Lawley and Maxwell (1971). These data comprise a correlation matrix of nine ability tests administered to 72 children.

FOOD • These data were gathered from food labels at a grocery store.

BRAND$	Shortened name for brand
FOOD$	Type of dinner: chicken, pasta, or beef
CALORIES	Calories per serving
FAT	Grams of fat
PROTEIN	Grams of protein
VITAMINA, CALCIUM, IRON	Percentage of daily value of vitamin A, calcium, and iron
COST	Price per dinner
DIET$	*Yes* if low in calories; *no* if regular

FRACTION • These data comprise a fractional factorial design where data appear in only 8 out of 16 possible cells. Each cell contains two cases. Four treatment factors *(A, B, C, AND D)* predict one dependent variable *(Y)*.

GIRLS • Harman (1967). These data contain these measurements recorded for 305 girls: height, arm span, length of forearm, length of lower leg, weight, bitrochanteric diameter (the upper thigh), chest girth, and chest width.

GROWTH • Each case in this file represents a group of plants receiving the same dose *(DOSE)* of a growth hormone. *GROWTH* is the mean growth measure for each group, and *SE* is the standard error of the mean.

HELM • Helm (1959), reprinted by Borg and Lingoes (1987). These data contain highly accurate estimates of "distance" between color pairs by one experimental subject (CB). Variables include *A,C, E, G, I, K, M, O, Q,* and *S*.

HILO • These are hypothetical price data for a stock. *HIGH* is the highest price for that month *(MONTH AND MONTH$)*, *LOW* is the low price, and *CLOSE* is the closing price at the end of the month.

IRIS • Anderson (1935). These data measure sepal length *(SEPALLEN)*, sepal width *(SEPALWID)*, petal length *(PETALLEN)*, and petal width *(PETALWID)* in centimeters for three species *(SPECIES)* of irises (1=Setosa, 2=Versicolor, and 3=Virginica).

JOHN • John (1971). These data comprise an incomplete block design with three treatment factors *(A, B,* and *C)*, a blocking variable with eight levels *(BLOCK)*, and the dependent variable *(Y)*.

JUICE • Montgomery (1991). The number of defective orange juice cans *(DEFECTS)* found in each of 24 samples *(SAMPLE)* of 50 juice cans. Data are collected on each of three shifts *(TIME$)* with eight samples taken for each shift *(SHIFT$)*. *SIZE* is also a variable.

KENTON • Neter, Wasserman, and Kutner (1985). These data comprise unit sales of a product *(SALES)* under different types of package designs *(PACKAGE)*. Each case represents a different store.

LABOR • U.S. Bureau of Labor Statistics. These data show output productivity per labor hour in 1977 U.S. dollars for a 25-year period *(YEAR)*. Other variables are *US, CANADA, JAPAN,* and *EUROPE*.

LATIN • Neter, Wasserman, and Kutner (1985). These data comprise a Latin square design in which the response *(RESPONSE)* of a different square *(SQUARE)* was tested five days a week *(DAY)* for five weeks *(WEEK)*.

LEARN • Gilfoil (1982). These data demonstrate a quadratic function with a ceiling. They are from a study showing that inexperienced computer users prefer dialog menu interfaces while experienced users prefer command-based interfaces. *SESSION* is the session number, and *TASKS* is the number of command-based (as opposed to dialog-based) tasks initiated by the user during that session.

LONGLEY • Longley (1967). These data are economic data selected by Longley to illustrate computational shortcomings of statistical software. The variables are *DEFLATOR, GNP, UNEMPLOY, ARMFORCE, POPULATN, TIME,* and *TOTAL*.

MACHINE • These data are in the file *MACHINE* and represent the numbers *(N)* of conforming (RESULT is 1) and nonconforming (RESULT is 0) units produced by each of five machines.

MANOVA • Morrison (1976). These data comprise a hypothetical experiment measuring weight loss in rats. Each rat was assigned randomly to one of three drugs *(DRUG)*, with weight loss measured in grams for the first and second weeks of the experiment *(WEEK(1)* and *WEEK(2))*. *SEX* was another factor.

MINIWRLD • This data file is a subset of *OURWORLD*.

MISSILES • Jackson (1991). These data are a covariance matrix of measures performed on 40 Nike rockets. Variables include *INTEGRA1, PLANMTR1, INTEGRA2,* and *PLANMTR2*.

MJ20 • Milliken and Johnson (1984). These data are the results of a paired-associate learning task. *GROUP* describes the type of drug administered. *LEARNING* is the amount of material learned during testing.

MJ202 • Milliken and Johnson (Example 17.1). These data are from a home economics survey experiment. *DIFF* is the change in test scores between pre-test and post-test on a nutritional knowledge questionnaire. *GROUP* classifies whether or not a subject received food stamps. *AGE* designates four age groups, and *RACE$* designates Whites, Blacks, and Hispanics.

MOTHERS • Morrison (1976). These data are hypothetical profiles on three scales of mothers *(SCALE(1)* to *SCALE(3))* in each of four socioeconomic classes *(CLASS)*. Other variables are *A$, B$, C$, A, B,* and *C*.

NAFTA • Two months before the North Atlantic Federal Trade Agreement • approval and *before* the televised debate between Vice President Al Gore and businessman Ross Perot, political pollsters queried a sample of 350 people, asking "Are you For, Unsure, or Against NAFTA?" After the debate, the pollsters contacted the same people and asked the question a second time. Variables include *BEFORE$, AFTER$,* and *COUNT*.

NEWARK • Collected by the U.S. Government and cited in Chambers, et al. (1983). These data are 64 average monthly temperatures *(TEMP)* in Newark, New Jersey, beginning with January 1964.

OURWORLD • Variables recorded for each case (country) include:

COUNTRY$	Names of the 95 countries used in this data file
URBAN	Percentage of population living in urban areas
LIFEEXPF, LIFEEXPM	Years of life expectancy for females and males
GDP$	Group variable with codes "Developed" and "Emerging"
GDP_CAP	Gross domestic product per capita in U.S. dollars
BABYMORT, BABYMT82	BABYMORT = infant mortality rate for 1990; BABYMT82 = infant mortality rate in 1982
BIRTH_RT	Number of births per 1000 people in 1990
DEATH_RT	Number of deaths per 1000 people in 1990
BIRTH_82, DEATH_82	Number of births and deaths per 1000 people in 1982
B_TO_D	Birth to death ratio in 1990
HEALTH, EDUC, MIL, HEALTH84, EDUC_84 and MIL_84	Expenditures (in U.S. dollars) per person for health, education, and the military in 1990 and in 1984
POP_1983, POP_1986, POP_1990, POP_2020	Populations in millions for the years 1983, 1986, and 1990; POP_2020 is the population projected by the United Nations for 2020
GNP_82, GNP_86	Gross national product in 1982 and 1986
RELIGION$	Expenditures grouped by the religion or personal philosophy of those who govern the country
GOV$	Type of government
LEADER$	Religion of the leaders of countries
LITERACY	Percentage of the population who can read
GROUP$	Europe, Islamic, or the New World
URBAN$	Rural or city

MCDONALD	Number of McDonald's restaurants per country
LAT, LON	Latitude and longitude measurements of the center of the country

PAROLE • Maltz (1984). These data record the number of Illinois parolees *(COUNT)* who failed conditions of their parole after a certain number of months *(MONTH)*. An additional 149 parolees failed after 22 months, but these are not used.

PATTISON • 1987 JASA article by C. P. Y. Clarke. Clarke took the data from an unpublished thesis by N. B. Pattinson for 13 grass samples collected in a pasture. Pattinson recorded the weeks since grazing began in the pasture *(TIME)* and the weight of grass cut from 10 randomly sited quadrants, then fit the Mitcherlitz equation:

$$\text{GRASS} = \theta_1 + \theta_2 e^{-\theta_3 \text{TIME}}$$

PLANTS • SYSTAT created this file to demonstrate regression with ecological or grouped data. The variables are *CO2*, *SPECIES*, and *COUNT*.

PLOTS • The split plot design is closely related to the nested design. In the split plot, however, plots are often considered a random factor. Thus, different error terms are constructed to test different effects. Here is an example involving two treatments: *A* (between plots) and *B* (within plots). The numbers in the cells are *YIELD* of the crop within plots. These data also use *PLOT* and *PLOT(1)* and *PLOT(2)* as variables.

POLAR • These data show the highest frequency *(FREQ)* (in 1000 of cycles per second) perceived by a subject listening to a constant amplitude sine wave generator oriented at various angles relative to the subject *(ANGLE)*.

PUNCH • Cornell (1985). These data measure the effects of various mixtures of watermelon *(WATERMELN)*, pineapple *(PINEAPPL)*, and orange juice *(ORANGE)* on test ratings by judges *(TASTE)* of a fruit punch.

QUAD • Cook and Weisberg. This function reaches its maximum at $-b/2c$; however, for the data given by Cook and Weisberg, this maximum is close to the smallest x. In other words, little of the response curve is found to the left of the maximum.

RATS • Morrison (1976). For these data, six rats were weighed at the end of each of five weeks *(WEIGHT(1)* to *WEIGHT(5))*.

RCITY • Adapted from a Swiss Bank pamphlet. These data include 46 international cities *(CITY\$)*, the name of continental region *(REGION\$)*, average working hours per week *(WORKWEEK)*, working time (in minutes) to buy a hamburger and a large portion of french fries *(BIG_MAC)*, average cost (in U.S. dollars per basket) of a basket of goods and services *(LIVECOST)*, net hourly earnings *(EARNINGS)*, and percentage of taxes security paid by worker *(PCTTAXES)*.

REACT • These data involve yields of a chemical reaction *(YIELD)* under various combinations of four binary factors *(A, B, C, D)*. Two reactions are observed under each combination of experimental factors, so the number of cases per cell is two.

REPEAT1 • Winer (1971). These data contain two grouping factors *(ANXIETY* and *TENSION)* and one trials factor *(TRIAL(1)* to *TRIAL(4))*.

REPEAT2 • Winer (1971). This data set has one grouping factor *(NOISE)* and two trials factors: period and dial. The trials factors must be entered as dependent variables in a MODEL statement, so the variables are named *P1D1, P1D2,...,P3D3*. For example, *P1D2* means a score in the {period1, dial2} cell.

ROCKET • Components A, B, and C are mixed to form a rocket propellant. The elasticity of the propellant *(ELASTIC)* was the dependent variable. The other variable is *RUN*.

ROTATE • Metzler and Shepard (1974). These data measure reaction time in seconds *(RT)* versus angle of rotation in degrees *(ANGLE)* in a perception study. The experiment measured the time it took subjects to make "same" judgments when comparing a picture of a three-dimensional object to a picture of possible rotations of the object.

ROTHKOPF • Rothkopf (1957). These data are adapted from an experiment by Rothkopf in which 598 subjects were asked to judge whether Morse code signals presented two in succession were the same. All possible ordered pairs were tested. For multidimensional scaling, the data for letter signals is averaged across sequence and the diagonal (pairs of the same signal) is omitted. The variables are *A* through *Z*.

RYAN • This TSQ chart signals an out-of-control condition. *Y1* and *Y2* are the control variables and *SAMPLE* is the sample identifier.

SALARY • These data compare the low and high salaries of executives in a particular firm. Variables include *SEX, EARNINGS COUNT*.

SCHOOLS • Neter, Wasserman, and Kutner (1985). These data comprise a nested design where two teachers from each of three different schools are rated. *SCHOOL* indicates the school that the case describes. Each teacher variable *(TEACHER(1–3))* represents a different school; a value of "1" indicates teacher 1 for that school, "2" indicates teacher 2 for that school, and "0" indicates that the teacher does not teach at that school. *LEARNING* measures the teacher's effectiveness (the higher, the better).

SPIRAL • These data consist of a spiral in three dimension with the variables *X, Y,* and *Z*.

SPLINE • Brodlie (1980). These data are *X* and *Y* coordinates taken from a figure in Brodlie's discussion of cubic spline interpolation.

SPNDMONY • Chatterjee, Price (1977). In this data set, *SPENDING* is consumer expenditures, and *MONEY* is money stock in billions of dollars in each quarter of the years 1952–1956 *(DATE)*.

SURVEY2 • In Los Angeles (circa 1980), interviewers from the Institute for Social Science Research at UCLA surveyed a multiethnic sample of 256 community members for an epidemiological study of depression and help-seeking behavior among adults (Afifi and Clark, 1984). The CESD depression index was used to measure depression. The index is constructed by asking people to respond to 20 items: "I felt I could not shake off the *blues...,*" "My sleep was *restless,*" and so on. For each item, respondents answered "less than 1 time per day" (score 0); "1 to 2 days per week" (score 1); "3 to 4 days per week" (score 2), or "5 to 7 days" (score 3). Responses to the 20 items were summed to form a *TOTAL* score. Persons with a CESD *TOTAL* greater than or equal to 16 are classified as depressed. Variables include:

ID	Subject identification number
SEX	1 = male; 2 = female
AGE	Age in years at last birthday
MARITAL	1 = never married; 2 = married; 3 = divorced; 4 = separated; 5 = widowed
EDUCATN	1 = less than high school; 2 = some high school; 3 = finished high school; 4 = some college; 5 = finished bachelor's degree; 6 = finished master's degree; 7 = finished doctorate
EMPLOY	1 = full time; 2 = part time; 3 = unemployed; 4 = retired; 5 = houseperson; 6 = in school; 7 = other
INCOME	Thousands of dollars per year
SQRT_INC	Square root of income
RELIGION	1 = Protestant; 2 = Catholic; 3 = Jewish; 4 = none; 5 = other
BLUE to DISLIKE	Depression items
TOTAL	Total CESD score
CASECONT	0 = normal; 1 = depressed (CESD Š 16)
DRINK	1 = yes, regularly; 2 = no
HEALTHY	General health? 1 = excellent; 2 = good; 3 = fair; 4 = poor
CHRONIC	Any chronic illnesses in last year? 0 = no; 1 = yes

TETRA • These data comprise a bivariate normal distribution. Variables include *X, Y* and *COUNT.*

TRIAL • These data contain two variables, *MALE* and *FEMALE.*

TYPING • These data show the average speeds for the typists in three groups, using typing speed (*SPEED*) and a character or numeric code for the machine used *(EQUIPMNT$).*

US • State and Metropolitan Area Data Book, 1986; Bureau of the Census; The World Almanac, 1971.

POPDEN	People per square mile
PERSON	F.B.I. reported incidences, per 100,000 people, of personal crimes (murder, rape, robbery, assault)
PROPERTY	Incidences, per 100,000 people, of property crimes (burglary, larceny, auto theft)
INCOME	Per capita income
SUMMER	Average summer temperature

WINTER	Average winter temperature
LABLAT	Latitude in degrees at the center of each state
LABLON	Longitude at the center of each state
RAIN	Average inches of rainfall per year

USCOUNT • Taken from the *US* data. These data are the means of *PERSON* (personal crimes) and *PROPERTY* (property crimes) within *REGION$*. The *COUNT* variable shows the number of states over which the means were computed.

USSTATES • State and Metropolitan Area Data Book (1986). Variables include:

REGION and REGION$	Divide the country into four regions
DIVISION and DIVISION$	Divide the country into nine regions
LANDAREA	Land area in square miles, 1980
POP85	1985 population in thousands
ACCIDENT	Number of deaths by accident per 100,000 people
CARDIO	Number of deaths from major cardiovascular disease per 100,000 people
CANCER	Number of deaths from cancer per 100,000 people
PULMONAR	Number of deaths from chronic obstructive pulmonary disease per 100,000 people
PNEU_FLU	Number of deaths from pneumonia and influenza per 100,000 people
DIABETES	Number of deaths from diabetes mellitus per 100,000 people
LIVER	Number of deaths from chronic liver disease and cirrhosis per 100,000 people
DOCTORS	Number of active, non-Federal physicians per 100,000
HOSPITAL	Number of hospitals per 100,000 in 1988
MARRIAGE	Number of marriages in thousands in 1989
DIVORCE	Number of divorces and annulments in thousands in 1989
TEACHERS	Number of teachers in thousand
TCHRSAL	Average salary for teachers for the 1990 year
HSGRAD	Number of public high school graduates in the 1982-83 school year
AVGPAY	Average annual pay for a worker in 1989
TOTALSLE	Total sale
VIOLRATE	Violent crime rate per 100,000 people in 1989
PROPRATE	Rate of property crimes per 100,000 in 1989
PERSON	Number of persons who commit crimes
POP90	Population in thousands in 1990 as cited in the *New York Times*
ID$	Name of each state in the United States
COUNT	Number associated with the state
MSTROKE and FSTROKE	Risk of stroke per 100,000 males and females (adjusted to weight each state's various age groups equally)
INCOME89	Median household income in 1989
INCOME	Represents income in 1991

BUSH, PEROT, and CLINTON	Vote count in 1000 for each candidate in the 1992 presidential election
ELECVOTE	Number of electoral votes each state received in the 1992 presidential election
PRES_88$	Number of electoral votes each state received in the 1988 presidential election
GOV_93$	Newly elected governor's political party in each state after winning the 1993 gubernatorial races
GOV_92$	Winning political parties in the 1992 gubernatorial races
POVRTY91	Census Bureau's estimate of the percentage of Americans below the poverty level in 1991
POVRTY90	Poverty estimates for 1990
TORNADOS	Number of tornados per thousand square miles from 1953 to 1991
HIGHTEMP	Average high temperature
LOWTEMP	Average low temperature
RAIN	Average annual rainfall
SUMMER	Average summer temperature
WINTER	Average winter temperature
POPDEN	Population density
LABLON, LABLOT	Longitude and latitude at the center of the state according to the *World Almanac and Book of Facts*, 1992. Pharo Books, New York
GOVSLRY	Salaries for U.S. governors

USINCOME • These data use the average income *(INCOME)* compared to its region *(REGION)*.

USVOTES • This data file breaks down the votes for *CLINTON, BUSH,* and *PEROT* by *DIVISION$*.

WESTWOOD • Neter, Wasserman, and Kutner (1985). A spare part is manufactured by the Westwood Company once a month. The lot sizes manufactured vary from month to month because of differences in demand. These data show the number of man-hours of labor for each of 10 lot sizes manufactured. The variables are *PROD_RUN, LOT_SIZE, MAN_HRS*.

WILLIAMS • Cochran and Cox (1957). These data consist of a crossover design for an experiment studying the effect of three different feed schedules *(FEED)* on milk production by cows *(MILK)*. The design of the study has the form of two 3 x 3 Latin squares. *PERIOD* represents period. *RESIDUAL* indicates the treatment of the preceding period. Other variables include number assigned to the cow *(COW)* and the Latin square number *(SQUARE)*.

WINER • Winer (1971). This design has two trials *(DAY(1–2))*, one covariate *(AGE)*, and one grouping factor *(SEX)*.

WORLD • Global mapping. The variables include *MAPNUM, MAXLAT, MINLAT, MINLON, MAXLON, LAT, LON, COLOR$*.

Index

Index

Index

Index

W

windows

Index